# VERMEIL

## THE ESSENCE OF LEADERSHIP

### BY JEFF GORDON

STELLAR PRESS

**Vermeil: The Essense of Leadership**

© Copyright 2003 - Jeff Gordon
All rights reserved

Cover and book design by Tim Steele

ISBN    0-9708422-6-0

Printed in the United States of America

Published and distributed by
**Stellar Press**
634 North Grand Boulevard, Suite 10-C
St. Louis, Missouri 63103
877-572-8835 (toll-free)
www.stellarpress.com
e-mail:info@stellarpress.com

# DEDICATION

This book is dedicated to every coach, from youth sports
to the pros, that does it the right way.

# ACKNOWLEDGEMENTS

Boundless gratitude is owed to the men and women that covered Dick
Vermeil's NFL teams on a daily basis. They include Ron Reid of the
Philadelphia Inquirer; Jim Thomas, Elizabethe Holland and Bernie
Miklasz of the St. Louis Post-Dispatch; Adam Teicher, Ivan Carter, Joe
Posnanski and Jason Whitlock of the Kansas City Star and Rick Dean of
the Topeka (Kan.) Capital Journal. I'd also like to thank Gary Smith, Peter
King and Michael Silver of Sports Illustrated.

# CONTENTS

Introduction . . . . . . . . . . . . . . . . . . . . . . . . . . . . . . . . . . . . . . 1

Chapter One: Commitment . . . . . . . . . . . . . . . . . . . . . . . 5

Chapter Two: Ambition . . . . . . . . . . . . . . . . . . . . . . . . . . 23

Chapter Three: Toughness . . . . . . . . . . . . . . . . . . . . . . . 41

Chapter Four: Caring . . . . . . . . . . . . . . . . . . . . . . . . . . . . 57

Chapter Five: Introspection . . . . . . . . . . . . . . . . . . . . . . 75

Chapter Six: Thoroughness . . . . . . . . . . . . . . . . . . . . . . 95

Chapter Seven: Persuasiveness . . . . . . . . . . . . . . . . . . . 113

Chapter Eight: Perseverence . . . . . . . . . . . . . . . . . . . . . 125

Chapter Nine: Adaptability . . . . . . . . . . . . . . . . . . . . . . 141

Chapter Ten: Poise . . . . . . . . . . . . . . . . . . . . . . . . . . . . . 159

Chapter Eleven: Loyalty . . . . . . . . . . . . . . . . . . . . . . . . . 173

Chapter Twelve: Accountability . . . . . . . . . . . . . . . . . . 187

Chapter Thirteen: Passion . . . . . . . . . . . . . . . . . . . . . . . 205

Appendix: Dick Vermeil On Coaching . . . . . . . . . . . . 223

About The Author . . . . . . . . . . . . . . . . . . . . . . . . . . . . . 234

# INTRODUCTION

**B**ack in 1998, the St. Louis Rams were staggering through a horrific 4-12 season. Dick Vermeil's two-year old program appeared to be in ruins. Despite the relentless optimism of their coach, the Rams were getting worse instead of better.

Vermeil had been away from the sideline for 14 years, working as a pro and college football analyst on television and a motivational speaker on the corporate circuit. Football was still the same game, of course, but the players had changed substantially. During his coaching comeback, Vermeil clashed with potential team leaders and forgave chronic screw-ups. The long hours spent on the practice field yielded incessant player whining and little else.

So I joined the chorus of media types calling for Vermeil's head. Ripping Vermeil was unpleasant work, since he was so darned likable, but back then it seemed mandatory. The Rams stunk. This star-crossed franchise, the league's worst in the 1990s, seemed to crave new leadership. It was agonizing to watch these bumblers stagger through the National Football League, inventing new and more colorful ways to lose. Attendance was on the wane and the team's luxury suites would be up for renewal in a year.

Dick just had to go. He just wasn't viable in the modern NFL. On this, I actually found some common ground with noisy Tampa Bay Buccaneers defensive tackle Warren Sapp. "I mean, Dick Vermeil? Come on," Sapp had told Sport Magazine after the 1998 season. "The game has passed him by. I mean, he's coached since what, 1970s? It's just the good-old-boy system. They just keep recycling them. I mean, Dick's a great guy, but I don't think he's a great coach."

Vermeil's response to such criticism was simple. He told us to be prepared to eat our words.

So here we are. Vermeil got one more chance from Rams management and led the Rams on their storybook run to Super Bowl XXXIV and their dramatic victory over the Tennessee Titans. Then, after a brief "retirement" from coaching, he staged another successful comeback in Kansas City. He guided a lackluster Chiefs team back into contention within three years.

Count me among those who were very, very wrong. Rather than just throw some ketchup on a newspaper story and chomp away—the normal response to such a blunder—I wanted to do something a bit more constructive to acknowledge the error.

Hence this book on Vermeil's career, a profile that takes you along his coaching journey while zeroing in on 13 personal traits that made him a winner: commitment, ambition, toughness, caring, introspection, thoroughness, persuasiveness, perseverance, adaptability, poise, loyalty, accountability and passion. He evolved as a leader over the last 40 years, learning from the great coaches he worked for and worked with. But his highly personal approach remained the same at ever stop. When given time, it always worked. Vermeil has won coach-of-the-year honors at each step on the rung: high school, junior college, major college and the NFL.

Despite all this success, Vermeil showed little interest in publishing an autobiography during his career. Some day he hopes to produce a book of his motivational talks, since he kept the notes to every key team address he has ever made. But he doesn't see his own life story as all that compelling. "I've always considered myself an ordinary person surrounded by extraordinary people," he says, "and I can't believe my biography would be that interesting."

Obviously, we disagree. Vermeil's story is both an inspiration and a lesson book. This would-be car mechanic from little Calistoga, California, became one of the coaching titans of his time. He overcame a spectacular a mid-career meltdown with the Philadelphia Eagles to live happily ever after. Returning to coaching in his 60s, he got back to the Super Bowl and won it all. He did all this while remaining true to himself, honest with his players and faithful to his friends and family.

In a vicious business overrun with tyrants, weasels and back-stabbers, Vermeil left a trail of lifelong friends. Just about everybody who spent serious time working with him or under him loves him. "I can't say enough about Coach Vermeil," says Tennessee Titans defensive end Kevin Carter, a member of the Rams' 1999 Super Bowl team. "All those players who were with him in the past would tear up when they talked about him. I thought, 'These guys are corny.' But man, after playing for him, when I talk about him, I tear up too."

After that Rams triumph, former Eagles tight end John Spagnola spent 10 days wrestling with a congratulatory note he sent his old coach. In the end, he simply wrote: "Thanks for teaching me that dedication, hard work, teamwork and devotion to family are the true keys to success and happiness. We are all better football players and men for having known you."

Not only did Vermeil become an outstanding leader, he became a noted teacher of leadership. Few football coaches have ever spoken so eloquently on the topic. So this book also includes an appendix of Vermeil quotations on the keys to successful coaching. Many of his thoughts can be applied to any sport—or any business, for that matter.

"A lot of coaches are afraid to get close to their players," says New York Jets coach Herman Edwards, who played for Vermeil in Philadelphia. "But Dick proved you can foster a relationship with players and still make them accountable. That's going to be his legacy. It won't be so much the Super Bowl he won or the championship games he's been involved in. His legacy will be all the players he's touched and the impact he's had on them. He molded them and helped them along their careers. And I'm one of them."

A reporter once asked Vermeil if he ever did write an autobiography, what word would appear most often.

"Maybe 'care,'" Vermeil said. "Care about the people that give you the responsibility to do the job, care about the people you work with, care about the organization you represent, care about your team, your community. Once you get going in this business, whether you want to or not, you become a symbol."

How did Vermeil live up to that challenge? Spectacularly well, as the chapters that follow will tell.

# CHAPTER ONE
# COMMITMENT

*"Everybody I grew up around worked. All the kids. They worked at the vineyards, the orchards or in their dad's butcher shop or the bottling works. That was the way of life, the world I was exposed to. I thought that's how everybody lived."*

-Dick Vermeil

Had circumstances been different, Louie Vermeil would have become a terrific football coach. He played the game at San Mateo High School and competed ferociously, earning all-conference honors as a lineman in the 1920s. He was a squat, burly man who proved height doesn't matter much on the gridiron. Power matters. Ferociousness matters. Precision matters.

Around Calistoga, California, which sits 30 miles north of San Francisco at the tip of the scenic Napa Valley wine country, folks called him "The Bear" and afforded him plenty of respect. His toughness became part of the local folklore. One time, a car fell on him while he was working in his garage. He called out to a co-worker, who rushed in and used a jack to lift the car off him. Louie shook off the mishap and returned to work without seeking medical attention.

"My dad was what you would call a local legend," said Al Vermeil, his youngest son.

Louie could have played at a higher level. He had a scholarship offer to play college football, but he had no interest in higher education. In fact, he never even finished high school. His dream was different: He wanted to turn his grandfather's barn in Calistoga into an automobile repair business. Louie wanted to strike out on his own.

So the Owl Garage was born.

He worked day and night to build a successful business. But football still called him into the fields, so he played for Calistoga's town team in the mid-'30s. Back before football games were televised—back before there was anything remotely like the pro football we see today—folks gathered to watch their men face the next town's men. "Some had never played high school football before," said Dick Vermeil, Louie's oldest son. "My dad had, of course, and a couple of guys had. One guy had played college football. So they put a team together."

Louie remained passionate about the sport. He would have made a wonderful Lombardi-style field marshal. He would have inspired a high level of commitment from his charges. He would have coddled nobody. Just ask his sons. Dick and Al played football for Calistoga High School, as did the middle son Stan. Their father coached them every day.

"As a player, you never played well enough," Dick said. "I don't know if he ever said, 'You played well enough.' He was always a nut on fundamentals. Just tackling, blocking, like the old-school guys."

Louie would have molded the young men in his charge. He would have asked the boys to give more than they believed possible. "About the only way you could get a compliment from my dad was to play well," Dick said. "He critiqued every snap."

The Vermeil boys realized that Louie knew the topics he preached. No gaffe passed unnoticed as he studied the game from the stands. Every missed block, blown tackle or bonehead decision was duly noted. And they would hear about it when they got home. "He always understood what was going on in the games," Al said. "He could really break the game down."

From time to time he gave the boys a personal football demonstration. Stan, a lineman like his dad, still remembers the time Louie tried to show the proper way to pull out and block on a sweep. He asked Dick to serve as the blocking dummy. As Louie approached with a head of steam, Dick wisely stepped out of the way and Louie bulldozed a gazebo-like structure in the back yard.

Louie did a little coaching in a more formal setting. In addition to helping lead the town team, he spent a couple of autumns helping the Calistoga High program before the task fell to teachers with proper certification. Years later, the sons would listen to men come by the Vermeil place and fondly recall Louie's days on the sideline.

Everybody agreed that Louie would have been a natural for that profession. "He always said he lived his life the way the high school coaches taught him to play the game, with the same methods and morality and work ethic," Dick said.

"He would have fit the mold at that time," Stan said. "He would have been a terrific line coach, maybe even a head coach."

Rather than become a famously successful football coach, he would raise one. Dick Vermeil, born on October 30, 1936 in Calistoga, learned how to work—really work—from his most demanding dad. His passion for football, his hunger for perfection, his capacity to persist toward a goal when a more reasonable man may have folded . . . Dick's key personality traits came from his upbringing.

The Napa Valley vineyards drew the Vermeil ancestors to this spectacular countryside. His great-grandfather on the Italian side of family came to make his own wine. And his grandfather on the French side of his family also enjoyed making his own brand wine.

Louie and his wife Alice settled into a home just 100 feet from the garage, raising their three sons and daughter Laura, their oldest child. Louie's grandfather purchased this house after the 1906 earthquake. It became something of a local landmark, since the writer Robert Louis Stevenson once lived there.

Today, Calistoga is a popular destination for day-trippers and vacationers who come to lounge in the spas, soak in hot mineral water and mud baths, find respite in the quaint bed and breakfasts, take wine-tasting tours, shop at the tony boutiques and ogle the "Old Faithful Geyser."

But there was nothing fancy about Louie's world in the 1930s and '40s. He fixed cars all day and all night. His garage was a low-tech place. Old cars and car parts filled the yard in front of the barn. That building, Dick recalled, looked like an old Tennessee still. Inside this rustic wooden structure, Louie literally pounded out his living by bringing cars back to life. He worked methodically to complete each project. It was called the Owl Garage because Louie worked around the clock, despite the posted business hours of 9 a.m. until 6 p.m.

Vermeil's key personality traits came from his upbringing.

Sometimes, Louie would fall asleep at the dinner table, then go back to work later in the night. Down the way at the Church of Our Lady of Perpetual Help, the clanging of repairs in progress could be heard at all hours of the night and day.

"You'll laugh, but as a young man I was fascinated by the thought of working 24 hours straight," Louie once said. "I did it, too."

Calistoga relied heavily on the Owl Garage for transportation in the 1940s, during the war years. Factories were making tanks instead of cars and car parts. So Louie had to do his own machine work to craft the parts he couldn't order. Cars backed up outside the Owl Garage while Louie did the painstaking work. "I had a Model A pickup that sat out here a whole year before I could get to it," Louie said.

During the war era, Louie hung blackout curtains over the windows and continued working at night—ignoring the occasional air raid warnings.

Money was tight through the depression and through World War II and he accepted barter. Stan recalls going with Louie to deliver a car and getting poultry in return. "Six chickens," Stan said. "That was a pretty good deal."

While growing up, Dick never saw his father's hands completely clean of the oil, grease and grime of his trade. He almost never saw him take it easy. "I do remember seeing him once, in swimming trunks, at a picnic on the Russian River," Dick said. "Hell, I didn't know he'd float."

All those years, he never saw his father take a real vacation, save the pilgrimage back east in 1946 to see the Indianapolis 500 automobile race.

By the time the war ended, Louie was exhausted. During that trip to the big race—made in a rebuilt '35 Ford convertible with a high school football teammate—he gave serious thought to selling the garage and finding something less strenuous to do. But when he got back to Calistoga, he felt refreshed and ready to resume his life's work.

Once the boys were old enough to use a wrench adroitly, they were expected to pull their weight in the garage. Even during the boys' high school football days, when they returned home from away games after midnight, Louie expected them to report to work first thing the next morning. Even if the boys had a Friday night dance to attend, Louie expected them to follow him back to the garage if there was still work to do.

In the garage, the Vermeil boys learned about commitment. The work ethic developed under the hood day after night after day became a cornerstone for their success later in life. "You carry your identity all your life," Louie told his children. "Remember what your last name is. Don't dishonor it."

Dick's education about the real world began shortly after grammar school ended. He was too young to play high school football, so he had lots of time to help Louie in the garage. "My parents lied about my age to get me a driver's license because I was driving the tow car," Dick recalled. "I was 14.

Farm kids were able to get a driver's permit at the time because they worked on farms, the orchards, the vineyards. My dad said, 'That isn't fair, I need your help in the garage, so you should get a license too.'"

> The work ethic developed under the hood day after night after day became a cornerstone for their success later in life.

The Vermeil boys learned to how to work meticulously until a task was finished, and finished well. "His philosophy was simple: Work until the job is done," Al said. "He always said there were three ways to get things done: the wrong way, the military way and the right way. He told us to do it right the first time."

Louie was a harsh judge of rightness. One time Dick rebuilt an engine and Louie ordered the expansion rings behind the piston rings set at a particular tension.

"Did you set the rings at the right tension?" Louie asked.

"I think so," Dick said.

"What do you mean, 'You think so?'" Louie said before proceeding to make Dick tear the engine apart, step by tedious step, only to discover that he had, indeed, set the expansion rings at the correct tension.

"Half the time you spent working in that garage was spent making sure you pleased him, because he was the guy who set the standards," Dick said. "It didn't matter if you thought it was good enough."

When the job WAS done well enough, the best the boys could hope for was an affirmative grunt or perhaps an "OK." The words "great job" never came out of his mouth. Still, Dick relished the opportunity to work side by side with his father. This was his chance to earn approval. This was the one place he could really connect with his dad. He could share his father's pride in his craft. He could really understand what made him special.

"Working in the garage was hard, but it was fun," Vermeil said. "The only way I ever knew my father was through working with him. It was a way that you could please your dad because it was tough to please him. It was a way to be involved with him."

The Vermeils didn't go on hunting or fishing expeditions, as other families did in the Northern California outdoors. Their recreation time together came at the local speedway and other race tracks in the region. Louie's main diversion was an extension of his work. He built sprint and midget racers and took them on the circuit, employing local drivers and later, his son Stan. Dick joined the pit crew and shared in the excitement of race day. They were at race tracks every weekend, either competing or watching others race.

Louie became a leader in the sport, becoming president of the Northern California Auto Racing Club, an official at Calistoga Speedway and a fervent promoter of sprint car racing in the region. He volunteered thousands of hours at the local speedway, watering down the track, sharing the maintenance work and getting the place ready for races.

Never one to let a job go unfinished, he helped keep the sport vibrant in that part of the country. This dedication earned him induction into the

National Sprint Car Hall of Fame, located in Knoxville, Iowa. He was inducted in 1995. He is enshrined with some notable company, including Mario Andretti, Johnny Rutherford, Bobby Unser, Gary Bettenhausen, Eddie Rickenbacker, Parnelli Jones, Pancho Carter and Barney Oldfield. Also, his old circuit has remembered him with the Louie Vermeil Award, given annually to the greatest contributor to racing.

Dick shared his father's passion for racing. This was the really fun part of the automobile business. "Being raised in the old garage, and around race cars, sprint cars, midgets, it was exciting," Dick said. "All kids love cars and all kids love speed. All my dad's outside friends from that little garage were in auto racing. So I was in that I environment, in pit crews as a teenager, and watching my dad's car run."

The Vermeils traveled to races around Northern California, then retreated to the nearest Italian restaurant for their post-race meal. There, they relaxed and assessed that day's adventure.

Growing up, Dick's predominant dream was to race in the Indy 500. When asked some 50 years later to name his favorite athlete when he was growing up, he didn't name a pro or college football player. Dick named a local race driver, Fred Agabashion. He also counted Andretti among his idols. He loved the racing scene, the challenge of building a fast car and the thrill of high-speed competition.

"You prepare as meticulously as you possibly can, put all the hours in," Dick said. "We used to work all night and race the next day, then one little thing can get you beat. The big difference there is, when you make a mistake and go offside, you're into the wall."

When a cheerleader named Carolyn Drake fell for him at Calistoga High, she knew that she, too, would have to spend a lot of time around cars. That was the Vermeils' world. If she wanted to spend significant time there, she would have to learn how to handle a wrench, too.

"We used to work on his car, a '36 Ford coupe, together," she said. "I learned how to change a carburetor. I was hanging around his house all the time. We were in high school. We were high school sweethearts. It was just like something out of the TV show 'Happy Days.'"

Back then, Dick was the Fonz. He was the cool kid at school. Everybody expected him to make his living in the garage and perhaps race hot rods. He had to have a nice set of wheels in high school—after he really did turn 16—so he plunked down $15 earned at the garage to buy that Ford Coupe that was as old as he was.

Carol quickly saw that Dick almost enjoyed working on the car more than the vehicle itself. He savored the opportunity to rebuild it and truly make it his own. Carol joined in, restoring the car's interior while he worked on the transmission and engine.

Like the Fonz, Dick was a natural leader who attracted followers. Stan, who is 11 months younger, said Dick always took charge of the neighborhood games. Hide and go seek, baseball, whatever the kids played—he would be the one maintaining order.

Unlike the Fonz, Dick was also an outstanding athlete with big aspirations. He was a good baseball player and he trained hard to run the middle-distance events in track. He also played basketball and served as quarterback of the high school football team, despite standing just 5 feet, 7 inches tall.

After arriving at Calistoga High School, new coach Bill Wood quickly saw that Dick was the young man to lead the team. "It was just his enthusiasm, his desire to win," Wood said. "He inspired a lot of players, also."

He was a rugged athlete, one that battled on through injuries like a concussion and a charley horse that left his thigh purple and swollen. Dick treated the latter injury with a mud bath and just hobbled on the best he could. "Back then," he said, "there were no trainers."

Vermeil was the perfect player to run the new offense Wood installed. It was the same "F Series" offense the College of the Pacific ran when Wood played there with quarterback Eddie LeBaron. It demanded a quarterback with quick feet and clever ball-handling skills. "You would ride the fullback all the way into the line, then pull the football out and hand-off," Wood said. "It takes really good footwork."

Football helped bring Carol and Dick together. The sport bound their families long before they were born. Carol's father had played with Louie on the Calistoga town team, even though he hadn't played high school ball. So the Drakes were all right by Louie.

Their families remained close over the years, so their coupling seemed inevitable. Calistoga High School had just 129 students, including 29 in the senior class that graduated Carol and Dick. These two were inseparable, with Carol coming to the Vermeils for supper on Saturday and Dick visiting the Drakes on Sunday.

As the kids got older, the Vermeil home became one of Calistoga's community hubs. Alice was a wonderful cook and Louie was a gracious host. "He had a real compassion for people, too," Dick said. "He liked people."

Still, he had an ominous image to uphold — remember that his nickname was "The Bear"— so he sometimes growled at Dick's high school classmates. "He used to scare a lot of people," Dick said with a laugh. "Sometimes I think he did it on purpose. All my friends were afraid of him." Except for Carol. She always sat right next to Louie, as the guest of honor. From the very start, she was one of Louie's favorites.

Dinner was often an event at the Vermeil home, since Louie and Alice threw open their door in the Old World tradition. This was a time to chat, share and celebrate friendships. "The greatest experiences I had growing up were sitting around the dinner table raving about my mother's cooking," Dick said. "My folks' kitchen was always open to everybody. Sit down, share a glass of wine over dinner. There was always somebody else at the dinner table."

Sometimes it was the customer whose car wasn't quite finished in the garage. Louie would invite him in for dinner, then head back out to finish the job and get the man on his way. Sometimes it was Dick and Stan having their high school teammates over for a pre-game meal or an informal post-season banquet.

Alice enjoyed hosting as much as she enjoyed cooking. She was a very social woman with a knack for reading people. She routinely welcomed relative strangers into her home for dinner and learned all about them before they left. Alice was the source of the gregarious, sentimental side of Dick's personality.

She also had a feisty side, which served her well being married to Louie for so long. She was every bit the character that Louie was. "To live with my dad all those years, she had to be very tolerant," Dick said. "He was a wonderful person and very giving, but tough."

Alice had the same traits. She could take a needle, but she could give it back. "They were a unique couple, very funny together," Stan said.

One night, Louie and Alice got onto the topic of physical fitness as they sat on the back porch of their home. As was his custom, Louie sat in his large "king's chair," a huge thing that had once graced a hotel lobby. From this throne, Louie raised doubts about his wife's upper body strength.

"You can't do a push-up," Louie said.

"Yes I can," she insisted.

Instead of just arguing, 43-year-old Alice got up, dropped to the floor and did 10 pushups.

She could push the kids hard as hard as Louie. Al recalled hitting .488 in baseball during his junior season at Calistoga. But after he went hitless in four at-bats in a big game against a neighboring high school, he came home to one very upset mom.

"What was wrong with you today?" she sniffed.

She might have been a worse loser than Louie, if that were possible. "She was a front-runner, I know that," Dick said. "She didn't like me as much when I lost. My dad could understand losing a little better. My mom didn't like it."

Such feistiness was passed to all the children, even Laura. She was a great athlete who sprinted past all of the boys at her eighth grade picnic.

Like her brothers, she developed a strong competitive spirit. She had to, just to keep up with everybody. Or pass everybody.

Just as Alice was tougher than she seemed, Louie was more mirthful than he let on. He had a wonderful sense of humor and could laugh at himself. Dick and Stan used to chuckle at the stories they heard in the garage, the tales of how Louie pulled pranks on fellow mechanics.

The old "fill the tool box full of manure so it gushes out when the box is lifted" trick? Louie apparently loved that one, to hear him talk about it. As a younger man, he apparently spent plenty of time rough-housing with the other fellows.

But when it came to raising his boys, Louie didn't joke around. In those days, fathers believed it was their responsibility to toughen up their kids for the real world. They had survived the Depression. They had seen boys go off to war and not come back. Today's touchy-feel style of parenting was definitely not in vogue then. Fathers were supposed to be stern. And being stern came naturally to Louie.

"I'd come home and tell him I threw three touchdown passes and he'd say, 'Good, go change a flat,'" Dick said.

There was friction between father and son, given Louie's flair for unleashing a withering tirade. "He invented the phrase, 'verbal abuse,'" Dick said. "I was 16 before I realized my real first name wasn't Dumb Bastard. You don't erase those scars."

One time, Vermeil actually quit working in the Owl Garage for a week. Louie had belittled him with especially profane diatribe and Dick finally walked away.

"My mother stuck her head out, I remember this, she was on the back porch of the house, she said, 'Louie, you can't talk to my son like that.' He was chewing my ass out like I had just thrown four interceptions in a row."

Louie bragged about Dick to everybody around town, but rarely in front of his son. Sports Illustrated writer Gary Smith explored this topic with Louie after Dick's first retirement from football in 1982.

"I was a critic," Louie said. "I didn't want him to think that life was easy. I'd praise him behind his back to everybody. I never realized how much he wanted me to praise him. Hell, my dad worked until he was 86 years old and whenever I worked for him, I'd bust a gut."

Dick's senior season in high school ended with a 14-7 loss to St. Helena's in the conference title game. Rainy weather made running the "F series" offense most difficult. Stan recalls that the field was virtually flooded. The rain was torrential. "One thing I learned is that when it's muddy, that system doesn't work as well," Wood said.

After that painful loss, the team gathered at his house for a final get-together. But Dick was too upset to join his teammates and spent the night crying in his room. "I know Dick still feels bad about that game today," Wood said.

Dick blamed himself for the defeat, a perspective Louie failed to discourage. Dick had to track down an errant center snap in the muck. Fearing that he wouldn't be able to get the punt off, he tried to run instead. He was stopped short of a critical first down and this loss of field position doomed Calistoga to defeat.

"Shoulda punted," Louie told him afterward. "You had the time."

Such was life in the Vermeil household. Louie's harsh approach precluded his boys from growing up spoiled. Dick never looked for special treatment from teachers, relatives, neighbors or anybody else and he learned to accept punishment like a man. "The people I have respected the most in my life were some of the toughest people I have ever had to deal with," Dick said. "I remember Mrs. Ford; she slapped the heck out of me. I got smart and I remember her and respect her."

Ah, Mrs. Ford. She was Alice Vermeil's eighth grade teacher. Then she had Laura, Dick and Stan, too, as the years passed by. "She wasn't the principal, but she ran that school," Stan said. "She had an 18-inch ruler. You behaved in her class."

Dick was starved for support, too, and he got it from Wood, who also coached him in track. At Calistoga High, the teachers and administrators just figured Dick was going to work for his father in the Owl Garage. They weren't troubled by his poor academic progress. "I didn't have any desire to go to college," Dick said. "My mom and dad didn't graduate from high school and education was never really stressed. But hard work was stressed and responsibility and these type of things. I never thought about going to college."

Given his taste for arduous detail work, Dick he could have become one heck of a mechanic. "My father never said it," Dick said, "but I knew he wanted me to stay and lead the way in the garage."

But Wood loved Vermeil's charismatic personality and pegged him as a natural coach. In turn, Dick saw Wood as somebody he wanted to emulate. He was an impressive figure, a former college standout that also coached the freshman team at the College of Pacific before moving into the high school ranks. Wood took the Calistoga job to help his mother-in-law cope with the passing of her husband. The school was fortunate to have him.

"Great person," Vermeil said. "If it wasn't for him, I wouldn't have gone to college."

Dick appreciated the impact he had on him and the other players. He made coaching look like the best job imaginable. He began dreaming of a life beyond the Owl Garage, a life where he could teach and lead teams and stay around sports forever.

Once he decided he wanted to coach, he resolved to be the best. He would take on the project head on, just as he had done so many times in the garage. One day while walking on the high school's cinder track, he had a pivotal conversation with Wood about a career in coaching. "If I'm going to do it," he told his mentor, "I'm going to do it right."

Louie had passed on his opportunity to play college football, pursue an education degree and become a coach. His ambition was to build a thriving business. Faced with a similar decision—to join the Owl Garage or stay in sports—Dick chose football.

He was a better athlete than a student, despite his lack of size. Major colleges weren't after him to play quarterback, but he was good enough to play at the junior college level for nearby Napa College. There, he could begin to play catch-up with his schoolwork while making an impact on the football field for a team with fewer than two dozen players on the roster. A sports-writer dubbed him the "Calistoga Comet" during his Napa College days.

**Louie's harsh**

After one year there, Vermeil decided to play for College of the Pacific, Wood's old school. But he didn't find the situation to his liking and he returned to Napa College for a second season.

**approach**

He took a pounding playing quarterback. Once Vermeil was knocked so cold that Stan, a freshman on the team during Dick's second season, was terrified that his brother was seriously injured. At one another point, Dick ended up on crutches. But he couldn't stand being sidelined in street clothes, so he dressed out and sat on the bench for a big game at Shasta. When his coach looked for someone to replace his quarterback, he spotted Vermeil in uniform and figured the kid could play. So into the game Vermeil went, cracked ankle and all.

**precluded his**

**boys from**

**growing up**

**spoiled.**

"I've never seen so much tape on an ankle in all my life," Stan said.

Napa College won seven games during his sophomore season and Louie and Alice were able to attend the home games to watch Dick and Stan play. "With Dick in the huddle, you just had confidence," Stan said. "He displayed confidence, not cockiness. He could motivate people without yelling and screaming at them."

During this year and a half, Dick continued working for Louie at the

Owl Garage. A typical day might have him up early for the start of his
class schedule at 8 a.m. Then it was on to football practice in the afternoon. Then he came home to work in the garage until midnight. Then he
would put in a couple of hours of studying before getting back up and
starting all over again.

"He developed the ability to push on," Al said.

Carol and Dick got married after his second season at Napa College,
during the semester break. He was 19 at the time and ready to move on
down to San Jose State University to continue his higher education. Wood
was a bit disappointed that Vermeil didn't end up at his alma mater. (That
school already had an exceptional quarterback that Dick would run into
down the road, a fellow named Tom Flores.)

Dick arrived for the spring semester in 1956 as a walk-on for head
coach Bob Bronzan. He immediately made a good impression and
worked his way onto the depth chart. "He gave me a scholarship at the
end the first spring practice," Dick said. "I was the third quarterback my
junior year."

Bronzan was an offensive innovator whose staff included an eager
graduate assistant named Bill Walsh, who would become a coaching
legend in his own right. Walsh quickly took a liking to Vermeil. "He had
tremendous energy and was really competitive," Walsh said. "There was
some Joe Montana in him. I just don't think the arms and legs were long
enough. He had everything else."

His early days at San Jose State weren't terribly hectic. "When we got
married, Carol worked for the first year," Dick says. "It was a breeze. I
had a summer job. It was nothing. I worked in the garage. Then all of a
sudden our first son, Rick, was born and she didn't work after that." To
allow Carol to stay home with the baby, Dick had to work side jobs.

He worked nights at the garage while going to school—he had a key to
let himself in after the others had left for the day—and also served as the
unofficial auto mechanic for the coaching staff. In this day and age, such
an arrangement would violate NCAA bylaws. "Without a couple of
things like that," Dick said, "I might not have made it. With today's strict
rules interpretations, that would be cheating."

Al recalled his brother having some magical moments during that first
season at San Jose State. Dick came off of the bench during the homecoming game against Denver University late and led his team to a touchdown. Then he kicked the extra point, kicked a successful onside kick and
marched his team to another score during the 35-26 loss. That game was
memorable to Dick for a less glorious reason. "We had a riot at the end of
the game, a big fight," he said. "Our right guard, Stan Keith, was a black
kid and it got ugly at the end of the game there." Widespread integration

of major college football was still more than a decade away.

After that 2-7-1 season, Bronzan moved on to join the coaching staff of the Philadelphia Eagles. Robert Titchenal took over the Spartans' program. Vermeil started the season as the back-up, then moved up to starter during the 3-7 season. The new coach put in a new scheme that allowed Vermeil to exploit his quick feet. "He switched the offense to sort of a split T and I fit that a little better," he said.

As a junior, Vermeil threw just 11 passes all season and rushed for just 11 yards. As a senior, he completed 43 of 84 passes for 580 yards and a touchdown and also rushed the ball for another 109 yards. He shared the punting duties with two other kickers, averaging 31.1 yards per attempt. He also returned a couple of punts and scored an extra point. The bigger star on that team was Ray Norton, who once held the title of "World's Fastest Human" and later played for the San Francisco 49ers as a running back.

The concussion problem that dogged Vermeil earlier in his playing career resurfaced during that final season in San Jose. He was knocked out of the second-to-last game of the season, during a 13-6 loss at Fresno State. "They weren't going to let me play my last game in college football," he said. "Our last game of the year was against the University of Hawaii in Hawaii. I wanted to go, so they let me play. But they said no more football."

Vermeil played in that final game and San Jose State won 12-0 in Honolulu, allowing him to end his playing career in 1957 as a winner.

He graduated with a bachelor's degree in physical education in 1958 and got his master's degree in physical education in 1959. Walsh read Vermeil's thesis on football and stayed in touch with him as both began their climb up the coaching ladder. In fact, while working on that master's degree, Vermeil planned to do his student teaching under Walsh at a Bay Area high school. But Bill moved up to Stanford as an assistant coach before they could reunite.

Bronzan gave his former student the highest possible praise in his brief letter of recommendation for potential teaching and coaching jobs. It read, "I would like my son to grow up to be just like Dick Vermeil."

Vermeil began his coaching career as an assistant coach at Del Mar High School in San Jose in 1959, working under head coach Bill Walker. By now, the Vermeils had their second son, David. Dick also served as the head track coach and he taught freshman English and freshman orientation. His salary that year? A whopping $5,300.

From there, he moved on to Hillsdale High School in San Mateo, California, as head coach in 1960. The school's athletic director had attended Bronzan's coaching clinics over the year and asked the former San Jose State coach for a recommendation on whom to hire. Bronzan suggested Vermeil and called his former student to see if he would be interested.

"I said, 'Are you kidding me? Darn right I want to.' At that time, Hillsdale was one of the most modern high schools in the United States," Vermeil said.

The Vermeils arrived with three children, daughter Nancy coming aboard in 1960. During this period of his life, Dick continued working at the garage in San Jose in addition to handling a variety of other jobs, such as laboring in a food warehouse, digging swimming pools and driving an ice cream truck.

Carol chipped in by mowing the landlady's lawn to lop $5 off the month rent, from $55 to $50. "Having three little kids all very close in age, I was busy," Carol said. "But that was our life. That's just the way it was."

This was the start of something very big. Vermeil hit Hillsdale like a whirlwind, captivating the young men at the school with his frenetic approach. "He was the best motivator of young people I've ever seen," said Homer Zugelder, Hillsdale's basketball coach at the time. "They'd run through walls if he had told them to. He had kids doing things they had never done before."

The Hillsdale football team was required to participate in regular weight training sessions, with the new coach right by their side. The players didn't mind doing the extra work because Vermeil was working so tirelessly himself. He convinced them to share his zeal for winning games and building a program. His energy was infectious.

The school's old leather helmets were quickly replaced with hard shells. He encouraged parent groups to form and raise funds to provide support. He recruited scouts to attend rivals' games and produce detailed 50-page scouting reports. He found a cameraman to begin filming games. He brought in a team chaplain.

Writing for the Washington Post, former Hillsdale High student Jay Mathews described Vermeil's arrival at the school as the new football coach:

> Then the inspirational posters appeared in the locker room and I began to get a sense of what the boy coach was up to. Vermeil had enlisted the school's wildest student artist, Jim Learn, to fill huge sheets of old newsprint with caricatures of linemen and running backs drooling and grimacing and look - ing as if they would reduce Capuchino High, the reigning league champions, to pulp. Some posters had Vermeil's watchwords in two-foot high letters, "DESIRE, DETERMINATION AND GUTS."

Hillsdale was a nice school at almost the exact center of the San Francisco peninsula and the American middle class. Most of the students did their homework, but nobody expected any geniuses. The school had a few ambitious teachers, but nobody quite like Vermeil. The athletic teams had modest goals, winning some games and losing others. The new coach thought that was awful.

On Monday nights, the Vermeils brought the team to their rented house in Redwood City to review game films. Carol baked a cake to honor the player of the week, and the team members became part of his extended family. Dick and Carol got know the players as individuals, tracking their progress through school and providing guidance beyond the team of football.

"It sort of runs your life," Carol said. "In a small-town situation, high school football is what everybody did on a Saturday night. It was exciting and fun."

Don Leydig was a sophomore when Vermeil arrived at Hillsdale. He watched, with amazement, as his new coach transformed the program. The players were handed thick play books to memorize. The diagrams looked like advanced geometry.

"His plays had names and numbers, 'blast,' 'rip' and 'explode.' There was the 'slam-right counter trap' that he opened every game with," recalled Bob Christopherson, another of the team's stars. "This was like another class. We had to study this and some of it was complex and we actually wrote (plays) on our forearm pads."

No detail was overlooked. If the forecast called for rain on game day, Vermeil practiced all week with footballs pulled from buckets of water. When the weather turned, he lectured the players about wearing caps for their walks home so they wouldn't catch cold. To foster team unity and give the players a treat, he arranged to have them work as ushers at a Stanford football game.

To motivate the teenage boys, he started using acronyms to teach them life lessons. He would write a word like "discipline" on the chalkboard. Then he would match an adjective to each of the letters to drive home an inspirational point. Vermeil also took unusual measures to settle the team's nerves before big games. He would play Ray Charles records in the locker room.

Louie took great delight in his son's progress as a coach. "His first big thrill was when Hillsdale beat Burlingame High School badly, like 42-0," Dick said. "Burlingame was the team that had beaten my dad's team in the championship at San Mateo High School. He never forgot that. He came down to that game. It was only about an 85-mile trip to come down from Calistoga to where the game was played. You would have thought we had just won the Super Bowl. It was just unbelievable how excited he was when we beat Burlingame like that."

Hillsdale went 6-3 during Vermeil's first season and he earned coach-of-the-year honors in the conference. The next season, in 1961, the school went unbeaten and won the league title. Leydig was named most valuable player in the league and made the saving tackle in the 12-7 victory over Capuchino in the championship game.

That was one of Vermeil's most memorable Thanksgiving Days ever, an event that would foreshadow events four decades later. "We're leading 12-7 and our opponent's got the ball first and goal," Dick recalled. "But our kids shut them down in four plays and won the championship."

Leydig considers that title a classic over-achievement. Hillsdale was not blessed with great players. This team was not exceptionally big, fast or strong. "On that team, I think there were two of us that got Division I scholarships," said Leydig, who went to Stanford and played freshman football before quitting the game to concentrate on his studies. "It wasn't this group of tremendous athletes. The guys would have done anything for him, because you knew that he cared so much, plus he was doing the little things that helped you win."

How well-schooled was this team? When NFL Films sat down with Leydig and Christopherson to get their reminiscences about Vermeil for an ESPN special, they were still able to bark out the names of the offensive plays that their coach had taught them 40 years earlier.

Even in his earliest coaching days, Vermeil made a personal connection with his charges. Leydig remembers Vermeil coming to study hall to pick him up and take him for treatment on his sprained ankle. He remembers the coach driving him to an awards dinner in San Francisco, then hustling him back home so he could attend Hillsdale's formal Christmas dance.

"I can remember him lending me his car to go home and get my cleats," Leydig said. "It was a blue Ford. That was the first or second time I ever drove a clutch car."

As Hillsdale's current principal, he realizes that such a gesture is unheard of today. Educators have to maintain a safe distance. He laughs at the memory of driving his coach's car. "You'd have to sign 35 different insurance waivers," Leydig said, "and you'd still worry about sending a kid off campus."

Vermeil reached out to all the kids, not just his stars. As a sophomore, the decidedly non-athletic Mathews had him as a teacher in a physical education class.

"PE was not my favorite class," Mathews wrote. "I was severely undersized and clumsy. I had not reached puberty and was not entirely clear about what that would mean. But Vermeil, unlike other gym coaches, did not pick on clueless larvae like me. He was encouraging and funny and direct. I sort of liked him."

Vermeil's motivational flair made him a successful high school swimming coach, too. When the school asked him if he could pick up the team, he didn't flinch. "And I don't even know if he can swim," Zugelder said. "The swimming program at the school was a very, very good one. The kids went through AAU programs before they came to the school and most of them had had stroke coaches."

After agreeing to take the team, Vermeil demonstrated his ability to delegate authority. Since he knew very little about this sport, he set aside his own ego and called on a well-regarded local coach, Ray Taft, to do the real teaching. Vermeil organized and supervised the program. He set the goals and did the motivating. Soon, the Calistoga High team was winning meets and setting records. "They were the toast of the town," Zugelder said. "And he didn't know anything about swimming."

Vermeil's success as a swimming coach makes him chuckle today. He noted that he had a much better won-loss record coaching the swimming team than the football team. "We won the varsity championship there every year for three years in that league," he said.

He looks back on his high school coaching tenure as one of the most satisfying jobs he has ever had. He got into the business because he marveled at the influence Bill Wood had on his players. At Hillsdale, he experienced that same achievement himself.

"No football coach in the country is more important than the high school football coach," Vermeil said. "Having experienced it myself for four years, I know the values. As a teacher, you can never really, totally evaluate your contribution until years later, how long-lasting your contributions to people are. You just never know how you touch somebody, or what impression you leave with them."

He looks back on his high school coaching tenure as one of the most satisfying jobs he has ever had.

Vermeil was only at Hillsdale for only three years, but he didn't treat the job as a stepping stone to bigger things. Though his eyes were on far higher targets, he threw himself into this job. "Hillsdale High School playing Capuchino for the championship on Thanksgiving Day was every bit as big an event as the Rose Bowl and the Super Bowl for me, at that time in my career, and it meant just as much to me," Vermeil said.

Those three years taught Vermeil some tough lessons that he carried to higher levels. He discovered that sometimes a coach just doesn't have good enough players to win. He took his lumps during his third year.

"I was 24 years old and I was really thinking I was a difference maker," he said. "The next year, all of these kids graduated. We won four games. It was startling. It was a startling blow to my ego, to be honest with you, because I was so full of myself and so excited about what I could do as a football coach. It made realize that players win games, not coaches."

That setback didn't deter him. Vermeil harbored no second thoughts about the direction his life would take. He realized he was meant to teach and lead young men on the football field. He wasn't meant to spend his life under the hood of a car.

"Working in the garage was hard, but it was fun," Vermeil said. "But maybe, that's why I work so hard now. So that I wouldn't have to go back to being a mechanic."

But would he have ended up as a mechanic? Years later, a visitor would suggest Vermeil would have ended up owning a chain of garages. Eventually, he would have built an empire to preside over.

Vermeil disagreed. "I'd probably have been dead because I would have driven race cars," he said. "And if you have the same goofy compulsion or competitiveness to win, in those days, they didn't have roll bars and all that other stuff. I've seen guys killed. I've often said, 'I'm sure glad I didn't end up being a race driver.'"

So is Wood. He enjoyed going to the races at Calistoga Speedway and watching Louie's car run. But one time Wood saw Stan Vermeil spinout in front of the pack and narrowly avoid a catastrophe. The mishap startled him. "I was thinking, 'My God, Stan, you've got to get out of this racing stuff," Wood said.

Such close calls made Dick feel better about his decision to pursue coaching instead. He became too consumed by his new dream to act on his childhood fascination with racing. He was on a different sort of fast track, one that would eventually carry him to the very top of his profession.

# CHAPTER TWO
# AMBITION

*"He'll never be done. When he's dead, that's when he'll be done."*

-Carol Vermeil

Stanford University coach John Ralston immediately recognized that Dick Vermeil was a go-getter. While coaching at Hillsdale High, Vermeil routinely sat up front at Ralston's coaching seminars, furiously scribbling notes. Then Vermeil would go home and organize those notes into a book.

Carol typed the text for him and Vermeil drew all the diagrams. Dick would make several copies of the finished product, sending one back to Ralston and giving other copies to his friends in the coaching community. He began building an encyclopedia set on coaching.

This is how he thrust himself to the forefront in this ultra-competitive profession. Each year brought another wave of eager young coaches into the business, each looking to curry favor with the giants like Ralston. Vermeil sought to stay one step ahead of them all.

"When you got a copy of those notes, you couldn't believe what you were reading, it was so well organized," Ralston said. No matter how much the Stanford coach had rambled and strayed off the topic, Vermeil's notes made the address seem crisp and coherent.

Vermeil did the same at other coaching clinics in the region. Zugelder recalls going to the University of Nevada to hear, among others, the legendary Clemson coach Frank Howard. As always, Dick took copious notes, organized them and had Carol type them up. Then he sent the book to Howard. Some weeks later, the phone rang at the Hillsdale High gym office.

"This is Coach Howard," said the man on the other end in a thick southern drawl. Zugelder figured one of their friends was just calling to goof on them. No, the man insisted, this was really Frank Howard.

"I want to talk to Coach VER-mil," Howard said. So Zugelder got Vermeil on the phone.

"Your notes are better than my play book," Howard told him.

Vermeil's vigor started to unnerve his peers. Who was this guy? Why couldn't he just kick back, listen, jot down a few notes and be like everybody else? "He was notorious," said long-time NFL and collegiate coach Mike White, another avid clinic attendee in those days. "Well, I don't know if that's the word. But he was famous."

He got so good at taking and organizing notes that college coaches would ask him for copies of his notes from other coaching clinics.

"They'd send me $25 for the notes or something, and that was big money," Vermeil said. "The Bud Wilkinson-Duffy Daugherty Coach of the Year Clinic was going around the country, and they hired me to transcribe the lectures because they had the same speakers at each stop. They paid me $125. I could not get over that I was going to make $125."

Then he sat down and did the math. Clinic organizers sold Vermeil's summaries to the coaches, 1,200 to 1,400 strong. "They were making a hell of a profit out of my $125," Vermeil said.

Soon, Vermeil would become known for more than his publishing skills. The self-assured Vermeil set high goals after graduating from San Jose State. His inner drive was stuck in overdrive. Many former college football players find a good teaching and coaching job, settle down in the community, raise their family there and live contentedly. That was definitely not the career Vermeil saw for himself. He couldn't sit still. He would never allow himself to become stagnant.

"He used to say when he was coaching in high school, 'My goal is to be a head football coach at a major university,'" Zugelder recalled. "He said that the day he arrived."

In 1963, Vermeil left Hillsdale High School to become assistant coach at San Mateo College, a junior college across town. "I loved the kids," Vermeil said, "but you end up thinking, 'God, wouldn't it be fun if you didn't have to teach P.E., take roll and all the other things?'"

Vermeil spent one season at San Mateo, then, at age 27, became head coach at Napa College. His junior college alma mater hired him for $8,000 a year. This was a huge step for him and his growing family, since the Vermeil's bought their first home for $19,500.

Of course, they didn't have the $19,500, or even the 10 percent down payment required. Louie and Alice didn't have that sort of cash and neither did Carol's folks. But Dick did have a prosperous uncle, a Stanford grad, who was able to front them the money.

They figured they would be there a while as Vermeil set out to build a junior college juggernaut. As it turned out, they would live in their first house for just six months.

With his brother Al starring as one of his key linemen, Dick finished 7-2. Napa College lost just once in conference play, 14-7 to Santa Rosa in the decisive game, and Dick was named the conference coach of the year. This was the best team the school had fielded since 1955, when Dick starred as the team's quarterback

"He got the whole community behind us," Al recalled. "That was probably the best football team they ever had there."

Louie enjoyed the season tremendously. Napa College played its home games on Friday and Saturday nights, and he could attend every one. Dick gave the program a quick but thorough makeover. He managed to round up a handful of impact recruits, although his roster was still half the size of some conference rivals. He planned out thorough weight-training and practice regimens and raised the team's expectations. His own enthusiasm spurred booster enthusiasm, rallying the community around the formerly sleepy program.

Looking to instill more pride, Vermeil ordered new uniforms and helmets with new colors: gold and green, Green Bay Packers colors. Suddenly there was a buzz about Napa College football.

"They were getting nobody to the games," Al said. But by the end of the season, Napa was drawing standing-room only crowds of 5,000.

Vermeil was fiery, tireless, demanding and caring. Players who broke the new rules were punished swiftly. Yet he also took players under his wing, including little brother Al.

Al stood only 5 feet 8 inches tall, but he became a weightlifting fanatic as a teenager and a forceful football player. He had created his own weight room in Laura's garage and had his high school teammates over to lift. Laura often fixed the whole gang pancakes to fuel their workouts.

"Al was one of the best football players, pound for pound, that I ever coached," Dick said. "My gosh, he was benching 400 pounds as a junior in college. If Al was six-foot-two and 220 pounds, he would have played in the NFL for 10 years."

As it was, Al was able to play at Utah State and embark on a coaching career of his own. He worked at the high school level for 10 years, then moved up to work for various professional teams as a strength coach. But he wouldn't have advanced had Dick not stayed after him at Napa College.

Al recalls walking off the field exasperated after a particularly frustrating, mistake-filled practice session. As he left, he muttered something about quitting football. He was at wit's end. As he made the 30-minute drive back home to Louie and Alice in Calistoga, he stewed the whole time. He hadn't been home long when the phone rang. It was Dick, offering a concise bit of encouragement.

What exactly Dick said has been forgotten over the years, but the impact was huge. Dick knew that he couldn't let the poor practice linger with Al. He couldn't let the frustration build overnight. With his timely phone call, Dick encouraged his brother to turn the page and come back ready to work.

When he went to Napa, Al figured he would be immune to Dick's motivational magic, since he had been around him all his life. Al had even moved with Dick and Carol for a stretch, when Louie believed a change in scenery might spur better classroom performance. Al practically idolized his big brother.

"I never had to search for heroes growing up," Al said. "I just had to look around the dinner table. I learned the right way and the wrong way to do things."

But despite this familial bond, Al found himself being swept up by his brother's pep talks. He was moved as much as those teammates who were experiencing them for the first time. "Since he was my brother, you wouldn't think the emotionalism would affect me," Al said. "But it did, like the rest of the players."

Dick's success at Napa College—combined with a timely recommendation from Bill Walsh, now on Stanford's staff—earned him a phone call from Ralston on January 28, 1965, on the Vermeils' wedding anniversary. Ralston offered him $8,500 to coach the freshman team and assist with the varsity squad. Dick practically jumped through the phone line to grab the job.

"How soon do you want me there?" Vermeil asked.

This job wasn't about money, it was about opportunity. Instead of sitting in a lecture hall listening to Ralston, he could learn from the master from the inside of his program. He could work side by side with some of the top young coaches in the business, men like Walsh, White and Rod Rust.

Ralston quickly realized he had made a good hire. Vermeil wasn't just a grandstander. He was willing to do the work necessary to advance his career. He cheerfully put in the endless hours demanded at the college level, laying the groundwork for recruiting, planning drills, breaking down opponents and looking at lots and lots of film. Vermeil fed off the energy of his fellow assistant coaches, some of the best and brightest in the business.

"The offensive staff room had blackboards on the wall all the way around," Vermeil said. "Bill Walsh would come in and start on the left and put his ideas on the board, and he would go all the way around."

Ralston followed Walsh around, pondering the tactical ideas presented by his cocksure aide. Then Ralston would start erasing them, even as Walsh was drawing up still more of his ambitious Xs and Os. "We'd be sitting there, laughing like hell," Vermeil said. "We thought we could do everything. We drove him crazy."

Vermeil impressed Ralston with his direction of the freshman team and graduated to a coordinating role with the offense a year later. "He moved right into the offense, just did an exceptional job, and called our plays from the press box," Ralston said. "I got really taken by the guy. He presented himself so well, he was so attentive to things, he loved to talk football."

Stanford proved the perfect environment to grow. These assistant coaches pushed each other and enjoyed great camaraderie. A year after Vermeil arrived, Jim Mora arrived from Occidental College to join Ralston's fraternity. Vermeil happened to be on a recruiting trip in the area when Mora was hired, so he stopped by and helped him pack up his moving truck.

**'I never had to search for heroes growing up,' Al said. 'I just had to look around the dinner table.'**

This staff bonded during the long hours toiling in the coaching office, building friendships that would last a lifetime. And away from the office, they could tear it up pretty good.

Vermeil, Walsh and White formed their own rat pack. White has fond recollections of trips over to Calistoga, to see Dick's folks, taste some wine and soak in the mineral baths. One thing would lead to another and soon the guys were performing dives and handstands. "All the people in there for medicinal purposes would stare at us," White said.

Carol Vermeil, Marilyn White and Geri Walsh formed a sisterhood of sorts while their husbands were off studying game films, mapping out tactics and plotting the takeover of college football. They raised their families together and, like their husbands, remained friends for life.

Ralston never had to prod his ambitious assistants; if anything, he had to reel them in from time to time. He marveled at their energy and ambition. He admired their willingness to do the grunt work of college coaching. "They were in the office at seven, they would never leave the place if there was something that they could get done or work toward," Ralston said. "And brilliant minds. You just knew these guys were going to be great head coaches."

For the time being, though, they were just assistant coaches—and Ralston impressed Vermeil with his ability to manage their considerable egos. These weren't "yes" men. They all believed they had the answers. Sometimes the young lions started to claw each other. Ralston allowed each assistant coach make his imprint on the program, but he also maintained his firm control. Uprisings were quelled, disputes resolved quickly.

"I learned how to tolerate different personalities," Vermeil said. "I learned how to organize. John would never stay mad at anybody. He would always take somebody he was mad at and make him a good friend. He never allowed a misunderstanding to materialize and blossom into a one-on-one war. I learned that there's lots more things to organize than just Xs and Os and John was good at all those things."

Ralston also taught Vermeil a great deal about player relations. This is a particularly critical skill at the college level, where athletes are still maturing and developing. "He's a tremendous people guy," Vermeil said. "John always saw what's good in somebody. No one else could see it, but he could see it. Invariably, he would bring it out in a person. He was a very good judge of talent."

A prime example was quarterback Jim Plunkett. Vermeil helped recruit him out of James Lick High School in San Jose. (At the same time, Dick also recruited quarterback named Mike Holmgren from San Francisco's Lincoln High School, but lost him to USC once Plunkett committed to Stanford.)

Just before Plunkett's freshman season in 1966, doctors discovered a tumor in his thyroid gland. After surgeons removed the tumor, they determined that it was benign and Plunkett was cleared to play football as long as he wore a clamp on his neck to protect the scar.

Then Plunkett pulled both groin muscles and struggled through a poor freshman season. Ralston suggested a switch to defensive end, but Plunkett said he would transfer rather than switch. Ralston relented, but had him sit out the 1967 season as a "red shirt" while getting up to speed in the office. In 1968, Plunkett began blossoming into a star on Vermeil's watch and Stanford was on its way.

This success helped Vermeil continue his upward climb. In 1969, after four productive years on Ralston's staff, Los Angeles Rams head coach George Allen contacted him when he was on the road recruiting in Southern California. Vermeil figured the call was another prank by his buddy Zugelder. But, it really was Allen and he beat out two other finalists to become the NFL's first special teams coach.

"I really didn't want to leave Stanford," Vermeil said. "I was coaching the offense and had Jimmy Plunkett. We were going to be pretty good. We had Gene Washington at wide receiver. I just felt it was an opportunity to grow. And I went from, like, $8,500 a year to $13,000. That was a big jump."

The job with the Rams was a cutting edge assignment. Other coaches scratched their heads when Allen made special teams play such a priority, but he proved to be a visionary. "Special teams will help lead us to the Super Bowl," he insisted. The kicking game, he said, should never be considered "a necessary evil."

Vermeil credits another assistant coach on that staff, wide receivers coach Howard Schnellenberger, for helping him learn that assignment. Vermeil had done some punting and place-kicking in college, but he had never really taught the kicking game. He didn't have much background in return and coverage tactics, either. Schnellenberger had come to the Rams from Alabama, where Bear Bryant kept the Crimson Tide ahead of the curve on special teams. Schnellenberger shared some of the basics.

"I credit Howard for giving me some roots," Vermeil said. "Then you just take off and be creative, learn yourself. You didn't have a lot of competition because there weren't a lot of people in the league doing it."

Working under Allen gave Vermeil a strong taste of what coaching pro football was all about. The demands were extraordinary. In a league full of perfectionists and detail freaks, Allen set the standard for contingency planning. His obsessive game preparations bordered on insane.

"Every time you win, you're reborn," Allen liked to say. "Every time you lose, you die a little."

Mostly, the Rams lived in 1969. They rolled to an 11-3 finish and won the NFC West. Vermeil found working for Allen a fascinating experience.

"He was a neat guy," Vermeil said. "He'd give you these elaborate studies to do and breakdowns as a coach. 'Give me a breakdown of the three-yard split by the tight end in Baltimore.' You would go through every freakin' game they played on film—no computers—and chart it all. And you'd give it to him. I found out later he would just put them in his bottom left-hand desk drawer and then never look at them. He did these things to stimulate his coaches."

Some of the veteran Rams coaches were tired of getting stimulated. They found excuses to decline his invitations to dinner, to avoid getting grilled on the game plan. They even went out of their way to avoid Allen on elevator rides, lest he catch them unprepared for a line of questioning.

On one ride, Vermeil recalled, the conversation went something like this:

"Did you check the sun?" Allen asked.

"What do you mean, Coach?" Vermeil said.

"Well, you are coaching my punt and kickoff returns, aren't you?'

"Yes."

"Have you told them where the sun will be at three o'clock during the game? Will they have to shield their eyes?"

Vermeil was stumped, as he would often be by Allen. But he never hid from Allen, preferring to soak up as much knowledge as he could during his first season of pro football. He realized there was more to coaching than he realized, like the sun angles for kick returners. He learned that no matter how much detail was put in a game plan, there were always more nuances that went uncovered.

Given Allen's life-and-death approach to football, Vermeil worked overtime to avoid special team fiascoes. Decades later, he could laugh about a 9-7 Rams victory at Chicago. It seems safety Ed Meador, the holder on the place-kicking unit, told Vermeil that a fake field goal would catch the Bears napping. But Vermeil didn't want the last word on such decisions and took the matter to Allen.

"What about a fake field goal?" Vermeil asked the coach. "We think it's there."

"No," Allen said. "Kick it."

But Meador didn't want to hear this. He ran out and called the fake field goal. The Bears covered the play well, and Meador couldn't throw, so he ran and made the first down by the nose of the football. On the sideline, Allen turned to Vermeil and said, "That's what I like, players that take the initiative."

Vermeil had dodged disaster. He knew that if the brazen play had backfired, there would have been hell to pay.

Hungry for broader responsibilities, Vermeil left after one season. He went across town to join UCLA and run the offense under coach Tommy Prothro. Allen tried to talk Vermeil out of making the move, even as he was cleaning out his desk and clearing out. But Vermeil viewed this as another unique learning opportunity, another rung on the ladder to grasp. During his years at Stanford, he had scouted UCLA and studied the program closely.

"I was amazed at how well they played considering how limited their talent was," Vermeil said. "I thought, 'I know they aren't that good, but they win anyway.' I wanted to learn how they did it. The only way to learn was to go be there."

He was willing to pay a personal price to switch jobs. Suddenly life wasn't so convenient. Carol and the kids were comfortable in Huntington Beach, near the Rams training facility, so he kept the family there and commuted to the UCLA campus. That left him with a brutal drive to and from work.

When he settled into his new job, it didn't take long to understand Prothro's success. This program featured tightly organized practices with an unyielding emphasis on fundamentals. The Bruins could grow their own talent to fill holes on the team.

"He could take average kids and make them better football players," Vermeil said. "He was head coach, but he didn't coach the offense or the defense. But he did the organization, he did the practice schedule, he set the tempo, he controlled the discipline, he controlled the leadership of the organization. And when he walked around, the drill tempo changed."

With Prothro in the vicinity, the Bruins ran a little faster and hit a bit harder in practice. The coach had an intimidating presence, allowing him to maintain firm command of his program. He kept his assistant coaches on edge as well.

"I was scared to death of him when I was working for him," Vermeil said. "And if you made a mistake as an assistant coach, uh, oh, would he rip you. Right in the huddle. The whole team would know the offensive coordinator made a mistake."

The Bruins slogged to a 6-5 finish that season. Vermeil was looking forward to pushing the Bruins offense to greater heights, but circumstances changed. When Rams owner Dan Reeves fired Allen after the 1970 season—the two had clashed constantly, despite Allen's success—Prothro took the job. UCLA gave Vermeil some consideration as Prothro's replacement, but figured he was too young and hired Pepper Rodgers from the University of Kansas instead.

Vermeil followed Prothro back to the Rams as the special teams and quarterbacks coach, ending his 105-mile round-trip commute. Prothro lasted two seasons at the helm, going 14-12-2, before he became a casualty of a bizarre franchise swap.

Reeves died and Baltimore Colts owner Carroll Rosenbloom convinced Robert Irsay to buy the Rams from his estate and then trade the team for the Colts. Once he got control of the Rams, Rosenbloom decided change was in order. Prothro was fired. Rosenbloom was impressed by Vermeil's potential, but figured he wasn't ready for the job at the age of 36.

"If you were a little older," Rosenbloom told him at the time, "I'd make you head coach."

Naturally, Vermeil didn't want to hear that. "I told him, 'I'm old enough.' Which I wasn't. They didn't offer me the job and they shouldn't have," Vermeil said.

At the time, however, the snub stung. Vermeil swallowed hard and remained with the Rams for one more season, working under old-school legend Chuck Knox. This single year became one of the most memorable of his career. Knox was a taskmaster, like Allen, but he also knew how to have a good time. When the work was done and the game was won, Knox knew how to celebrate. He knew how to laugh. Not every coach does.

"It might have been as much fun as I've ever had in any year since I've been coaching football," Vermeil said. "I remember some of the big wins we had; we'd always celebrate them as a staff. We'd go out to dinner, drink some Napa Valley wine, hoot and holler, raise a little hell. With Chuck, every accomplishment was something to be shared."

Knox also reinforced Vermeil's notion that he had to be himself while coaching. Nothing could be gained by putting on an act or blowing smoke at the players. He was direct and his coaches and players could respect that.

"He's a very down-to-earth, honest man," Vermeil said. "That's so important if you're a coach. You have to be yourself. If you can just be yourself, then you will be consistent with your approach. When you start changing this and that, you get into trouble."

The Rams raced through the 1973 season with a 12-2 record, winning the NFC West and earning a shot at the Dallas Cowboys in the playoffs. UCLA, suitably impressed, called Vermeil in December and offered him its head coaching job. He was just 37 at the time and looked even younger.

Vermeil credits Prothro for getting him the job. He hadn't spoken to his former boss since his dismissal from the Rams, but, out of the blue, Prothro called to tell him the UCLA job was his for the taking.

Athletic director J.D. Morgan considered hiring him in 1970. Now, after consulting with Prothro, whom he still respected, Morgan was ready to offer him the job. All Vermeil had to do was go take it. He flew up to an athletic director's meeting in San Francisco, interviewed with Morgan, got the offer, accepted the assignment, came home and told Carol he was now the head coach at UCLA.

"How much money are we going to make?" Carol said.

"I don't know," Dick said. "I never asked."

This was the opportunity Vermeil spent 15 years working to earn. He had met his goal of becoming head coach at a major university, and an excellent football school at that. His salary was $27,500. The Bruins had won 17 games the previous two seasons under Rodgers, but it had been nine years since they'd been to the Rose Bowl, which at the time pitted the Pac 8 champions against the Big 10 champs.

Vermeil accepted the job offer while the Rams were preparing for the playoffs, so he couldn't hurl himself into the job. He could only supervise the program from across town. When the Rams were done working, Vermeil would drive across town and interview the assistant coaches that wanted to remain.

Since his typical NFL work day lasted until midnight, these sessions were held in the wee morning hours. Incumbent assistant coach Carl Peterson recalls that his introduction to Vermeil came at about 2 a.m.; the meeting provided a glimpse of what his life would become.

Vermeil named holdover Lynn Stiles his defensive coordinator and assistant head coach, to keep things humming until the Rams were done. After the Rams lost their playoff game to the Cowboys 27-16, Vermeil celebrated Christmas by plunging himself into his new assignment.

Rodgers had assembled an all-star coaching staff, and much of it remained, including Stiles, Peterson and future head-coaching stars Terry Donahue and Dick Tomey. Vermeil had watched them work during spring practice, while he was still with the Rams, and was impressed with their ability. To add to this mix, he would also summon his old friend Mora to help out.

Vermeil's first challenge was to adapt his offensive philosophies to the personnel he inherited. "Pepper had been a wishbone coach," Donahue later recalled. "Dick was left with wishbone personnel. He didn't want a wishbone team, so he went to the veer." This offense used some of the wishbone run principles but also gave him some capacity to throw the ball.

The assistant coaches quickly discovered they were on a ride unlike anything they experienced before. Once Vermeil took over on a full-time basis, he called his first staff meeting for 6 a.m. and worked the group until 1 a.m. the next day. This was how coaching at UCLA was going to be. It was official: The new coach was a maniac.

Vermeil never stopped moving. His energy extended to the realm of fitness, since he had remained an avid jogger since his days at Hillsdale. The assistant coaches were stunned when he rounded them up for their first five-mile run. Naturally, he left them all in his wake.

"I just think if you're in a physical business, you better be a good example," he said. "I don't feel good when I don't work out."

There was nothing phony about this guy. He asked his staffers to work around the clock, but he worked even harder. He pushed his players very hard on the practice field, but they could see how hard he pushed himself. He was willing to lead the charge, which is why he got such a strong response from his charges.

He also established that no matter how much he punished his team with long, grueling, full-contact practices—pushing plenty of young men past their brink—he really did care for the troops. When Vermeil came aboard, one of the very first things he did was visit tight end Gene Bleymaier after Bleymaier underwent shoulder surgery. The lad was blown away, since he had never played a down for him.

"He didn't know me from Adam," Bleymaier said. "But there he was."

Running back Theotis Brown vividly remembers the impression Vermeil made on him during the recruiting process. Vermeil wanted him to sign with the Bruins, but only if he was ready to excel in class. He noted that Brown had just earned a C on a biology paper.

"Somehow, I don't even know how, he found out," Brown said. "And he told me if I was going to make a commitment, it had to start in the classroom. He said, 'This isn't about football. It's about life.' He showed he cared about me, and not just because I could run up and down the field."

Sometimes, though, the Bruins had to remind their coach that they were students. They did need some time for schoolwork. When classes started, the players asked him to back off the two-a-day sessions so they could get their schedules in order. He relented, but just a bit.

Left and right, key players went down with injuries or staggered home exhausted as Vermeil kept demanding more. To win, the Bruins had to learn to go longer, run faster and hit harder every single day in practice. The surviving players could find some consolation from the price the coaches were paying, which was greater still.

> Vermeil worked so many hours during the season that a friend drove him home so he wouldn't nod off at the wheel.

"I can remember scenes from my UCLA days that will stay with me a long time," quarterback John Sciarra said. "For instance, I was working in the equipment room during the summer one year, and I would get there about seven o'clock in the morning. Now, this was in the off-season and lot of times, Dick Vermeil's car would be in that parking lot when I got in. And he'd been there for a while already."

Vermeil worked so many hours during the season that a friend drove him home so he wouldn't nod off at the wheel. On at least two occasions, family members found Stiles asleep in his car in his driveway. Some of the Bruins assistants moved into a nearby Holiday Inn three nights a week to buy a little extra shut-eye.

Sciarra watched Vermeil outpace all his assistant coaches, even go-getters like Stiles and Peterson. "Carl and Dick went recruiting one night in Santa Barbara and when they got back, Carl asked Dick if he'd just stay at his house instead of driving him home because it was late, about two in the morning," Sciarra recalled. "So Dick stayed with Carl. Carl fell asleep, and the next thing he knows, there's a knock at the door. It was Dick. It was 6 a.m. and Dick already had shaved, showered and had on a suit."

Such episodes brought the coaches closer. Vermeil had a way of getting people to work as hard as he did and somehow enjoy it. His enthusiasm was infectious. His optimism was empowering. He believed he could win by outworking his rivals and he convinced his staff that it was true.

In Vermeil's first season at UCLA in 1974, the Bruins clawed out a 6-3-2 record with a young and somewhat undermanned team. Those players willing to sacrifice themselves stayed and played. Those that didn't, left. This season was spent raising the expectations for those in the program and those coming in from high school.

But there was still much to do. The Bruins season ended with a 34-9 drubbing from their cross-town rivals, Southern Cal. UCLA was just going to have work harder in the weight room, harder in spring football and harder in next summer's camp to get better. And Vermeil was going to have to push himself harder, too. That gave him credibility with the players.

So did the fact he cared about them. Vermeil took the time to develop relationships with his players. He built mutual trust. He recalls letting tight end Rick Walker miss practice time to tend to family matters. He knew Walker, he knew his family and he knew that Walker was sincerely concerned about problems back home.

"He pulls no punches," Sciarra said. "He pushes you harder than you've been pushed. And I still look at him as a second father. It wasn't always about football. It was about all the other things, the commitment, the conviction, the passion, the emotion, the loyalty, the things in people you look for that make you want to say, 'That's somebody I want to know.' That's Dick Vermeil."

He still had some things to learn about being a major college head coach. Given his emotional nature, he struggled with public criticism. He sought the advice of UCLA basketball coach John Wooden.

"When he spoke, boy I listened to him," Vermeil said. "He said, 'Dick, all the great things they write about you, most of them aren't true, and all the bad things they write about you, most of them probably aren't true either. So why get involved in either, just keep your focus on what you have control of.'"

With her husband going a mile a minute in his dream job, Carol Vermeil was left to fend for herself with Rick, David and Nancy. During his second season at UCLA, Dick stopped a game film when he spotted David in a sideline shot.

"My God!" Vermeil exclaimed. "Has David ever grown in a year!"

That was enough to make the other coaches wince. "He said it was the only time he saw his kid on the sideline," Peterson said. "Not during the game, when he was there with him, but on film a year later."

David Vermeil took his father's dedication in stride. But Dick's oldest son, Rick, did not. He was in high school while his dad coached UCLA, and like so many kids that age, he soured on his father for a while. "It's tough to walk a middle road with a dad like him," Rick would later say. "I rebelled. I resented him because he could work so hard and was so driven and so successful. He'd say be home at ten, I'd be home at three."

Such rebellion was a natural response. In return, Vermeil pushed his son, but not toward a breaking point in their relationship. Just as Louie allowed Dick to choose his own life course, so Dick did with Rick.

"He never pushed me into sports," Rick said. "He just wanted me to best I could at whatever I did."

Vermeil didn't work around the clock just to get out of the house or put on a show for his peers. He spent that time efficiently, accomplishing twice what some peers did. His meticulous game plans gave the Bruins the belief that they were better prepared than their opponents. They gained confidence from their knowledge of their foes.

"When I went into a game as a quarterback in college, I always had a strong game plan that I'd feel very confident about," Sciarra said. "You don't know how much that means for a quarterback. He can really make a quarterback look good. I don't think I would have been an all-America if not for Vermeil."

The Bruins opened the 1975 season with a 37-21 victory over Iowa State and a 34-28 victory over Tennessee, both at home. Then UCLA stumbled with a 20-20 tie at Air Force and came home to take a 41-20 thrashing from powerful Ohio State. The team was at a crossroads. Which direction would the season and the program turn? By winning 31-21 at Stanford and 37-23 at Washington State, the Bruins got back on a winning track. Then they beat a very strong California at home, 28-14, to give them the belief they could be special this season.

The Bruins followed with a loss to Washington, but they clobbered Oregon and Oregon State. Those victories gave UCLA a chance to play USC with the Pac 8 title and Rose Bowl berth on the line. A victory would also give them another crack at No. 1 Ohio State.

And win the Bruins did, 25-22, despite fumbling 11 times and losing eight of them. Vermeil was beside himself on the sidelines during this near-disaster. "Wendell Tyler was a fumbler and he fumbled it," Vermeil would later recall. "Then I went to my next running back, Carl Zaby, and he fumbled. Then I went to my next running back, Kenny Lee, and he fumbled it. I remember turning to my coaches and saying, 'We had a black guy fumble it, a white guy fumble it and an Oriental guy fumble it. Let's go back to the best running back and see what he'll do.'" That best back was Tyler, who rushed for 130 yards on 17 carries in the game.

Despite that victory—or perhaps because of the sloppiness of it—the Bruins weren't given much of a chance against Ohio State in the Rose Bowl. A few weeks before the rematch, Vermeil and Sciarra were in New

York for an awards banquet. Also at the dinner were Ohio State coach Woody Hayes and his great running back, Archie Griffin. Officials joked with the Buckeyes contingent about giving them the national championship trophy right then and there, to save some trouble. Such banter left Vermeil simmering.

"I remember Dick being pretty upset," Sciarra later recalled. "He was kind of on a mission."

Vermeil was determined not to blow this payback opportunity, so he resolved to reach still higher levels of preparedness. So he and his coaches worked. Even on Christmas Day, they worked.

"Dick gets us out there and works us harder than you can imagine," Sciarra said. "Two-a-days. Full pads and a lot of hitting. For a bowl game."

As became his custom as a head coach, Vermeil had an advisory panel of key players who were free to meet with him to express team concerns. Sciarra was on this committee, along with teammates Oscar Edwards and Wally Henry. They pled their case. The troops, they told their coach, were exhausted. The team was reaching the point of rebellion. The players were ready to break. Couldn't he give them a break instead?

Vermeil was unmoved. After listening to their summation, he gave them a response they didn't want to hear.

"Guys, let me tell you something," Vermeil said. "I'll go out there to Bruin Walk and get students, if I have to, to play this football game. I'm not embarrassing myself.

"If you don't want to work, leave. If you do want to work, you make sure everybody is dressed and out there when they are supposed to be." Sciarra and his co-leaders hobbled back to the locker room, tails between legs. The Bruins cheered their return, assuming they had straightened out Vermeil.

"Then we say, 'Wait guys, it's not good news. We didn't get anything done," Sciarra said. The Bruins moaned. They knew Vermeil would work them even harder, and he did.

As the game approached, Vermeil endeavored to psyche them up. Shortly before the Rose Bowl, he had actor Tom Laughlin of "Billy Jack" fame address the team. Laughlin, a major Bruins booster, laid it on thick.

"Tom told us that not only were we going to win, but win so big that he was giving Ohio State 10 points," Vermeil said. "I thought he had lost his mind."

Ohio State flexed its considerable muscle in the first half of the Rose Bowl. Yet the Buckeyes held a meager 3-0 lead despite controlling the ball for 20 of the first 24 minutes. Ohio State reached the UCLA 25-, 33-, 32-

and 21-yard lines, but extracted just one Tom Kleban field goal from those drives. The stubborn UCLA defense kept the game in hand, but the Bruins offense was going nowhere against the stout Buckeyes.

Vermeil scrapped his ground-oriented game plan.

"We're throwing it," he told his team at halftime.

Sciarra came out firing, firing 16- and 67-yard touchdown passes to Henry, and UCLA scored 16 unanswered points in the third quarter. Sciarra's passing opened up the ground game, and Tyler clinched the 23-10 victory with his 54-yard touchdown run in the fourth quarter.

"Dick made the adjustments we needed at halftime," Sciarra says. "We weren't supposed to win that game, but we did."

'I remember watching him walk off the field,' Tose said. 'There was something in his manner that suggested the type of leadership we were looking for.'

History will recall Vermeil's winning effort as one of the great coaching performances ever. Ohio State's talent advantage evaporated right there on the field.

"They had the Heisman Trophy winner, Archie Griffin, but Dick had a plan and a structure," Brown said. "We knew exactly what they were going to do. I remember with about one minute left in the game, Woody Hayes walked over to Coach Vermeil, shook his hand and said, 'Good job. You beat the hell out of us.'"

This was a triumphant moment for the Vermeil family, which assembled en masse to watch the victory. Even Louie got choked up. At the airport as he and Alice prepared to fly home, he did something a bit out of character. He praised Dick directly.

"He looked at Dick and had tears in his eyes," Al Vermeil recalled. "He said, 'This is the greatest day of my life.'"

Louie believed the hard-nosed Hayes was the greatest coach, so for Dick to beat him was the ultimate. The upset cost Ohio State its expected national championship. Oklahoma earned the title by beating Michigan in the Orange Bowl. Sooners coach Barry Switzer was glad to see Sciarra and Bruins teammate Randy Cross when they arrived in Honolulu later in January to play for him in the Hula Bowl.

"From the time I got off the plane, he was patting Randy and I on the back, buying us cocktails and dinner just about every night," Sciarra said.

"He kept thanking us for the national title."

Vermeil's success caught the eye of Philadelphia Eagles owner Leonard Tose, who was in the market for a savior. His football team had been an embarrassment since the 1960s. Perhaps a top college coach could turn the thing around, somebody like Harvard's Joe Restic or taskmaster Frank Kush at Arizona State. He tried to lure Joe Paterno, but failed.

Tose and his general manager, Jim Murray, had already been screening candidates for the job when they decided to tune in to the Rose Bowl. They were impressed by UCLA's victory and they sensed that the youthful Bruins coach was something extraordinary.

"I remember watching him walk off the field," Tose said. "There was something in his manner that suggested the type of leadership we were looking for." George Allen, now coaching the Washington Redskins, also recommended Vermeil. Tose had great admiration for Allen and often sought his advice on football matters.

Vermeil was initially reluctant to take the Eagles job, since it would mean leaving his Bruins coaches behind. Carol and the kids had grown quite comfortable in Southern California. They had spent their entire lives in that state.

"I thought I was going to be there the rest of my life," Vermeil said. "By the end of my second year, we were the best football team in the country. There were a lot of special kids on that football team."

There were plenty of reasons not to leave UCLA. "Dick said to us, 'I can't go now. I want to be a NFL coach, but if I go now, I won't be able to take all of you. I'd need veteran pro coaches up there.'" Peterson recalled. "He's absolutely the most loyal man I've ever met. We said, 'My God, Dick, this is financial security. You've got to talk to him.'"

Tose and Murray finally sold him on the job. Ultimately, the challenge was too enticing. Though Vermeil's ambition had always been to become a major college head coach, his earlier NFL stints had shown him that pro football was the big show. His hesitance to head East melted away.

Vermeil was ecstatic when he called his parents to tell them that he was now an NFL head coach. Louie did not gush with pride and praise for his son. Ever the old-school father, he berated his son for abandoning UCLA without fulfilling the terms of his contract.

But Vermeil's ambition would not let him pass on the NFL opportunity that had eluded him three years earlier. He didn't mind that the Eagles hadn't made the playoffs since 1960. He didn't mind that Philadelphia went through five coaches in the previous 14 years while posting a 64-123-9 record. He didn't mind that he was inheriting a roster that stunk, or that a significant load of future draft picks had already been squandered.

"Dick called when he got to the Eagles and said, 'There are players at UCLA who could come in here and start,'" Stiles said. "He took over a team in disarray and at the bottom of the heap."

Walsh watched Vermeil's ascension with admiration. His former colleague had become the golden boy of coaching. His success left Walsh second-guessing his own performance.

"You go through life wondering if your approach and judgments are the right ones," Walsh said. "Dick and I were assistants at Stanford together. Then I worked as an assistant with Oakland, Cincinnati and San Diego, while Dick became the UCLA head coach and won the Rose Bowl. Then, as head coach at Philadelphia, he rejuvenated that program. I always wondered if I could come close to doing what he did. Could I turn on that energy and drive? I visited with him a lot, asking him how to do it."

When Vermeil looks back over his climb through the ranks, he, too, is amazed by his rapid ascension. He is grateful that great coaches like Ralston, Allen, Prothro and Knox believed in him and took the time to teach him. He is grateful for his association with Walsh, White, Mora and the other emerging coaches.

"That is what's great about America, if you work hard and have a passion about something and a compassion about people at the same time, good things many times can happen to you," he said. "So many people have been good to me, provided me with opportunities."

# CHAPTER THREE
# TOUGHNESS

*"When I played for Dick, I was fearful and I was scared. As long as you play with fear, you're always going to play at your best."*
-Former Philadelphia Eagles running back Wilbert Montgomery

**D**efensive end Carl Hairston arrived in Philadelphia not long after Vermeil did, as a seventh-round draft pick in 1976 from the University of Maryland-Eastern Shore. He came to training camp at Widener College with the first wave of Eagles hopefuls, the late-round picks and obscure free agents summoned to compete with the incumbents for NFL work and bring new life to the franchise. This was a cattle call in the truest sense.

Hairston was a prototypical Eagles job candidate that summer. No major college football programs recruited him out of high school. In fact, he drove furniture trucks for two years after graduating. He made decent money behind the wheel, $300 a week, but he still loved football. A recruiter for Maryland Eastern-Shore spotted him in a pool hall and wondered if he still wanted to play.

He did, and four years later the Eagles summoned him to battle for a NFL job. Teammates didn't call Hairston "Big Daddy" back in '76. He was just another guy, one of the dozens trying to beat impossible odds.

Camp began early that summer, on July 3. Vermeil created his own version of "Survivor," pitting the players against each other in head-to-head combat. That first day, the Eagles practiced for two and a half hours in the morning and a merciless three and a half hours in the afternoon. After each practice, they ran and ran and ran. This immediately eliminated the least-conditioned aspirants from job contention.

Back at the players' dorm, the scene resembled a fire drill. Players were hastily gathering their belongings and fleeing. The competition began thinning out immediately. "All you could hear were suitcases being thrown down the steps," Hairston said. "There were cabs out in front. We had about 10 guys leave that night."

Vermeil set an extreme pace for his coaches, too. He tackled this challenge with his familiar single-mindedness and he made his assistant coaches follow suit. Carl Peterson, who left the UCLA coaching staff to become one of Vermeil's aides in Philadelphia, loves talking about the second day of their first Eagles camp.

It was July 4, 1976. The whole country was celebrating its bicentennial . . . except the Eagles. While the players lay strewn about their dorm rooms, the coaching staff was digging into its review of the two practice sessions and their planning for Day 3. Outside, a massive fireworks display in the school stadium was creating quite a distraction. Vermeil became agitated. His staff tried to calm him by pointing out that the United States was celebrating its 200th birthday. This was extraordinary day for the nation.

"Carl," Vermeil growled, "you go out there and tell those people to tone it down."

What was a bicentennial celebration when there was training camp to run? Vermeil was willing to push himself and his assistant coaches to unseen levels. He knew, in his heart, that such dedication could yield big results.

Vermeil prodded the Eagles coaches and players with same motivational tactics he used back at Hillsdale High School, Napa College and every stop thereafter. He gushed optimism every waking hour. His fiery pep talks covered a wide range of topics, often far afield from football. He stayed in his players' faces during practice, moving between the stations, alternately urging, chastising and praising the troops. He was constantly in motion, constantly imploring. This wasn't how many NFL coaches behaved, but this was the Vermeil way.

"The day he came in, my reaction was, 'Where in the hell did they get this Harry High School coach? I can't believe we have somebody this crazy and gung ho,'" veteran linebacker Bill Bergey said.

But platitudes alone couldn't turn the Eagles around. Lethargy, complacency and resignation had poisoned this team. Vermeil wanted to cleanse those traits from the veterans he inherited. They would sweat out the toxins. Sometimes they would vomit the toxins. They would develop more mental and physical toughness, or they would move along and make room for somebody with a stronger will. At every turn, the weary veterans saw youngsters like Hairston eager to take their jobs.

"We were dog meat when he first came in," Bergey said.

"We weren't the Eagles anymore, we were the Beagles," said John Bunting, another veteran linebacker that survived and flourished.

During that first camp, the two-a-day practice sessions lasted twice as long as the Eagles ever experienced. The stretching session alone lasted for 45 minutes. Then the high-tempo individual drills with the blocking sleds, tackling dummies and more lasted another 45 minutes.

"If somebody got sick, they just moved the drill somewhere else," Hairston said. "If somebody went down, the next guy stepped up. Back then, it was no-holds barred football."

Then it was time to pit the offense against the defense in various combinations, with full contact and heavy hitting. Offensive linemen pounded on defensive linemen. Linebackers creamed running backs. Safeties hunted for the heads of receivers. Every day, twice a day, the Eagles beat on each other. And between drills, the players could not remove their helmets to cool off, not even during the water breaks.

"There were rules for everything," Bergey recalled. "Your chinstraps had to be buckled at all times. The practices were forever. We were in pads every day. There was unbelievable discipline."

Then came the capper: The post-practice running. The players would have to stagger through 10 "dashes" of 110 yards.

This regimen—the drills, the hitting, the running —was designed to test each individual to see who would break. "His basic philosophy in training camp was to bring us right to our knees," Bergey said. "He would take everything out of us early, then ease up near the end and try to bring us back in time for the season."

'We were dog meat when he first came in,' Bergey said.

Vermeil needed about 45 players to play a regular season game, but invited 120 to training camp and let Darwinism take over. This competition would identify the veterans worth building around, like Bergey and Bunting.

"My whole attitude was that I wasn't going to let this little Frenchman beat me down," Bergey said. "I'll hang with it. He won't break me."

This is how he would locate some eager newcomers, like Hairston. "I knew I had to have good work habits and practice hard every day," Hairston said. "What really helped was working against the older offensive linemen. I'd jump in when they lined up, because I knew the coaches would be looking."

Hairston made a mark in the full-contract drills, winning skirmishes with the older guys. "He stood out right away, his ability to butt and take on a run block," Vermeil said. "He had a strong pop. He just exploded into a guy. He disengaged instantly. He was great in pursuit."

But such performance took all he had. The morning practices typically left Hairston too tired to eat lunch. He crawled back into his dorm bed and took a nap before the afternoon's torture began. About three weeks into his first camp, Hairston neared his own breaking point. On the practice field, Vermeil accosted him. "You've got no chance in hell of making this football team," he yelled.

Hairston mulled that over for a while. If he had no chance, why was he killing himself twice a day in this heat? But Vermeil had pushed his pride button. Like Bergey, he resolved not to buckle. So as the wannabes fell by the wayside, Hairston battled on. And Vermeil never backed off.

"They don't take Marines and train them on a beach with ice cream in their hands and then tell them to fight," Vermeil explained. The way he figured it, every play in a football game features 11 individual wars. He wanted each Eagle to be prepared for that war. He demanded that they play with desperation. He saw no other choice, because rebuilding the Eagles would be an epic project.

The franchise had not enjoyed a winning season since 1966. Coming off a 4-10 debacle that got coach Mike McCormack fired, the Eagles needed new leadership at every level. The team had made many disastrously short-sighted moves in the 1970s, including spending receiver Harold Jackson and two first-round draft picks to acquire quarterback Roman Gabriel in the very twilight of his career.

The Eagles spent another first-round pick for Mike Boryla, who, as it turned out, was definitely not their quarterback of the future. An increasingly desperate McCormack had decided to forsake the future, ala George Allen with the Washington Redskins, and shoot for short-term success. He missed. The Eagles football men took to gambling with personnel the way owner Leonard Tose gambled in Atlantic City, and the results were just as disastrous.

"When I got there, all they had done was lose," Vermeil said. "(Tose) kept firing coaches. He'd fire the coach in the middle of the season. Fire the general manager. He's a very volatile guy. And as I moved around the community, he wasn't very popular. Nobody's popular when you lose with the Eagles. Everybody is guilty."

Although McCormack left Vermeil with a decent core of talent, led by respected veterans like Bergey, Bunting and offensive lineman Stan Walters, the Eagles lacked depth. And how could Vermeil rebuild that depth without high draft picks, which had been lost in ill-advised trades?

Vermeil realized he might need several years to turn the program around. The Eagles had to rebuild the organization from scratch and rebuild some players from scratch, too. To do this, Vermeil would need a relentless staff. Although the bulk of his UCLA coaches elected to stay in the college ranks—the Bruins replaced Vermeil with young assistant coach Terry Donahue—he lured Peterson to Philadelphia to assist in this project.

"It may have been as bad as any situation in the last 40 or 50 years," said Peterson, who spent his first Eagles season as an assistant coach before moving up to administrative aide and then personnel director. "The future wasn't very bright. We did not have first or second draft choices for the first three years we were there and we did not have a third-round choice for the first two years we were there. In our first draft, our first pick was in the fourth round. It was a very ugly situation. They were beat up, they were down. Talk about a losing attitude, there was a lot to overcome."

Vermeil's right-hand man at UCLA, Lynn Stiles, also agreed to join the Eagles' crusade. But before Stiles could settle in, San Jose State offered him its head coaching job and he grabbed it. "I knew it was going to be a tough road there," said Stiles, who eventually returned to Vermeil's staff in 1979. "Dick had to battle, because he couldn't just go out and get players in that situation because they didn't have any draft picks. It was really the cesspool of the NFL."

That first staff also included Johnny Roland, Chuck Clausen, Dick Coury, Bill Davis, John Idzik, Ken Iman, Duane Putnam and John Mazur. It was not unusual for the staff to work well past midnight preparing for the next morning's practice. Nobody ever got a good night's sleep.

"In the old days, you didn't have videotape," Vermeil said. "Everything was film and you had to wait for that to be developed. We didn't advance plan as many practices. We went more day to day, so that always took time, and then the film would get there from the afternoon practice and you stay up and watch all the film. It would be 2 or 3 in the morning every day."

Even during the day before preseason games, the Eagles fought through a full-contact practice in the morning and a full practice, minus the pads, in the afternoon. Those Eagles that managed to survive the first training camp felt compelled to celebrate. Never had they paid such a price on the practice field. The veterans who met the challenge demanded a party, so Bergey brought the proposal to the new coach.

"Just try to end it by midnight," Vermeil said.

"Coach," Bergey said, "that's when we were planning on starting the party."

Vermeil shrugged, figuring the players would learn their lesson soon enough.

The Eagles carried on all night, then straggled onto the practice field the next day reeking of alcohol. Vermeil knew his troops were a bit ragged, but he couldn't tolerate a ragged practice.

"How was the party last night?" he asked Bergey.

"It was really good, coach," the linebacker said.

"Good, Bill, because now we're going to have a really good practice."

He showed no sympathy toward the hungover, running the pitiable

Eagles for about four hours in the heat. The players regretted every last ounce of their overindulgence. With drill after drill, Vermeil reminded the players of the new reality in Philadelphia. Mediocrity would not be tolerated. The urgency to improve would be felt every single day of work. There would be no days off after celebrations. The players had to show up every single day ready to go.

"We paid for it," Bergey said. "Dick never mentioned it again, and we never had another training camp party."

The tone was set for the program. Vermeil was not going to back off, not ever. Walters engaged his coach on this topic one time and got nowhere with his plea.

"We're killing ourselves in practice," Walters complained to his coach.

"I'm looking for the last five players on the team," Vermeil said.

This, Walters believed, was madness. "He's killing the first 40 to find the last five," he thought to himself.

"It didn't make sense," Walters recalled. "Now, looking back, if you're running any business, you have to make sure that weakest link is strong."

Vermeil was convinced that hard work could solve just about any problem. The long hours he served at UCLA wouldn't be enough in Philadelphia. He would have put in longer hours still. Hanging in the Eagles locker room was this sign: "THE BEST WAY TO KILL TIME IS TO WORK IT TO DEATH."

Hanging in his coaching office was a photograph of Allen, whose preoccupation with football—and every minute aspect of his operation—bordered on insanity. Next to the picture was a note from Allen: "You have prepared yourself well. You are a winner."

Defensive lineman Manny Sistrunk came to the Eagles in 1976 from the Washington Redskins, where he played for Allen. Naturally, folks wondered how these two strong-willed coaches compared. "George tried to outsmart the other teams and concentrated on having no mistakes," Sistrunk said. "Dick believes in hard work to make up for mistakes. He works us a whole lot harder than George did with the Redskins."

Vermeil cherished the advice Allen gave him when he took the job. "Do it your way," Allen told him, "because you're going to get fired anyway. If you do it somebody else's way or are influenced too heavily by some other group or individual and lose, you're going to be upset with yourself because you didn't do it your way."

So he did it his way. Vermeil tried to manage every small aspect of the operation. Everything had to be just right, even if he had to make it right himself. He could not compromise. He tended to every detail at Hillsdale High School and Napa College—and that trait stuck with him as he climbed the coaching ranks.

"When I got to the NFL, I wanted to call every play and make every decision," Vermeil said. "I wanted to run the offense and coach the quarterbacks."

This proved incredibly time-consuming, since Vermeil was a perfectionist. "If the average man works 48 hours a week, the average NFL coach works 96," he said at the time. "To gain an edge, you go to extremes."

To the chagrin of his assistant coaches, Vermeil seemed to get his second wind after dark . . . and still had plenty left after midnight. In time, Vermeil would give up trying to commute to his suburban Philadelphia home during the week in the regular season. He wasn't trying to be a hero; he was just using common sense. The commute back and forth to his home would eat up 90 minutes. That's 90 fewer minutes he would have to sleep . . . or work some more.

He toiled into the early morning hours, so Carol would be sound asleep anyway when he got home. What was the point of making the drive? Even if Vermeil would have gone home, there would have been no time for idle chit-chat over coffee in the morning. So Vermeil slept in a hotel across the street from Veterans Stadium. When he realized that ate up too many minutes, he just started sleeping in his office. He could pick up another half hour of work time.

Over the years, one feature writer after another romanticized Vermeil's work ethic. His image as the hardest working man in football created some backlash from his peers. What were the other NFL coaches doing at this time, cutting out early to go bowling?

"Vermeil got under my skin by making a big deal of sleeping at the stadium and saying that he worked 16 hours a day," Dallas Cowboys general manager Tex Schramm would say later during Vermeil's tenure in Philadelphia. "I know what other coaches do and they just don't talk about it."

Vermeil reminded reporters that he was merely following the lead of his mentors. "I've worked for a lot of coaches, George Allen, Chuck Knox, John Ralston, Leeman Bennett, and they all worked hard," Vermeil said at the time. "They just don't admit it."

Vermeil started every day by drawing up his "to do" list for the next 24 hours. He drew up similar lists for Carol to follow at home and for his personnel guys in the office. Like Allen, he thought about little else but his team during the fall. He began carrying a pocket tape recorder everywhere he went in case a new stratagem popped into his head. He kept one near his bed or his office couch, in case he awoke with a new idea.

"During the season I can't think about anything but football," he explained. "Am I obsessed with winning? Absolutely."

Once the real games began, there was no respite for the Eagles. They went full-tilt in practice, full contact in full gear. The Eagles didn't stage two-a-day practices—not with all that classroom work to do in preparation for the game—but their regimen was grueling nonetheless. Those veterans who didn't bail out in the first training camp began to buy into the program. They were tired of losing. They were weary of serving as a doormat for the rest of the league. They didn't enjoy hearing the jeers in public.

"Everyone, players and fans, had hit such a low point, that you were hoping Vermeil could get the job done," Walters said. "Nobody even had a wait-and-see attitude. We had to get out of this rut."

Perhaps the Eagles really could outwork their rivals. Their new coach was restoring their pride. He was making them believe in themselves again. Each completed week was an accomplishment, a verification of their manhood. The surviving players kept meeting the challenge.

The victories were coming Monday through Saturday, if not on Sundays. Vermeil's tenure began on a painful note, with the Eagles absorbing the first of many beatings from the Dallas Cowboys, 27-7. They bounced back to defeat the New York Giants 20-7, then they played Washington into overtime before losing 20-17. In their fourth game, they squeezed out a 14-13 victory over Atlanta to even their record at 2-2.

Then reality hit. Their schedule was murderous, featuring nine winning teams, including that season's Super Bowl combatants Oakland and Minnesota. The Eagles lost eight of their last 10 games during Vermeil's initial season. During a span of four late-season losses, they scored just 17 points. Boryla wasn't getting much done at quarterback, despite having the 6-foot, 8-inch Harold Carmichael to throw to. The Eagles didn't score more than 20 points in a game until their season finale against the expansion Seattle Seahawks.

Sundays were bleak in Philadelphia. Jaded fans heaped abuse on their energetic new coach, ending the honeymoon. Fans gathered behind the team's bench and waved dog bones at the players. Veterans Stadium was a brutal workplace. At one point, Vermeil nearly went into the stands after hecklers.

"I wasn't used to being called a 'dumb ass,' of being told, 'Why don't you go back to UCLA where you came from!'" Vermeil said. "When I heard that and saw this guy, I jumped into the stands and started to go after him."

Fortunately, he was subdued by former Eagle great Chuck Bednarik before the situation got out of hand.

Progress that season came on a less tangible level. The team had a better mindset and a greater work ethic, if not a better record.

"We didn't win one more game than we did the year before," Bunting said. "We were the same. But people knew something was happening. Because we played hard for 60 minutes instead of half the time."

Unwilling veterans exited, creating room for hungry youngsters. Talent didn't interest Vermeil as much as attitude in those early days. Players who wouldn't go full tilt were replaced, regardless of their skill. He focused on hearts and minds. He could add faster legs and stronger arms later.

Back then, there was no salary cap, so there were no repercussions for axing somebody who had signed for big money. Cleaning house was a much simpler process. Players either met the challenge or they left. They either conformed or got cashiered. No player kept his job for economic reasons. Everybody had to earn his place on his team.

"He was going to break us down as much as possible and pick us up in his own way," Bergey said. "Right from the start, he was a very demanding coach. The players we had then resented it; they didn't want to work. But he kept saying, 'This is the way we're going to do it.' He wanted to instill discipline from the first day he arrived."

He believed he could add the right players once the framework was in place. Running back Wilbert Montgomery arrived for Year 2 of the Vermeil regime as a sixth-round draft pick out of little Abilene Christian in Texas. He was exactly what Vermeil was looking for, another overlooked small-college battler who was willing to pay the steep price needed to win. But the reticent Montgomery was overwhelmed at first, so much so that he kept a suitcase packed at his first training camp, waiting to get cut and sent home.

On the other hand, cornerback Herman Edwards, who arrived as an undrafted free-agent in 1977, provided the instant impact sought for the Eagles' secondary. Edwards' lack of speed made him suspect in the eyes of some NFLscouts, but Vermeil loved his work ethic and his self-assured personality. While at UCLA, he had tried, and failed, to lure Edwards to Westwood

Vermeil went after Edwards again once his college career was over. Since the Eagles didn't have any high draft picks, they had to find good young talent wherever they could. Peterson had always liked Edwards and was eager to sign him before another NFL club did.

So, after Edwards made a visit to Miami, Peterson put the full press on. He flew to San Diego and intercepted Edwards has he arrived home from the Dolphins look-see. Peterson made the same sort of recruiting pitch he made time and again at UCLA.

He coaxed Edwards into flying back to Philadelphia immediately to meet with Vermeil and the Eagles staff. Peterson bought Edwards a first-class ticket so he could join him at the head of the jet and talk football. Peterson talked up Vermeil's plans and how Edwards could become a cornerstone for the rebuilding program.

"All I wanted to do was sleep because I'm tired from flying all over the country," Edwards said.

After a two-day mini-camp, a suitably impressed Edwards signed and flew back to San Diego. He didn't check the ticket the team provided him. When he got to the airport, he went to his scheduled flight and looked for his seat in the first-class section.

"But they tell me, 'No, son, you're in the back, in row 28. I'm like, 'What happened?'" Edwards said.

Every Eagles camp under Vermeil would be the same: Merciless.

As soon as he got him, Edwards phoned Peterson to report the travel snafu. Peterson told him there was no snafu. "Recruiting's over," Peterson told him. "Now you're a player."

There was no chance that Edwards would turn soft on the Eagles. He brought the fiercely competitive temperament the Eagles needed. During one memorable practice, the offense sent four deep passes in row his way. Finally, Edward had seen enough and let the offensive unit know about it.

"Keep it coming guys," Edwards yelled defiantly. "Keep throwing my way."

None of the passes were completed. Edwards would never have to speak up during practice again. "I was just a free-agent guy, but I had lots of confidence," Edwards said.

After his first week of practice, Edwards walked up to Carl Peterson. "If I don't make this team and start," he said, "you should cut me. I don't just want to play special teams."

Peterson was taken aback. "You're kidding," he said.

"I'm not kidding," Edwards said.

The Eagles also acquired quarterback Ron Jaworski from the Rams. Vermeil had worked with him in Los Angeles, when Jaworski was a raw, deep-throwing rookie from little Youngstown State. He believed he could become a quarterback worth building around, unlike Boryla. Jaworski had started just nine games in four years in L.A., so he would have to grow into the job as the Eagles grew. But Vermeil was fascinated by his potential and he was weary of wrangling with Boryla.

Vermeil knew exactly what he wanted from his next quarterback. "A real competitive guy," he explained. "Mentally and physically tough. He establishes rapport with people quickly and assumes responsibilities."

The 1977 training camp was a duplicate of the '76 camp. When Edwards arrived, there were 21 other defensive backs bidding for work. The team needed only seven or eight.

"You have to remember, today, you have maybe 80 guys in camp," Edwards said. "Back then, we would have 120 guys come out, and Dick would make them run the first day just to chase off a few guys. After a day or two, 30 or 40 guys would quit. Back then with Philly, it was like the Marines."

Every Eagles camp under Vermeil would be the same: Merciless. In each camp, tempers would flare as the hitting got harder. Once the sessions got up to top speed, all hell broke lose.

"After about the second or third day of practice," Hairston said, "fights broke out all over the place. The thing about Vermeil, he'd jump right in the middle of guys and try to break them up. Dick (seems like) 5-foot-3 at the most, and he'd jump in between guys and all you could see was guys swinging over the top of his head. Lem Burnham and Stan Walters fought every day. Every single day. We'd just wait for it to happen."

To amuse themselves, the players made small wagers on when exactly the fights would break out. "It might be in one-on-one pass rush," Hairston said. "It might be on 9-on-7. I might be in 'team' (scrimmage). But we knew Lem Burnham and Stan Walters were going to fight."

At one point during this camp Vermeil became so agitated that he blew his whistle, called the team together and informed them that were staring the whole session over again, right from the stretching. The Eagles were an hour into the practice, so they would be on the field for four hours.

The competition to make the team was savage enough to keep most campers on edge. Edwards will never forget the morning he learned he made the team. After the final preseason game, he waited for "The Turk," the Eagles staffer that notified players to bring their play book to the coach's office. At this camp, "The Turk" slipped written notification under the door of the player's dormitory at shortly after 4:30 a.m.

"I used to wake up at 4:30 and I'd listen for that," Edwards said. "You'd always know when a paper was slipped under somebody's door. You can hear a lot at 4:30 in the morning."

On this morning, a paper slid into the room housing Edwards and roommate Skip Sharp, a fifth-round draft pick. Edwards sat the edge of his bed, staring at the paper and Sharp slept sound. Finally, he mustered the courage to look at it. Sharp was the one going home.

Edwards couldn't believe it. Sharp, after all, was the highest draft pick in camp. So Edwards got dressed and ran down to the locker room, which was about a half mile away. "I was thinking, 'Maybe they made a mistake,'" he said. He entered the locker room at 5 a.m. and saw that his name was still above the locker and his gear was still in it. Edwards had made the cut. He started the first game he played and quickly became a team leader.

"He was a student," Vermeil said. "He worked at it physically, mentally and emotionally very, very hard. His teammates respected him. He was a good communicator. He was a great practice guy, a great after-practice guy, a great before-practice guy, a great meeting guy and a great team guy."

There were no quick fixes back in the 1970s. Bad teams couldn't lure proven players from top teams with big free-agent contracts. And the Eagles were still a few years away from having a full set of draft picks again. So they had to redouble their efforts if they were going to get better.

"We had a different kind of free agency in the 1970s," Montgomery said. "Those free agents were reject players. So Dick felt the only way we could win was through hard work. If we didn't make mistakes, we would be the better-conditioned team. We'd win the fourth quarter."

Vermeil never let up, not even the day before games. In today's NFL, the day before a game, teams walk through some strategic points in gym shorts while trying to visualize how the game plan will play out. But the day before a game was just another full practice day for Vermeil. On Saturday, the players strapped on the shoulder pads, put on their helmets and went to work.

"Everything was high tempo," Montgomery said. "What he called light tempo was like a cheetah trying to catch his prey. It was all out."

When Peterson moved up from the coaching staff into an administrative role in 1977, he began hearing from the weary Eagles. Carl seemed like such a reasonable guy. Couldn't he convince Vermeil to tone it down a notch? Walters, Bergey, Carmichael and the others would complain that Vermeil was wearing them down and shortening their careers.

The pleas were always the same. So was the response: There was no point debating the matter with Vermeil. There was still too much work to be done.

The 1977 season brought much better efforts, but only marginally improved results. Many bad things happened, like a 17-14 loss to the Redskins that featured three missed field goals by Horst Muhlmann and a blocked Spike Jones punt that handed Washington the tying touchdown. Muhlmann's third miss, from 31 yards out with 22 seconds left, would have forced overtime. It, like the others, was swept away by a sudden gust of wind. Clearly the football gods were toying with the Eagles.

But at least some progress was being made. The Eagles finished that season with two victories at home, 17-14 over the New York Giants and 27-0 over the New York Jets, to improve their record to 5-9. Vermeil finally turned his rookie running back loose during the last two games of the season.

"The coaches were banging on my ear to play him, play him," Vermeil said. "I wouldn't play him because I didn't think he was quite ready. So, he returned the opening kick for a touchdown. Then he went in the last two games and went over 100 yards rushing. All of a sudden, we won the last two."

Jaworski made plenty of mistakes in 1977, but he was fearless. He loved throwing the ball downfield and taking shots at the secondary. He didn't cower after suffering interceptions. He played with a broken thumb and made no excuses about the decline of his passing skills. That's what convinced the coaches that he could be special. He remained confident and resilient through a trying season.

New defensive coordinator Marion Campbell switched the 4-3 defensive scheme to a 3-4, which better suited the team's limitations on the line. Finding defensive ends that could both stuff the run and rush the passer was difficult. The 3-4 allowed the Eagles to get by with three run-stoppers on the line, since the pass pressure could come from the linebackers.

"It's easier to find 220-pound linebackers than it is superior defensive linemen," Vermeil said. "It's also easier to play pass defense."

Skeptics regarded the "30" defense as a college scheme, one that couldn't work in the NFL. Only a few pro teams used it. But the four-linebacker set kept the Eagles competitive. The Eagles could keep almost any game close. "The defense could keep them down," Vermeil said. "We just couldn't score. We couldn't score against a wind storm."

Opponents began noticing a large and painful difference with this team. "They beat you up," Dallas Cowboys linebacker Thomas "Hollywood" Henderson observed, "but they don't beat you."

The Eagles were building character and gaining confidence through the competitiveness of the games. They knew they were winning a lot of one-on-one battles on the field. They could see the respect they were gaining from their opponents across the line.

"That's the strongest memory I have of that 5-9 season," Walters said a few years later. "It was the year that built this team, the camaraderie, the spirit and a certain toughness. Out of the nine losses, we were leading in seven of them in the third quarter. We'd play our hearts out, but the other team's talent would win in the end. I'd look around the locker room and see my teammates totally spent. Eyes sunk back in their heads. We'd lost another close one."

Vermeil's response was always the same. He told the players to keep their heads up and to battle on.

"And we did," Walters said. "Talk about a team that could have been demoralized fast. But every game we were in it. That was a nice feeling. Players on other teams knew we were coming on, if nobody else did. You'd see our special teams running down the field. Just flying. Then the other teams, with their talent and speed, would catch up and knock 'em all over the place. And our guys would get up and go again. We'd have guys get blocked three times on the same play. It might not have looked good, but we had people trying. And caring."

Jaworski earned more and more responsibility from Vermeil. He repaid this faith by putting in coaching-like hours while preparing for games. He could sense the turnaround coming and he wanted to help lead it. He would leave the stadium at 5:30 p.m. most days and head home for dinner. Then he would retire to his home office and pop some more film into his projector. He knew that Vermeil would be calling at 11:15 or 11:30 to go over what he saw in the films.

Vermeil was thrilled to have a quarterback who took his job as seriously as Jaws did. He and Boryla had clashed. Gabriel, the old pro, was literally on his last legs. Jaworski was the future and he was willing to put in the hours required to learn.

"He has a very good football head," Vermeil said during that season. "Nothing is complicated to him football-wise. He's always thinking football. It's his whole life. He's not a guy thinking about getting a law degree. To some guys, football is a way to make a lot of money, a good living quickly. They enjoy doing it, but they picture themselves doing something else as quickly as they can."

Hard work became a year-round objective of the Vermeil program. The Eagles became a pioneer in between-seasons conditioning. When Vermeil arrived, only seven Eagles lived in the Philadelphia area all year. So the team began paying incentives to players that stayed in the area and lifted weights with their teammates. Few other teams did that.

"We demanded the players raise their level of off-season work," Peterson said. "We worked on improving facilities and worked closer with the players individually. What happens is, you start getting a few new players, and then a few more and soon, a player not taking part feels like he's on the outside looking in."

The Eagles were learning how to become as meticulous as their coach. This wasn't easy, because Vermeil seldom left a loose end lying behind. One time, a blizzard hit the Philadelphia area, and Vermeil couldn't work his team outdoors. So, he took the Eagles by bus to suburban Widener College and arranged to run some drills in the school's gymnasium.

Trouble was, the gymnasium wasn't exactly ready to hold a football practice. When the players arrived, desks were arranged on the floor for students to take their final examinations. Vermeil didn't flinch.

"Men take your pads off, we have to move the desks back," he told the team.

So the Eagles moved the desks to the side so they could get a 90-minute practice in. When they were done, they were headed for the bus when Vermeil stopped them.

"Oh, no," he said. "We have to move the desks back."

The players grumbled.

"I'm like, 'You got to be kidding me,'" Edwards said. "And he wants them straight like they were. We're lining desks up. By then, we're all laughing. Everybody did it. There wasn't one guy who didn't move a desk or help. We're weren't mad at the guy. That was Dick. That's what he did. And you loved the guy."

In time, Edwards would strive to emulate Vermeil's thoroughness. He sought to lengthen his own attention span. To train himself to be more methodical, he began assembling toy military models. For him, assembling these models provided the same foundation that garage work gave Vermeil.

"The tediousness of building models and putting those little pieces together with such detail, painting every eyebrow on every soldier, helped my attention to detail," Edwards said. "I never thought of building models when I was a child. But for two years as a player, I did. I'd start a project and tell myself, 'Don't quit, don't stop until it's done right.'"

Such was the impact Vermeil had on his players. They ultimately respected the fact Vermeil pushed himself as much as he pushed them. They knew he was trying to give them every opportunity to succeed. "You see he's working hard, so it makes everybody want to work harder," Carmichael said. "And the way we work harder brings everybody together. We know we're in it together. We might as well be one, do it as one."

Vermeil pushed himself to physical extremes. He hadn't changed a bit since his days at UCLA, when he literally ran his staff ragged. Just as he set aside time for his daily conditioning run while coaching the Bruins, he made his daily run with the Eagles. Players that tried to run with him couldn't keep up. They watched him run laps around Veterans Stadium and shook their heads. He ran the first mile in a certain time and the last mile in a certain time, every time. Why didn't he just give it up and get a pot belly like most other coaches?

"He would work himself to death," Montgomery said. "Coach Vermeil would have shin splints from all that running, and it wouldn't make any difference to him. I believe that that leg, from running with the shin splints, still bothers him from all the pounding."

Vermeil was also willing to pay a personal price for success. Later in his Eagles regime, he wouldn't even pull himself away from his work to celebrate Christmas. He suggested putting a Christmas tree in his office and having the family come there to open gifts. Instead, the Vermeils chose to celebrate the holiday later, once the Eagles were finished playing.

Later in life, Vermeil would regret ignoring domestic matters to concentrate on football. But during his run in Philadelphia, it was the only way he knew how to operate. Carol and the kids would have to live their lives without him in the late summer, fall and early winter.

Nancy and David moved to the Philadelphia area with Dick and Carol, but Rick originally stayed behind in California. He went to a junior college and UCLA, then he left and came back to Villanova. David also went to Villanova and Nancy attended Penn State. Pennsylvania would become the Vermeils' home.

With the kids heading their way and Dick tied up at the office, Carol was often on her own. "It gets lonely and I get the blues," Carol said during a 1977 interview. "I wouldn't be human if I didn't. But as Dick progressed in his career, I resolved it within myself that I had to share him with the team and with the public."

Her ability to accept Dick's schedule prompted Eagles assistant coach Bill MacPherson to nickname her "St. Carol." She allowed him to be a workaholic and maintain some semblance of a family life, too. She knew her husband was going to plow on, regardless of the strain his job placed on his family. He was a coach, after all, and he only knew one way to do his job.

"I've got three kids in college now and I passed up a lot of time with them," he said later in his Eagles tenure. "Instead, I invested it with other people's kids. Deep down, it's hard for me to justify that. But from the point of satisfaction, it's been worth it. I'm a driven guy. I need to know that I've done a good job, given myself every opportunity to succeed. If I had to do it all over again, I'm sure I'd think about what I was doing. But I might do it the same way."

# CHAPTER FOUR
# CARING

*"He makes you happy to win. That's what football is all about."*
—Former Philadelphia Eagles running back Louie Giammona

They were coming. The Eagles knew it and Dick Vermeil knew it. But when? When would Vermeil's tears start to flow? That element of the unknown brought some intrigue to Vermeil's team addresses the night before big games, especially games against the Dallas Cowboys. Eagles veterans turned these speeches into a game.

Herman Edwards, Claude Humphrey and Carl Hairston would sit in the back of the meeting rooms on Saturday nights wagering desserts on just when their coach would show his affection for them. "If" was not the question. "When" was the issue. The currency of choice was pie a la modes.

"I bet you two pie a la modes that within five minutes it's going to happen," Hairston or Humphrey would say.

"You guys are crazy," Edwards would reply.

And sure enough, within five minutes, Vermeil's eyes would be welling up with moisture.

"Any time a player was getting an award, you knew it," Edwards said. "The pie a la modes were getting bet."

Such outpourings of emotion became routine as he grew closer to his team. This was the flip side to Vermeil's personality, the softer side that inevitably caught the new players off guard. The same coach who subjected his players to cruel and unusual practices also loved them like they were his sons. The same coach that would run his players ragged during training camp, causing them to lose all control of the bodily functions, would also have them over to the house for a party.

"You could go back to any of his ex-players in Philadelphia, and not one guy would say they hated him," Wilbert Montgomery said. "We believed in him. We'd go to parties at his house and he'd come to our house. It was a family-type relationship."

Edwards was immediately taken by this. He had bounced around from the University of California to Monterrey Peninsula Junior College to San Diego State during his college career, but Philadelphia would become his football home.

"He had a big influence on me as a player right away on how he responded to players, to me, off the field and on the field, and how he created a family atmosphere, somewhat of a college atmosphere in Philadelphia," Edwards said. "He was close to his players. He came into the league at a time when that was not the thing to do. But he came out of a college atmosphere and he created that atmosphere in Philadelphia."

Veterans like Bill Bergey responded, too. His first coach in the league had been the taciturn Paul Brown. "There wasn't any contact between him and us that was not football related," Bergey said. "He's a guy we could never get close to."

Once an Eagle passed muster, Vermeil sought to build a stronger relationship with that player. He conversed with him about his life, his upbringing, his family and his expectations. He asked how he was doing off the field. Perhaps he would have him over to his home for dinner. Maybe he'd throw some steaks on the grill and Carol would bake a cake, just as she did for Dick's high school football players and swimmers.

How could he motivate a player if he didn't know his dreams and his fears?

"The thing about Dick is that he doesn't coach everybody the same way," Bergey said. "Some players he had to chew out. Others, he'd pamper a little bit. Some, he wouldn't say anything to. But he had the unique, innate ability to relate to all kinds of personalities. That's really pretty special in a coach."

There was no façade with Vermeil. When the Eagles acquired quarterback Ron Jaworski from the Rams in 1977, Vermeil asked Ron and his wife fly in for a visit. Rather than go to a four-star restaurant, Vermeil took the Jaworskis to a decidedly blue-collar institution in South Philly, The Triangle restaurant.

"We don't go to the Le Bec-Fin or one of those highfalutin' places," Jaworski said. "We go to The Triangle. That's the kind of guy Dick is. He wanted me to see what the real Philadelphia was all about. And at the same time, it was his way of showing us what he was all about."

Vermeil was the same coach who would toss his car keys to a Hillsdale High player who needed to run home for something he forgot. He was the same coach who knew what his UCLA recruits did on their last high school history test. He was trying to inspire people, not football players.

"I don't think I've ever changed my philosophy on how to coach since high school," Vermeil said. "You're still working with people. A lot of these guys in the NFL are still kids, just with more money. The basic things that people need to excel exist at 26 just like 16."

He refused to believe that the NFL was just a mercenary league, as his colleagues had warned him when he left the college ranks for good. He still believed they played for the love of the game, not the opportunity to make money.

When his players started to learn, evolve and succeed, he gushed with pride. With the gushes came hugs and tears. In return, the players came to believe in themselves, their coach and the program. Football, to Vermeil, wasn't a series of games. It was a crusade. It was winning over hearts and minds. That's what drew him into coaching and that's what drove him to the highest levels.

"As athletes, we all want to achieve something for ourselves," Bergey said. "But with Dick, you go way beyond that. You play for 'The Cause.' That's why our teams played so well in the fourth quarter. We could reach down for something extra, something that other teams did not have. We had it because Dick helped put it there."

Once the Eagles embraced this cause, the players began to take on even more work than Vermeil gave them. For instance, John Bunting began convening off-hours meetings for the linebacker corps after Wednesday practices. The players would gather for pizza and go over their assignments and challenges for the game ahead. They gathered even though they had spent all day either looking at game film or working on the practice field.

Because he cared so much, Vermeil was able to push his players so hard. The players didn't despise him. Some coaches make themselves a negative rallying point, inspiring their team to come together and win to spite them. Vermeil couldn't operate that way. He didn't believe in "creative tension" in his workplace.

Many coaches wrestle with how close they can get to their players. Can they become close to them and remain hard on them as well? Can they know them as people and yet handle them as business inventory? Many NFL coaches prefer to leave some emotional distance between them and their players. The personal interaction is often left to the position coaches that work more intimately with the players day after day during meetings and practices.

Jaworski played for all sorts of NFL head coaches during his career. He saw some try, in vain, to maintain a barrier between themselves and the troops. But NFL players and coaches spend so much time together that relationships invariably form. In most cases, players figure out that the coach really does care, even if he doesn't act like it.

Vermeil had a paternal influence on Jaworski, who relished the support he got from his coach. Jaworski is reminded of this whenever he watches the old Eagles highlight videos produced by NFL Films. In each video, it seems, Vermeil was recorded comforting him on the sidelines.

"Don't worry, I'm not going to jerk you," Vermeil tells Jaworski.

"You're my quarterback."

More than once, Vermeil started over toward the stands to confront Jaworski's hecklers at Veterans Stadium. Vermeil consistently expressed his support through the media, too, trying to keep the heat off Jaworski as he learned. He publicly chastised fans for giving the quarterback such a rough ride.

On the other hand, Vermeil would call Jaworski in the day after a bad game and tear apart his performance piece by painful piece. He held nothing back. After building a bond with his players, he tested that bond to make sure it was strong.

"Dick is the most forthright and honest person you'll ever find," Jaworski said. "He won't always tell you what you want to hear. He's going to tell you the truth. Now, some people don't want to hear the truth, they can take it the wrong way. But he's always been a guy who will tell you like it is."

This trait allowed him to draw a firm line on his players without losing them. He didn't play mind games with them, making them guess where they stood. "He showed me that you could be a disciplinarian, you could be hard, but you had to be fair to your players," Edwards said. "And if you were fair, and you constantly communicated with them, they trusted you. You trusted them. You could be successful."

This fairness often led to generosity. As Edwards became a top cornerback in the league, Vermeil tore up his contract and gave him a raise. Then he did it again two years later as Edwards continued to star.

Team morale was critical to Vermeil. He was always looking for new ways to nurture the team's camaraderie. As long as his team was progressing, he didn't stop his players when they blew off a little steam. He could laugh as easily as he cried or yelled.

During the 1978 season, the Eagles were getting a bit uptight with a big game against Dallas looming. So Bunting, sidelined by a knee injury at the time, decided to loosen things up. He donned sneakers, a vintage leather helmet and a jockstrap — and nothing else — and rode an electric cart onto the Veterans Stadium field for practice. It was freezing cold and snow was piled up on the sidelines, but Bunting was undaunted. He flew down the ramp at about 35 miles per hour. Bunting circled the field, waved to everybody, then drove back toward the locker room to stave off frostbite.

As the Eagles developed some character, Vermeil allowed the team to develop some character. A classic example was his nephew, Louie Giammona, the son of his sister Laura. Like Dick, Stan and Al, Louie wasn't a big guy but he had lots of heart.

At first, the Eagles were skeptical of Giammona. He was the coach's nephew, after all—although Louie swore he hardly saw him while growing up, since Dick was off coaching. Also, Giammona didn't look much like a NFL running back. So he resorted to mood-lightening pranks to win over his teammates. He did some extreme things to endear himself to the Eagles, like biting the head off a dead bird.

"These guys would ease the feelings of the team," Montgomery said. "We knew we were going to be on the field for four hours. How could we get through this? Someone would do something crazy to make you forget about the four-hour practice so you could relax and have fun."

Vermeil hated cutting players he admired, especially hustlers like special teams captain Vince Papale. This guy was the underdog's underdog. He had been a track star at St. Joseph's University. On a dare, Papale tried out for the Philadelphia Bell of the World Football League and made the team, despite lacking any football experience. Later he made the Eagles, against all odds, as a special teams hit man in 1976. He job was to run down field as fast as he could and pound the kick returner.

*After building a bond with his players, he tested that bond to make sure it was strong.*

A couple of summers later, Vermeil realized he no longer had a spot for Papale. On the day he planned to pink-slip him, Vermeil arrived at 6 a.m. and began pacing around the stadium parking lot. Papale personified his Eagles program. He was the ultimate long shot. He didn't have much skill, but he cheerfully sacrificed his body for the team.

"How can I do this?" Vermeil thought over and over as his tears flowed again.

He loved Papale and everything he stood for. In this case, he was able to ease his anguish by giving Papale another go-around when injuries created a special teams opening a few weeks later.

The combination of relentless work and believing in the cause paid off in 1978, when the Eagles finally began to become viable contenders in the league. After opening the season with two tough losses, 16-14 at home to the Los Angeles Rams and 35-30 at Washington, the Eagles won three consecutive games for the first time in Vermeil's tenure.

Turned loose during his second NFL season, Montgomery became a star. Vermeil just kept sending him into the line. The Eagles won games by controlling the ball and grinding down their opponents. Vermeil brought in former UCLA quarterback John Sciarra as a special teams player and even designed some veer-type option plays for him to run, in case he decided to take his run-first philosophy to an unprecedented level.

The Eagles were boring, but Vermeil didn't apologize for the absence of entertainment value. He was conservative because he believed a careful approach gave his team its best chance to win. Why should he gamble when solid football won games? So Jaworski kept handing the ball to Montgomery, who would gain 1,220 yards on 259 carries that season.

After the three-game winning streak, the Eagles lost three of their next four games. That included a 24-14 loss at New England to a powerful Patriots team.

"Guys, we're playing a team that's better than we are," Vermeil told the team beforehand. "We really don't have a good a chance of winning today. As a matter of fact, if we played this bunch 10 times, we might beat them once. Guys, can you find that one way to beat them today?"

The Eagles couldn't, but they later put together their first four-game winning streak for Vermeil. In the midst of that run, they capitalized on one of the all-time blunders in league history on November 19.

The New York Giants led 17-12 late in the fourth quarter and simply had to run out the clock to win the game. The Eagles were out of timeouts. Play could not be stopped. The inevitable defeat would drop the Eagles to 6-6 on the season and greatly diminish their chances of making the playoffs. Jaworski went to the end of the bench and sulked.

But rather than merely instruct quarterback Joe Pisarcik to repeatedly take a knee, Giants offensive coordinator Bob Gibson sent in a running play for fullback Larry Csonka.

"I'm like, 'What?'" Pisarcik recalled.

The first play went like clockwork, with Csonka busting a nice gainer up the middle. When Pisarcik tried to take a knee on the next play, Eagles linebacker Frank LeMaster bowled over Giants center Jim Clack, who fell into his quarterback.

The teams scuffled after the whistle and the Giants coaches flinched. They didn't want to see Pisarcik get rolled over while taking a knee again. So Gibson switched up, going back to Csonka with the running play that opened the sequence. Pisarcik was puzzled.

"Man, why don't we just fall on it?" he thought.

That was the consensus in the huddle. No one was sure what was going on.

"Don't give me the football," Csonka told Pisarcik

The quarterback was tempted to overrule the call, "Pro Up 65," and just take a knee again, but he had been chastised the previous week for changing a play. So he followed orders. As the Giants got organized at the line of scrimmage, Edwards casually chatted with Giants running back Doug Kotar, who assured Edwards that his team would just fall on the ball.

Then Clack rushed his center snap with 31 seconds left in the game, catching Pisarcik off guard. Pisarcik didn't handle the ball cleanly, so as he turned he hit Csonka in the hip with the ball. It fell to ground.

Pisarcik tried to jump on the ball but it bounced up through his hands.

And then the incredulous Edwards arrived untouched to scoop up the ball at the Giants 26 and run into the end zone. Pisarcik sprawled on the field, closed his eyes and wished this fumble was just a dream. But it wasn't.

Vermeil wasn't surprised that the Giants decided to give the ball to Csonka, rather than simply taking a knee, but he was shocked to see the ball come loose. He joined his team's spontaneous celebration as Edwards crossed the goal line to give the Eagles a 19-17 victory.

And then he looked over to the Giants sideline. "As a coach you get really excited," Vermeil said, "but you can also say, 'Holy Cow, can you imagine how those guys feel on the other sidelines?'"

Not too good, as it turned out. Gibson would be fired the next day, effectively ending his football career. Head coach John McVay was fired after the season. But the Eagles were too busy moving forward to commiserate with their foes.

All those murderous training camp sessions, all those marathon game-week practices and of Vermeil's emotional pep talks were rewarded with an unbelievable stroke of luck. Edwards' touchdown would become a turning point for the franchise. The Eagles finally believed they were destined for better times.

Vermeil would often use this example to illustrate how good luck is often the result of preparation. He would note how defensive coordinator Marion Campbell had called an 11-man blitz, hoping to disrupt that fateful play. "We hadn't given up," Vermeil said. "That's why our right cornerback (Edwards) was in the backfield."

In the practice week that followed, Vermeil installed his "Herman Edwards play" for clock-killing situations. He placed a running back well behind the quarterback to play safety in case a bad snap caused the ball to pop loose. This would become the standard NFL formation for clock-killing situations.

Vermeil worked tirelessly to develop plans for every contingency. George Allen would be proud of him, but this commitment was starting to take a toll. Writing for Sports Illustrated, Gary Smith described what

Vermeil's life had become in Philadelphia:

*He set curfews for himself and broke them. He canceled vacations. He gulped coffee for breakfast, ate a Carnation Breakfast Bar for lunch and sometimes had a hoagie, while sitting on the toilet, for dinner. He'd try sleep - ing pills or hot chocolate or a glass of wine to get to sleep, and he'd still awaken wondering what Shula and Landry and Noll were doing. When he went home, his mind did not, and once dinner ended, he'd plug himself into stereo headphones and a Neil Diamond tape and collapse on the couch.*

But now he was getting results. The so-called "Miracle of the Meadowlands" lifted the Eagles spirits and helped them view themselves as a playoff contender.

"You never know what play's going to determine a game, so you finish each play like it's the one that's going to win the game or lose the game," Edwards said. "That's one of those things where being in the right place at the right time kind of lifted our team, propelled us to gain some confidence.

"I think the significance of the play was coach Vermeil inherited a football team that wasn't very good at that time. We were in a lot of close games our first year and we lost. We were 4-10. That next year, we were kinda floundering a little bit and we were always losing games at the end, and all of a sudden that play comes about, and I'm just in the right place at the right time. It's really significant how plays turn around your fortune."

The Eagles followed their fortuitous victory over the Giants with a 14-10 victory at St. Louis. A gut-wrenching 28-27 loss at Minnesota and a 31-13 flogging from the Cowboys put Philadelphia's playoffs hope in peril again. But in the final week of the season, they inflicted further punishment on the Giants, beating them at home, 20-3, to finish the season with a 9-7 record. Vermeil literally cried on Tose's shoulder.

"It's like a dream come true," he said, "just to be able to say we're winners."

They left Veterans Stadium unsure of their fate. They reported to Bookbinder's for the season-ending party, arranged in an upstairs room by the restaurant's owner. There, in the midst of their post-game revelry, they learned that circumstances fell their way. The right team won and the right team lost and they were in the playoffs as a wild-card team. At the height of this party, Vermeil donned Edwards' "Superfly" hat and danced with his players as the disco music pounded in the room.

He had done what he had set out to do, take a miserable, talent-poor franchise from the bottom of the NFL into post-season play. These Eagles should have stayed in the playoffs, too, but they blew a 13-0 lead over the Atlanta Falcons with five minutes to play. After the Falcons rallied with two touchdowns to take a 14-13 lead, Eagles kicker Mike Michel missed a 34-yard field goal with 13 seconds left.

Michel, a punter forced into kicking duties by Nick Mike-Mayer's injury, also missed an extra point and a 42-yard field goal earlier in the game. This is the same Mike Michel that had once whiffed on a punt, missing the football completely with his foot during a critical game against the Redskins.

"It's something I've got to live with all year," Michel said after this fiasco. "But I'll come back." Not as an Eagle, though. Vermeil has a big heart, but he can't tolerate egregious failure.

Despite the agonizing playoff demise, this was a hallmark season for the Eagles. Vermeil, the NFC's Coach of the Year, had proven that round-the-clock work and a touchy-feeling coaching style could pay off in pro football.

In the afterglow of this season, Bergey invited the Vermeils to his house for dinner. Midway through it, Dick welled up with tears. He told Bergey how touched he was. In all his years of coaching, a player had never invited him to his home for dinner before.

The 1979 season began with a crisis. Before the season began, Vermeil summarily dismissed running backs James Betterson and Mike Hogan when they were arrested on drug charges. His compassion had its limits.

"I had set down the rule long ago," Vermeil explained. "Even an association with drugs would not be tolerated. I hope they are both exonerated, but if I didn't do what I did, I'd be letting my team down." (The charges against Hogan were eventually dropped, and Hogan later returned to the team.)

He had done

what he had

set out to do,

take a miserable,

talent-poor

franchise from

the bottom of the

NFL into post-

season play.

Training camp was as tough as always. Just ask future Pittsburgh Steelers coach Bill Cowher, who tried to make that Eagles roster as a non-drafted linebacker.

"There were two-a-days and hitting both practices," Cowher recalled. "I made it to the last cut and, when I got cut, I wasn't sure if it wasn't a blessing in disguise because I felt like I had been through a whole season." Physically whipped, Cowher returned to college, earned his degree, did some more weight work and made the Cleveland Browns the following summer—after getting into that camp on an Eagles recommendation.

Vermeil didn't need any more underdogs in '79. He had a playoff-caliber team now. He had all the hard workers he needed, so set his sights on higher goals. To go deeper into the playoffs, the Eagles needed a more explosive offense. Vermeil decided to diversify the offense by granting creative license to new assistant coach Sid Gillman, perhaps the greatest passing guru the game has ever seen.

Some of Vermeil's colleagues wondered why he would summon a living legend to join the staff. Sid was literally old enough to be Vermeil's father; Dick was only six weeks older than Sid's oldest daughter. Wouldn't this undermine his authority? An insecure head coach might never have made that move, but Vermeil had no trouble sharing authority. He would count this hire as one of the smartest of his career.

"He became a coach's coach," Vermeil said. "He coached me. He coached my coaching staff. You can't always rely on having the best players."

Vermeil allowed Gillman to install a more daring passing attack during for that season. Gillman believed in throwing the deep pass to stretch out a defense, opening up the field for plays underneath. The pass could be used to open up the run; Vermeil always viewed offense as the run setting up the pass. He learned that axiom coaching under George Allen and Chuck Knox.

Gillman's arrival thrilled Jaworski. The Eagles offense would become less predictable. It would use more formations and get more potential receivers into the play. Jaworski would have more options—and the greater likelihood of catching a defense off-guard. And Gillman's influence on the head coach was just as exciting as the new play book.

Suddenly Vermeil embraced the value of a big-play passing attack. He trusted Gillman's vast experience, his legendary attention to detail and his ability to teach the game.

Gillman had compiled a famously comprehensive video library of the great quarterbacks executing every conceivable play. When Jaworski developed a problem that needed fixing, Gillman was able to show how the masters threw that particular type of pass or reacted to a particular defensive tactic.

Superior tactical preparation became a trademark of these Eagles teams. Vermeil's fanatical planning produced results and reinforced the staff's credibility with the players. His game plans were always dead on. That thoroughness made the workload more acceptable. The Eagles were reaping the fruits of their labor, just as their coach said they would.

"We didn't always agree with Dick's methods, but when we were celebrating victories on Sunday nights, we didn't complain," Jaworski said. "I never remember seeing a defense I wasn't completely prepared for. But everybody dreaded Mondays, even after we won."

Because Vermeil made them go right back to work. And no matter how well the Eagles played, their coaches had identified lots of things they did wrong. There was no let up on the team, even as the Eagles rolled to a 6-1 start in 1979.

They won a couple of tough games against the New York Giants, 23-17 and 17-13, and beat New Orleans, Pittsburgh, Washington and St. Louis in close games. Despite the improvements in the passing game, Montgomery remained the team's offensive staple. He would carry the ball an amazing 338 times and gain 1,512 yards in the 1979 season.

"Not to give the ball to Wilbert 25 or more times a game would be dumb coaching, like driving a car in second gear," Vermeil said. "Wilbert could go again on a Wednesday after playing on a Sunday. If I had another Wilbert, I'd have each run the ball 15 times."

A three-game losing streak, capped by a mistake-filled 24-19 loss to the Cleveland Browns, put the Eagles' post-season hopes in peril. Philadelphia had the game in hand until Montgomery fumbled not once, but twice as the Eagles were just trying to run out the last five minutes.

But then the Eagles got back on track, winning five of their last six games. The turnaround began with their first-ever victory in Texas Stadium, a 31-21 win over the Cowboys. Knowing how badly their coach wanted to beat the legendary Tom Landry, the Eagles gave Vermeil the game ball. Landry had owned the Eagles for a long, long time and had won his first six games against Vermeil. Naturally, Dick's tears flowed.

"You can't always rely on having the best players."

"This is the most meaningful thing that ever happened to me," Vermeil said. "We've been through some tough times the last few weeks, but now I think you will see us getting better and better and better."

That victory became a milestone for the Eagles, since Dallas was the franchise standing between them and title contention. Vermeil based his entire program on beating the Cowboys. Landry was the NFL's top coach. His team was "America's Team." Dallas set the standard that all organizations aspired to. Vermeil marveled at the Cowboys' discipline on game day, especially on defense.

So the Dallas victory was enormous. The Eagles had reached new heights. Their 21-10 victory at Green Bay lifted their record to 9-4 and gave them their first undisputed division lead in 19 seasons. They found the view breathtaking.

"The first-place thing is only temporary. There are three games left," Vermeil said after the Packers game. "But the fact a lot of people knocked us last year, said we were lucky to make the playoffs, said I was too conservative. Well, it's a year later and we're right back. We've won nine games in 13 weeks. Last year it took 16. I'll sleep pretty well tonight."

The next week, the Eagles clinched their playoff berth with a 44-7 demolition of the Detroit Lions. "I thought it would take five years for us to become competitors, but we darn near did eight years of hard work in four years," Vermeil said amid the post-game celebration.

The Eagles lost a tough game against Dallas, 24-17, but finished 11-5 after edging Houston, 26-20, to close out the season. Then they rallied to beat the Chicago Bears, 27-17, in the wild-card playoff game, their first home playoff game in 20 years.

Jaworski suffered a rocky start in this game, prompting Eagles fans to turn on him again and Vermeil to bristle. The fans chanted "We want Walton!" and clamored for back-up quarterback John Walton. Vermeil wondered why they couldn't believe what he and his players believed. Why couldn't they see this team's remarkable progress? He blasted them for their negative behavior.

"I said to myself, these fans have been losers for so long that they better not turn back to losers too soon, before the game is over," Vermeil said. "Some teams are losers because the fans are on them. It should be a lesson for them, too. We battled out of a hole just as they were turning on is."

The Tampa Bay Buccaneers finally stopped the Eagles run with a 24-17 victory in the divisional playoff game. Vermeil learned a hard lesson about game preparation during this loss.

He prided himself in his attention to detail, but he overlooked an obvious factor before this game. The Eagles had practiced in the freezing cold of Philadelphia all week. Then they went south and had to play in the heat. After the Eagles warmed up, Vermeil knew he had a crisis on his hands. He shared the bad news with one of his assistant coaches.

"Coach, we are in trouble," Vermeil said.

"Why?" the assistant asked.

"Look at these guys, they are wringing wet," Vermeil said. "They hadn't perspired in a month and they look exhausted."

And they were. The Eagles fell behind 17-0 before getting acclimated.

"We were not real sharp and not the football team we had the ability to be," Vermeil said. "We caught up with ourselves and started playing pretty well, but it was too late."

Once again, a kicking fiasco sealed the Eagles' fate. This time rookie placekicker Tony Franklin decided, on his own, to attempt an onside kick. He compounded that mistake by not sharing his decision with his teammates. Apparently, he wanted the element of surprise on his side.

"He was going to recover it himself and make a gallant effort to win the game on his own," and incredulous Vermeil said. "It didn't work."

With the Eagles sprinting downfield to cover the kickoff, the Buccaneers had no trouble recovering Franklin's little squib kick. Vermeil fined Franklin $1,600, a lot of money in those days, and labeled it tough love.

"I believe a guy profits from a mistake directly proportional to the aggravation he felt after he made it," the coach later explained.

But the Eagles knew they were contenders now and they roared into their 1980 training camp with confidence. Their esprit de corps was at an all-time high. The Eagles relished their image as NFL castoffs trying to make it big.

The inner core of this team was an exclusive club. Newcomers were subjected to a bit of hazing. The incumbents loved to pull pranks on the new guys, sabotaging equipment and leaving booby traps around the locker room.

"You have to prove yourself worthy," Giammona said. "Becoming an Eagle takes time. You can't become an Eagle in four days. It's tough on a newcomer. No one says much to you. If you're not a good guy, if you don't fit in, you don't stay here. I remember when Jerry Robinson joined us in 1979. He was an all-American at UCLA and our first draft choice. But he was injured early in training camp and didn't get the respect of the players until he started to play. The veterans won't take you in and say, 'We love you.' It's up to the new guy to become an Eagle. But when you become one, it's fun."

Coaches had much more flexibility in building rosters in that era, so Vermeil was able to add good people as well as good players to his mix. He was also able to jettison players that didn't blend into the team mix.

"There's a lot of ifs all over the place in this sport," he explained at the time. "We've been very philosophical in regard to new people on our roster. We try to evaluate them personally, as well as players. We want character people. There are a lot of people with ability. It's whether you get it done or not that counts. I've always believed that attitude is important, and I couldn't enjoy coaching if I didn't enjoy being around the people I'm working with. I've been credited with being a motivator, but I think I'm a better evaluator. The key is to keep the right kind of people. I had about 18 to 20 guys on that team that you could bet your life on."

Given the presence of so many character players, Vermeil could be ruthless on those job aspirants found lacking. During this camp, Vermeil cut a kid named Mike Siegel on the field for blowing his blocking assignments. Right in the middle of practice, Siegel got the short haircut.

"Get him out of here!" Vermeil screamed. "I can't stand him any longer."

Siegel left, all right, stripping off one piece of equipment after another on his way off the field. This was a classic Vermeil story, an anecdote that all his veterans love to share.

"He fired the guy on the field," Carl Hairston says. "We thought he was just joking, but Dick said, 'Turn your equipment in.'"

Years later, Vermeil winces while recalling that story. He had subsequently run into Siegel at a TGI Friday's, where he was tending bar. Vermeil bought a beer from him. "I was wrong in doing that," he said. "As I look at it today, I made a fool of myself. Hey, the kid was giving all he had."

The Eagles opened the 1980 season with lopsided victories over Denver (27-6), Minnesota (42-7) and the New York Giants (35-3). After the win over the Giants, as reporters assembled in a meeting room for Vermeil's post-game remarks, the coach turned to the blackboard behind him and wrote 32/31 on the board. Then he circled it, smiling. The Eagles had crossed the .500 barrier for his tenure. He now had a winning record as a NFL coach.

After a 24-14 loss to St. Louis, the Eagles regrouped with a 24-14 victory over Washington. The Eagles trailed the Giants 16-3 during their second meeting, but rallied for a 31-16 victory. Giammona, filling in for injured Montgomery, shook off a costly early fumble to score a pair of second-half touchdowns. Vermeil regarded this comeback as one of the hallmark games of his regime.

Philadelphia finally earned its first victory over Dallas at Veterans Stadium, 17-10. "I wish I could tell you how I feel, but I cannot," Vermeil. "This was our No. 1 goal of the season, to beat Dallas at home. Before you can be a champion, you have to beat a champion."

The victories kept coming: 17-14 over Chicago, 27-20 at Seattle and 34-21 at New Orleans. Before that game, he took precautions to keep his confident veterans from having too much pre-game fun in the French Quarter.

"I told this team if we couldn't do down there and beat (the Saints), then we weren't a division championship-caliber team," Vermeil recalled.

"I don't care about Bourbon Street or Whisky Street or the broads or the hookers. We had to win and get the job done."

Bergey assured reporters that Vermeil's detractors were long gone. Those still playing for the Eagles believed. The leadership base on the squad was wide. Grumbling was almost non-existent. A hard-fought 10-7 victory over the Oakland Raiders was the Eagles' 11th victory in their first 12 games. Vermeil had managed to fire up his troops with the time-honored "no respect" pitch. That's all the guys were talking about afterward.

That victory, however, exacted a terrible physical toll on the Eagles. Many players suffered contusions, sprain and bone chips. The team lost its legs during the next month and lost three of their last four games.

The Eagles backed into the NFC East title on the tiebreaker formula. But with the divisional crown finally in hand, Vermeil feted the nine players who had stuck with the franchise from those bleak days in 1976: LeMaster, Bunting, Carmichael, Bergey, Walters, Charlie Smith, Guy Morriss, Jerry Sisemore and Randy Logan.

"For me, it was great to walk around the locker room and call these people champions," he said. "They were here when people were calling them losers and bums and throwing bottles at them. To call them champions was the greatest satisfaction I've ever had as a coach."

It was so great, in fact, that he allowed himself to go home for the holidays to spend time with Carol and the rest of the family. "It's the first time we've won something that I can spend some time enjoying," Vermeil said. "I'm going to put the Christmas tree up tonight. To me, that's exciting."

From afar, Bill Walsh admired the work of his long-time friend. He was amazed that Vermeil was able to do so much with so little so quickly. He had willed a moribund franchise to greatness. "There are other great coaches, but they had great organizations around them," Walsh said. "Vermeil beat them with his own guts and a few people who followed him. Players of his that he bragged about, I wasn't that impressed with. He convinced himself and them that they were great."

The Eagles rallied from a 14-0 deficit to defeat the turnover-prone Minnesota Vikings, 31-16, in their divisional playoff game, setting up a showdown with the Cowboys in the NFC Championship.

During a news conference during the week before that NFC title game, Vermeil spoke glowingly of the progress his regime had made. "I question whether anybody in this room would have bet $50 that we would do this within our five-year program. I doubt even if I would have," he said. "I'm proud of what we've accomplished. But to come this far and not get it done would be a letdown."

He prepared the team maniacally, escaping the cold to practice outdoors in Tampa for four days leading up to the game. When the team returned to Philadelphia, it got a boisterous hero's welcome at the airport from a mob of Eagles fans. But Vermeil refused to let his team get ahead of itself. All week, he challenged his offensive linemen, calling them "a bunch of fat asses." He reminded them that their performance against Minnesota would not be sufficient to beat the Cowboys.

Walters said he and his fellow offensive linemen took Vermeil's motivational speeches to heart. They did not want to play like a bunch of fat asses against the Cowboys. "He got us after practice one time and told us to stop pouting and get serious," Walters said. "We had been challenged to match up to their front four, because that was the Dallas strength. If we could do a job on them, even neutralize 'em, everything would go well."

Once again, Vermeil exploited the "no respect" angle to inspire his troops to knock off America's Team. He told the Eagles that the Cowboys didn't really respect them. He said the Cowboys believed they would win because they were the Cowboys and the Eagles were the Eagles. But, Vermeil reminded the team, the Eagles were only inferior if they believed they were.

Looking to create some bad karma for the Cowboys, he made them leave their white uniforms home and wear their blue uniforms as the visiting team. The Cowboys seldom wore blue and seemed to suffer bad luck when they did.

Seeking every conceivable edge, he even activated little receiver/punt returner Wally Henry, who was still recovering from a vicious hit that cost him his spleen in late October, just in case. "The doctors said he'll be OK to play," Vermeil said, "but the doctors have never been hit by a Cowboy defensive back before."

When game day arrived, the Eagles couldn't wait to take the field. "I woke up at 5 a.m.," Morriss said. "I got it in my mind that we could intimidate 'em if we came at 'em hard, if we were physical."

The game was played in a bitterly cold Veterans Stadium. The wind-chill factor dipped to minus-17, although a few of the more fanatic ticket holders showed up with bare chests painted green. Vermeil worked his team into a frenzy as game time neared. "They're taking you for granted," he barked at the team.

When the Eagles hit the field, they were jumping around, beating on each other, eager to tear the Cowboys to shreds. They didn't feel the cold. Their adrenaline was pumping too hard.

"The thing that immediately pops into my mind was walking down the tunnel knowing 100 percent that we were going to beat the Dallas Cowboys that day," Bergey said. "That's how in-tune, how engulfed, how wrapped up the players were. There was no question in our minds. Dick gave us a real rah-rah speech right before the game. I remember looking around and thinking, 'We're going to win. There isn't one guy in this locker room who doesn't think we're going to win.' I just knew it. I knew it right away."

On the Cowboys' second snap of the game, Bunting anticipated a screen pass to Cowboys running back Ron Springs and crushed him for a seven-yard loss. Bunting was dropping back into zone pass coverage when he saw the Dallas linemen starting to set up the screen.

He sprinted across the line of scrimmage before the Cowboys blockers could set up and hammered Springs as he caught the ball in the flat.

"He absolutely undressed Springs," Bergey said. "I went crazy. We went on and absolutely kicked the hell out of them."

On the Eagles' second offensive play of the game, Montgomery ignited his teammates and the entire Veterans Stadium by bursting 42 yards for a touchdown. "Wilbert's run heated up the whole stadium, the whole city," Carmichael said

Montgomery would go on to grind out 194 yards on 26 carries, shrugging off a mid-week knee injury that threatened to sideline him for the game. Overall, the Eagles rushed for 263 yards with their offensive line dominating. The Cowboys never knew what run over them. "Why did we run so well?" Sisemore asked afterward, repeating a reporter's question. "We ran because we wanted to. We made up our minds we'd take it to 'em."

Walters battled through the game despite a back injury that left him nearly incapable of movement. At halftime he lay motionless on the trainer's table. He was moaning.

"Why?" he asked nobody in particular. "Why in the biggest game of my career, the moment I waited for all my life, is this happening? Why has this damn back gone and done such a thing now?"

Walters wasn't about to miss this opportunity to really pound on the Cowboys. So he allowed doctors to inject him with pain killers so he could continue waging his battle against Dallas pass rusher Harvey Martin. "Who knows how much longer I might have to wait for something like it again," Walters said. "That's why I had to get back in."

The Eagles defensive line was just as forceful in this game. "We just beat 'em, no flukes, no excuses, no nothing," noseguard Charlie Johnson said. "We dominated them and we intimidated them. That's right, intimidated them."

Years of grueling work resulted in a glorious victory for the Eagles.

With the game tied 7-7 at the half, the Eagles defense forced three turnovers in the third period and cashed them in for 10 points. They later tacked on a field goal for good measure, winning 20-7.

As the clock wound down, Vermeil was screaming at his team: "You're going to the Super Bowl! You're going to the Super Bowl!" As police horses ringed the field to keep the fans at bay, Vermeil hugged Leonard Tose and buried his head in his shoulder, again.

The Eagles left the field believing the margin of victory should have been much larger. Bergey boasted that the score should have been 55-0. Vermeil lamented their blown opportunities to score. The Eagles were a league power now and they expected to play like one in the big games.

"After we beat the Cowboys, some of us went out to dinner," Bergey said. "Everybody was whooping and hollering and having a good time. Well, it just hit me. I was looking around and I started to think, 'What am I doing? We still have another game to play.'"

# CHAPTER FIVE
# INTROSPECTION

*"I was afraid we'd get a phone call in the night saying he'd gone to sleep and hadn't woken up. Cardiac."*

-Al Vermeil

The big stage finally beckoned. By hammering the Dallas Cowboys in the NFC Championship Game, the Eagles carried Vermeil to the coaching pinnacle. They would play the Oakland Raiders in Super Bowl XV at the Superdome in New Orleans, Louisiana.

The Eagles had outworked an entire conference to earn this opportunity. Now they would try to outwork the Raiders. The Eagles arrived in New Orleans five hours earlier than the Raiders because Vermeil insisted on putting in a full workday.

The team went from the airport to the team hotel, dropped off its bags, then got back on the bus and headed to the practice field for what center Guy Morriss termed "a two and a half-hour blister." The tone was set for the week.

When the Raiders arrived, they gave reporters a quick wave and hit Bourbon Street after dumping their stuff at the hotel. It was time to unwind. "We cruised the French Quarter," quarterback Jim Plunkett reported after the team's first night in town. "But we didn't see any Eagles."

The media found the stark contrast between these two finalists irresistible. The game matched good against evil, the clean-cut Vermeil and his earnest laborers against renegade Raiders owner Al Davis's merry band of marauders. "We play cards in the locker room, we shoot dice," guard Gene Upshaw observed.

"This is an entirely different type of club," Raiders defensive end John Matuszak explained. "This is not the kind of team that would respond to Coach Vermeil. That's what makes this a good match-up."

Matuszak partied especially hard. One morning during the week, he woke up next to an unfamiliar woman, a massive hangover pounding his head. He pulled himself together and straggled back to the team hotel. When he wandered glassy-eyed into the interview room, late for a league-mandated media session, reporters hounded him for the juicy details of his nocturnal adventures.

"I'd love to give you a blow-by-blow account of the evening," he said, "but it's basically a blur."

So much for Matuszak's earlier proclamation that he would help keep the younger Raiders out of trouble during Super Bowl week. "That's why I was out on the streets," he reasoned. "To make sure no one else was."

Raiders coach Tom Flores tolerated the high jinks of his players, but he didn't endorse them. He vowed to fine them for each of their transgressions and backed it up by collecting $15,000 in $1,000 increments. Matuszak, for instance, was docked the standard $1,000 for wandering off on his overnight adventure. But the Raiders insisted on swashbuckling their way through Super Bowl week.

Reporters all but ignored Flores. With Vermeil's taskmaster reputation and the Raiders' hardy partying getting all the ink, he jokingly introduced himself at one news conference by saying, "I'm Tom Flores, coach of the other team."

Vermeil and Flores had faced each other before, on the football field back in 1957. While Vermeil was a quarterback at San Jose State, Flores was putting up huge passing numbers at the nearby College of the Pacific. Then both became highly successful coaches, working their way to the Super Bowl showdown.

Davis, the league's outlaw owner, relished the opportunity to sign out-law players. He left the chore of managing those miscreants to Flores, who stepped in when the beloved John Madden retired as coach. What if Vermeil coached the Raiders? What would he have done with Matuszak?

"I'd fine him $10,000 and send him home on the next flight," Vermeil said.

That comment made the Raiders laugh. Banish a curfew violator? Come on. If that were the case, Upshaw said, then there would have been nobody left on the Raiders' sideline to play the game.

The Raiders wouldn't see much of Matuszak until game day. Meanwhile, Vermeil kept his team under wraps outside of New Orleans at a hotel in a nondescript suburb near the airport. The Eagles had not come south for a holiday.

"I don't give a damn for parties, ceremonies, celebrations," a grim-faced Vermeil said. "To me, there's only one way to enjoy a football game, and that's to win it."

The hoopla was old hat for many of the Raiders, who beat Minnesota in Super Bowl XI four years earlier. The veterans helped the younger Raiders handle the circus-like atmosphere. Also, the Raiders featured some of the most notorious party animals in the league. They saw them-selves as Hell's Angels in cleats. The zoo-like atmosphere of Bourbon Street didn't intimidate them.

"We had our first practice 11 days before the game," one Raider told

Sports Illustrated. "Only 23 players showed up. One was in Peru."

The Eagles, on the other hand, adhered to a curfew and little free time. Vermeil ran them through a typically demanding week. On picture day, the Eagles did their meet and greet with the media, chatting it up with an army of newspaper, magazine, radio and television reporters. But after basking in the limelight, the Eagles were herded onto buses and given box lunches to eat before they got to their practice facility for another full practice. Nothing would stop Vermeil from working his team.

During the week, Herman Edwards got a call from a friend on the Raiders, Dwayne O'Steen, wondering if he could get free for a bite to eat. Edwards told O'Steen that he couldn't work out the logistics, since the Eagles were hemmed in at their hotel without transportation.

"What do you mean," O'Steen said. "You got a car. They provide players with cars, that's part of the deal."

The Eagles didn't realize this until the Friday before the game. Edwards and some teammates followed up on O'Steen's tip and, sure enough, there were the cars.

"Where the heck have you been?" an attendant asked Edwards. "These cars have been here all week."

The Eagles were disappointed, but not surprised by their discovery. "That's the way Dick was," Edwards said. "But you expected it. The thing about it was, when that guy told you something, you did it because you knew it was best for the team."

As always, Vermeil expressed his belief in the team as Sunday neared. On Saturday, he assured the players that they would reign as world champions. When they arrived at the Superdome for the game, they seemed to be in excellent spirits. Vermeil allowed Philadelphia Inquirer reporter Ron Reid, who had covered his Hillsdale High School teams back in California, into the locker room to capture the scene.

Here is how Reid recalled it:

> At the outset, most of the players sat in front of their cubicles, drinking Cokes, getting taped in the training room, reading or watching a college bas - ketball game on the TV set atop Harold Carmichael's cubicle.
>
> Vermeil came into the locker room smiling and relaxed, more like he was going to do one of his Cadillac commercials rather than coach the biggest game of his career. It seemed to fit the breezy mood of the moment that as Vermeil greeted his players, punter Max Runager was rubbing the callus of his left foot, with a jock strap.
>
> The cheers of the crowd could be heard in the locker room two hours before kickoff, while the Eagles watched a NBC pre-game telecast featuring the highlights of their 10-7 victory over Oakland in November. The sound of

*tearing adhesive tape went on for more than 90 minutes.*

*At 3:25 p.m., Eagles owner Leonard Tose brought Don Rickles into the locker room, hoping the comedian would ease some of the mounting tension. Rickles delivered his best line to Tony Franklin, telling the kicker, "If every - thing goes well, Tony, I'll shake your hand personally. If not, don't call me." A moment later, Carmichael stretched to his full 6-foot-8 height and knocked loose a ceiling tile.*

*With one hour to go, the locker room tension became all too apparent. Various Eagles used the bathroom half a dozen times within half an hour, the flushing toilets sounding like Niagara Falls.*

*At 4 p.m., Eagles offensive and special-teams players left the locker room. The defensive linemen and linebackers stayed behind, steadily becoming more frenzied. Carl Hairston, soul-slapping his teammates, grew more aggressive, anxious and moody by the second. Bill Bergey implored, "Make something happen every play!" When it appeared no one could endure another moment of pressure, the defensive players went on the field.*

*With 20 minutes left before kickoff, the Eagles returned to the locker room with loud cries of "The time is here! Start fast! Let's go to work!" Middle guard Charlie Johnson told his teammates, "We got to keep pounding, run their asses in the first half and make them drag 'em in the second. Beat them up. Keep pounding, pounding . . ."*

*Wilbert Montgomery told Franklin, "Don't be havin' no smile on your face."*

*Moments before the game started, Vermeil yelled, "OK, let's tighten up," and the Eagles listened intently to the final word from their head coach.*

*"If we win this thing together," Vermeil said in a voice choked with emo - tion, "no one guy is going to win it for us. If we win, we win it together. But we aren't going to lose! We're going to kick the hell out of the Oakland Raiders. The big thing, though, is controlling our intensity. Direct your intensity to help you win. You're ready to play a ball game. You're ready to be world champions. I just thank you for taking me along."*

But the Eagles had no pep after this talk. "When we finally got on the field," Bunting says, "we were exhausted emotionally and physically."

The players carried a look of dread into the game. The Raiders could see that their opponent was spent. "I remember before the game, talking to Derrick Ramsey out on the field," Morriss said. "And he said he could just see it in our eyes. We were beat. We were tired before the game even began. And here come the Raiders, the wild men of the NFL. I think for four days they did nothing but party. Then they got down to serious business."

The Raiders started fast, taking a 7-0 lead six minutes, four seconds into the game on Plunkett's two-yard touchdown pass to Cliff Branch. The

Eagles tried to respond, but an illegal motion penalty on Carmichael wiped out what could have been a game-tying touchdown pass to Rodney Parker.

With nine seconds left in the first quarter, Plunkett hit an 80-yard touchdown pass to Kenny King and the Raiders had a commanding 14-0 lead.

When the Raiders lost to the Eagles in the regular season, Plunkett, who played for Vermeil during two of his seasons at Stanford, suffered eight sacks. In this game, Flores shifted the protection scheme to area blocking instead of man-to-man to counter the Eagles stunts. Afforded time to throw, Plunkett kept making the big plays. Tactically and motivationally, Flores had his team better prepared than the Eagles were.

"Dick was a paramilitary type of guy then," Flores said. "His players were having two-a-days and moaning and groaning. And they hadn't changed (strategy) since our first game. They were a very conservative team that liked to run. We felt if we could get them to throw the ball, we'd win the battle."

His assessment was correct. The Raiders were able to harass Ron Jaworski into a terrible performance. Unheralded Raiders linebacker Rod Martin would pick off three of his passes, two on throws intended for John Spagnola. The first interception came just three plays into the game, and Martin's 17-yard return put the Raiders in scoring position at the Philadelphia 30.

"We were just in the doldrums," Spagnola said. "I could feel it. I couldn't put my finger on it."

With the Raiders leading 14-3, the Eagles had one last chance to stem the tide, but their final offensive drive of the second quarter died inside the Oakland 20, and Tony Franklin's 28-yard field goal try was blocked.

"We had a little something going in the second quarter," Vermeil said, "but we go in at halftime with three points instead of six."

The normally vibrant Eagles sat numb in their locker room at halftime. Their confidence and their energy were gone. They tried to fire up, but the embers had gone cold. "We weren't talking," Montgomery recalled. "We couldn't get it going. It wasn't the same. I just don't know what happened."

The Inquirer's Reid was also allowed to observe the halftime scene as the Eagles attempted to regroup. Here is what he wrote:

*"This ain't over by a long shot," one player shouted, and his urgency was repeated as various Eagles tried to exorcise the lethargy that marked their first-half effort. "We've been here before," said Hairston, who had a pizza-sized splotch of blood on his knee. Bergey begged for 30 minutes of fight and fellow linebacker Frank LeMaster said: "The defense has to set the tempo."*

*But the Eagles looked weary and stunned.*

*When Vermeil ended the offensive meeting and called the entire team into the middle of the room, the Eagles were slow to respond.*

*"That's just about the way we're playing," Vermeil shouted. "We've got no damn tempo! I believe we're a little uptight and tense. We do not look like NFC champs! Guys, we are playing for a world championship. Now let's go out and get it!"*

*With the shout, "Let's come back in here a winner," the Eagles left their locker room for the last time.*

The second half brought more of the same. The Eagles couldn't get their offense rolling; they mustered just 69 yards on the ground and kept the struggling Jaworksi in tough down-and-distance situations.

Plunkett made the big plays when he needed them and the Raiders rolled to a 27-10 victory. He completed 13 of 21 passes for three touchdowns and earned Most Valuable Player honors for the game.

The Eagles retreated to their locker room in a state of shock. "Anyone who says one loss cannot ruin a season, never lost a Super Bowl," Vermeil mused.

After the game, an inconsolable Bunting just sat in the shower...and sat, and sat, and sat. He was crying and he didn't want to come out. Rookie cornerback Ronyell Young tried to talk him out.

"Hey, J.B., no problem, man," he said. "We'll be back next year."

"Ronyell, this is my ninth year," Bunting said. "You have no idea how hard it is to get here."

Montgomery couldn't explain what happened to his team. The Eagles lost their fight. Their resilience evaporated. Try as they might, they couldn't gear up for one of their trademark comebacks.

"All year we were a second-half ball club," said Montgomery, who rushed for just 44 yards on 16 carries. "Today, it was like we gave up. It was a terrible feeling. We never got our motor running."

The Raiders played as if they had no worries in the world. After the game, the Superdome clean-up crew found peanut shells around the Oakland bench. The nonchalant Raiders had been snacking during the game.

Had Vermeil pushed his team too hard? That was an easy conclusion for analysts to reach, although key Eagles disputed it. Jaworski claimed the Eagles had terrific practices during the week and that he expected they would come out "smoking," as they almost always did.

Some players cited the natural letdown that occurred after beating the hated Cowboys. That game had meant everything to the franchise, given the abuse it had suffered at the hands of "America's Team" for many seasons. Perhaps they spent all they had left to beat Dallas after a grueling run to the NFC title game. Maybe they had nothing left to give.

People questioned whether the Eagles would have been better off carousing with the Raiders, but Bergey said, "The bottom line is we lost. You can't blame it on the cheerleaders. You can't blame it on the food. You can't blame it on not getting drunk on Bourbon Street, like the Raiders did."

The defeat devastated Vermeil. At first he concluded that his team just wasn't good enough to win it all. In the months that followed, however, Vermeil wondered if he should have been even tougher on his team while preparing to face the Raiders.

"I don't know, but I'm certain I have to act according to my impulses," Vermeil said. "I made a mistake along these lines in the Super Bowl game. There was all this attention focused on the game and it was our first time up there, and I thought that I'd better show the players that the coach was cool, calm and collected under the pressure.

"Well, the team reflects the coach. And I think my team got too sedated. What I was doing was artificial and it hurt the team. I'm convinced of that. Oakland kicked our butts all over the place. It didn't look like the same Eagles team that went 12-4 through the season."

Time did not heal the pain of this loss. Vermeil remained despondent. Sensing that his coach wasn't recovering, Bergey went to his house that winter for a heart-to-heart talk. They poured some wine and talked about the future. The linebacker wondered if the coach should go on beating himself up this way.

He owed nothing to the players, Bergey told him. "I told him it was OK if he wanted to get out of the game," he said.

But Vermeil wouldn't even consider that possibility. "He said he couldn't let his players down," Bergey recalled.

The Super Bowl defeat would dog Vermeil for the rest of his Eagles tenure. He failed to recharge during the spring and summer of 1981. During the next preseason, he was even testier than usual. With little provocation, he railed at Jaworski, one of his most trusted leaders. After a sloppy exhibition game, Vermeil snapped.

"Right now, the offense stinks," he said. "I'm concerned about the entire offense. I don't think Ron is as far along as he ought to be."

The harshness of his coach's tone baffled Jaworski. After all, this was the exhibition season. He had served Vermeil well through some difficult times. Did the coach have to dog him with the season still weeks away?

"Sure, it bothers me," Jaworski said at the time. "It's the constant total evaluation all the time. It seems like I'm always playing under a microscope. I can't ever relax and just do my thing. This is my eighth year in the league and I still feel I have to prove myself every game, heck, every practice. Sure, I'm still making some mistakes, but to say the offense stinks, well, that seems a little strong to me. If I were 21 or 22, I could see the constant criticism, but you would think after seven years in the league, they would know I could play."

Despite Vermeil's angst, the Eagles won their first six games in 1981, although Vermeil could hardly relax. For instance, he wasn't pleased after a lopsided 36-13 victory over the Washington Redskins in the fourth week. "In the first half we were outcoached and outplayed," Vermeil complained. "We weren't sharp mentally and we had no tempo."

Vermeil was similarly miffed after a 31-14 rout at New Orleans, which pushed the Eagles record to 6-0. "When we make a mistake, when we jump offside, it tees me off," he said. "It's my job to coach them on every snap, not just on those snaps on which we play well."

Despite Vermeil's agitated state, the Eagles seemed to be on track for another NFC title. They won nine of their first 11 games...and then the bottom fell out. The Eagles lost four straight games, scoring just 43 points in the process. Perhaps the strain of meeting greater expectations prompted them to buckle, although Vermeil didn't want to believe such a collapse was possible.

"We're snake bit," Vermeil said during the downturn. "Our football players believe we're a better football team now than last year. They have invested a great deal of time in the off-season and a lot of effort during the season to be a winner. You don't chip that out of the character of a person."

The trouble started against the Giants, a team they had beaten nine times in a row. Among the mishaps in the 20-10 loss was a botched fake punt in the fourth quarter. The normal long snapper, Mark Slater, had been a tight end on the previous play, so rules prohibited him from moving back inside to hike the ball on fourth down. Morriss had to fill in, and he missed the call. He wasn't aware that he was supposed to snap the ball to the up man, linebacker Frank LeMaster. He snapped it to punter Max Runager instead, and the flummoxed Runager chunked a

> "Dick was a paramilitary type of guy then," Flores said. "They were a very conservative team that liked to run. We felt that if we could get them to throw the ball, we would win."

nine-yard punt that led to the Giants' tie-breaking field goal.

The Giants clinched the victory on Terry Jackson's 32-yard interception return; he picked off a cross-field pass toward Charles Smith on a third-and-40 play. That left Vermeil kicking himself.

"That was probably a stupid call on my part," Vermeil said. "I knew they would be in that damn prevent defense and they just laid back there and picked off a fly pattern."

The Eagles controlled the clock with Montgomery rushing for 102 yards, but they lost anyway. Fans booed Jaworski and chanted "We want Joe," for Joe Pisarcik, who was now Jaworski's back-up.

A 15-13 defeat to the Redskins was particularly galling because the Eagles out-gained Washington, 416-176. Holder John Sciarra muffed a snap, keeping Tony Franklin from nailing a 24-yard field goal with 58 seconds left. The winning Redskins touchdown came on an interception return, after a tipped pass.

"My confidence is shaken," Vermeil told reporters. "I've never considered myself to be a great coach, but I think I'm a halfway decent coach. My record would indicate that. Whenever your team's losing, whatever kind of job you're doing, it's not good enough."

Before playing Dallas, Cowboys running back Ron Springs said things like, "I think the Eagles are cake, and we're getting ready to eat up that Christmas cake," but Vermeil's troops were unmoved by this bulletin-board motivational material. Their spirit was waning. Sciarra's dropped punt helped lead to a 21-10 loss to the Cowboys.

The Eagles managed to dismiss the miserable St. Louis Cardinals, 38-0, to secure a playoff berth, but their bid to repeat as NFC Champions died quickly, in a 27-21 loss to the Giants in the wild-card game. Kick returner Wally Henry, another of Vermeil's UCLA faithful, fumbled twice in the first quarter, and both mishaps led to touchdowns. The Eagles were down 20-0 before they knew what happened. Such blunders left Vermeil with a profound sense of déjà vu.

A season of frustration had come to a fittingly painful end. Philadelphia fans gave the Eagles a collective catcall, booing the whole team and Jaworski in particular at Veterans Stadium. In less than one year, the thrilling triumph of 1980 was all but forgotten by the ticket holders. Second-guessers taunted the head coach that built a championship team from rubble. After all he had done for Philadelphia —giving the city a winning football team after years of mediocrity—this is how people treated Vermeil?

"The only thing I can do is win the Super Bowl," Vermeil lamented. "Anything less, then I'm an idiot. Either my program isn't good enough or my quarterback isn't good enough or I should change my receivers."

Vermeil agonized over his team's slide. Getting to the top is extremely difficult, but the Eagles proved how hard it was to stay there. The tireless overachievers were now drawing criticism as failures.

"There's nothing as sweet as the first time you do it," he said. "After that, people begin to expect more from you. And maybe the pressure builds. Maybe that's why the losing streak of four straight was so bad. We began to lose confidence in ourselves, began to doubt ourselves and what we were doing."

Philadelphia sportswriters and sportscasters fueled the public unrest by suggesting Vermeil's hard-driving style was having a negative effect on the team.

"He'd put on this air as this tough little French sonofagun, but underneath he was more sensitive than anybody knew," Carl Peterson said. "He'd say he never read the papers. Bull. If he didn't read them, he'd say, 'What'd they say Carl?' For all his success, his confidence level wasn't always strong enough to pull him through."

The defeats devoured Vermeil during the 1981 season. He responded by pushing himself, his assistant coaches and his players even harder. Assistant coach John Becker recalls waking up with profanity on his lips, cursing the insanity of the long hours.

From his office on the West Coast, Raiders owner Al Davis would call Vermeil at 3 a.m. to talk football because he knew Vermeil would be at his desk working away.

"I couldn't turn the projector off," Vermeil said. "I just worked. I laugh when I say it now, but I worked anywhere to 3 a.m. to 6 a.m. and went to work at 8. I just could not turn my job off, and it got so the thrill of winning didn't satisfy me. Right away, I started worrying about the next game."

Assistant coach, Ed Hughes, would never forget a particularly torturous night of film study. Bringing a strategy session to a halt, Vermeil ran back a particular play 52 times. Fifty-two!

"I counted them," Hughes said. "He was trying to get ideas. The rest of us got ideas—we got the idea to leave." Fearing that he would suffer a heart attack working in Vermeil's pressure cooker, Hughes quit after the season.

Vermeil obsessed over details, making sure every little thing was just right. For instance, when an assistant coach failed to use a stencil to make sure the circles and squares in his play book section were perfect, Vermeil redrew the plays himself. This was symbolic of how he approached the job each day. Such thoroughness was taxing.

"Sometimes that kind of dedication can be a fault, not a strength," he admitted. "It's the worst after we lose. I keep thinking if I see enough films, I'll find out what went wrong and it won't happen again. The problem is, on Monday and Tuesday after a loss, I can't get the loss out of my mind and I can't concentrate on the game coming up. By Wednesday, I'm starting to see straight."

The agony of defeat was almost unbearable. "If I described what it felt like inside me to lose, you would write me off as a lunatic," he said. "They'd call me one-dimensional, but when I lost, it was the only dimension that people evaluated."

General manager Jim Murray tried to convince Vermeil to slow down, but to no avail. The Eagles assistant coaches couldn't make any headway and neither could veteran players like Bergey. Even the team chaplain couldn't convince him to change.

Carol Vermeil tried to draw a line. Looking to break the downward spiral, she convinced him to meet with a psychiatrist. But Dick wasn't quite ready to explore his soul with a stranger. He made an appointment but refused to open up.

"So," Carol asked, "how did it go?"

"Criminy, it'd take me a good week, at least, to straighten that guy out," Vermeil said.

This was a brutal period for the Vermeils. The team's reversal of fortune took a toll on Carol, too, "I'd be sitting on an airplane next to her after a loss, and she'd have tears in her eyes," Dick said. "I'd walk into my office after a ballgame and she'd be emotionally drained."

Carol's misery only made Dick more miserable. His response was to put in even more ridiculous hours.

"It was not a good time for us," Carol said. "He was possessed. It was like 'The Blob.' It came over him."

From his office on the West Coast, Raiders owner Al Davis would call Vermeil at 3 a.m. to talk football because he knew Vermeil would be at his desk working away.

Lynn Stiles, who rejoined Vermeil in 1979 after a stint as San Jose State's head coach, recalled leaving the office at three o'clock in the morning and seeing his boss still grinding away. After getting a few hours sleep at a hotel across the street, Stiles would return to the office to see Vermeil up and at it again.

"I'm in a meeting diagramming everything he said, because my mind is mush," Stiles said. "I was so tired I couldn't remember anything."

Vermeil would not, could not let up on his players. Even when he coached the college All-Star game, the Olympia Gold Bowl in 1982, he worked his team hard, to the chagrin of event organizer Mike Garrett, a former star running back.

"I'd promised these players a light week, a vacation," Garrett said. "The first day he has them killing each other and they're pulling me aside, saying 'This guy is crazy. You've got to cut this out or we're leaving.' My teammates called me 'Mr. Intense' at USC, and this guy was two octaves higher than me or anyone I've ever seen. He was personable, but I'd have been terribly afraid to play for him. You couldn't even drink a glass of water slow around him."

During that off-season, Dick and Carol both contracted hepatitis, which left him bedridden leading up to the NFL draft. Vermeil could hardly stand this. He had never been laid out like this before. He couldn't recall missing a day of work or school in his life, but for three weeks, he was flat on his back. Carol got medical clearance to get up and get out, but the doctor kept Dick confined to a bed. One day, Peterson got a call from the coach.

"Damn it," Vermeil said, "she beat me getting well."

Against doctors' orders, he reported to the Eagles' war room for the NFL draft. And he didn't laugh when his assistant coaches teased him by donning surgical masks.

"You sons of bitches," he said. "I don't think that's real funny."

But Vermeil pushed on, plotting a variety of changes to rejuvenate his team. Hoping to get Jaworski back on track, Vermeil called Sid Gillman back from his one-year retirement to clean up the quarterback's passing game. The Eagles drafted three receivers, including top pick Mike Quick, and brought 18 wide-outs to camp. Vermeil wanted to give the offense a fresh start and get it back to the level it was during the Super Bowl season. So he discarded the passing portion of his play book and started over. Page by page, X by O, he redid the whole thing by hand before the start of training camp.

Vermeil suffered a major blow when Peterson, his right-hand man, departed during the summer to become general manager of the Philadelphia Stars of the upstart United States Football League. Vermeil endorsed Peterson's exit and promoted Stiles into his old personnel director's spot.

Following the advice of those closest to him, Vermeil tried to ease up in his team in training camp that summer, but his adjustment was too little, too late. Nose guard Charlie Johnson, one of his most loyal team leaders, demanded to be traded. He just couldn't take being an Eagle any more. He couldn't pay the physical and emotional price. Day after day, week after week, year after year of head-to-head warfare during Eagles practices beat him down.

He suffered splitting headaches during the intense two-a-day sessions in training camp. Johnson wanted out before the 1982 camp, so Vermeil traded him to Minnesota. His departure became a precursor of doom for the program. If Johnson folded, how would the less-committed players hold up? He had been one of the bulwarks of the program. But if Vermeil couldn't change, then Johnson couldn't stay.

"His work habits were so strenuous on a person," Johnson explained. "You could never loosen up. You were afraid to make mistakes because of the pressure put on you. You would dread going into a meeting because you would get yelled at and screamed at. He would just go off on you. You can't do veterans like that. You can scream at them and curse them sometimes, but sometimes you just have to say, 'Correct it' and leave it alone.

"I felt the training and preparation were really tough. There was a lot of pounding, a lot of contact. The body could never heal. In this game, you need days off, and you need to back off during the week to get your body well. You were never really well. It started taking its toll and breaking down the momentum and enthusiasm of the personnel. Your attention span was gone. You were trying to block it out, just survive. It takes away from everything."

On defense, Claude Humphrey retired and linebacker Al Chesley lost his starting job, then got waived when he complained. Still, Jaworski tried to seem optimistic as the preseason unfolded.

"We all came back ready," he said. "This is the best camp we ever had."

But the 1982 season opened with a 37-34 loss in overtime to Washington at Veterans Stadium. Redskins kicker Mark Moseley kicked a field goal on the last play of the fourth quarter to force overtime, then kicked another field goal to win it. One of the Eagles' lowlights was a botched fake punt in the fourth quarter. The Redskins knew that LeMaster, the up man in the punt formation, was going to take the snap and run. They lined up their defense accordingly, but LeMaster went through with the play and got stopped. He should have checked off the play and ordered a punt.

"Evidently, I can't leave that responsibility to a football player," Vermeil complained. "I'll never do that again."

The Eagles rebounded to win their next game, 24-21 at Cleveland—but then the NFL players, seeking a new collective bargaining agreement, went on strike. Pro football shut down. In other league cities, some teams gathered to work out informally to stay in shape while their negotiating committee tried to iron out a new deal with the owners.

But the Eagles scattered. Relieved to be freed from their frazzled coach, the Eagles dispersed to their various hometowns. For a while, Vermeil came to the office and tried to stay busy, even though there was nothing to do. Leonard Tose did manage to order him home on weekends.

During those Saturdays and Sundays off, Vermeil actually enjoyed the break. He and Carol drove into the countryside of Pennsylvania, and he was awestruck by the autumn scenery he had never noticed before while holed up in his office reviewing game films.

Fans derisively chanted 'Strike! Strike!' at the Eagles and menaced them when they came off the field.

"When the league went on strike, the changing trees, the colors in the fields, amazed Dick," Carol said. "You know, I think he thought all fields were green with white stripes on them."

When the Eagles returned in November from the two-month long strike they came only in body, not spirit. Their edge was gone. Rather than talking about the upcoming game in the locker room and lunch room, the Eagles discussed the new collective bargaining agreement and the state of their industry.

"Some guys started turning Dick off," Jaworski said. "He'd get emotional and it was 'Here we go again.' The bang effect was gone. And we were so much more programmed than other teams, we couldn't just come back after eight weeks and start winning."

They lost their first game back, 18-14, to Cincinnati. Vermeil tried to shield his team from criticism, but this was an ugly scene. John Bunting, a member of the NFL Players Association executive council, was astonished by how agitated the Veterans Stadium crowd became. Fans derisively chanted "Strike! Strike!" at the Eagles and menaced them when they came off the field.

"For the first time in my life, I was scared coming off a football field after a game," he said. "What it basically came down to was witnessing a different type of hostility from anything I had ever seen before. I came here in '72, and I had tomatoes and oranges and other things thrown out on the field at us. That Sunday, there was a special viciousness in some, not all, of the people. And a lot of the people hanging over that tunnel where we go off the field were obnoxious, profane, obscene, using words you can't put in a journal. And there were threats made, threats on my person, threats to the team were made."

Things didn't improve next week as the Eagles fell, 13-9, at Washington. In the third quarter, a fourth-and-one play at the

Washington 18 was stopped.

Franklin clanged an extra point attempt off an upright, meaning that in the fourth quarter, the Eagles had to play for a touchdown instead of a field goal. Jaworski threw two of his four interceptions late in the game as the Eagles gunned for the end zone.

That loss left the Eagles in a quandary. "You start taking things for granted over time," Bunting said. "You lose the hunger. We have to get it back."

Vermeil wasn't thinking about his team's post-season prospects after this fiasco. He talked about getting back to square one, about just winning another game to restore some order. But next up was a 23-20 loss at home to St. Louis, dropping the Eagles to 1-4.

"You might as well go back on strike!" Tose yelled at the players after the defeat. For a lot of the Eagles, that didn't seem like such a bad idea. Once a close-knit family, the Eagles were now a dysfunctional mess. The players were mad at Tose and weary of Vermeil. When the Giants pounded the Eagles, 23-7, the Eagles had won just six of their last 17 regular-season games. Vermeil was left grappling with his composure. "It's not just the players who haven't done well," he said. "The coaches haven't done a very good job, either, including me. It would very easy for me to start pointing fingers, but I don't use that approach."

Vermeil's whole program was based on intensity. He worked Eagles harder than any team worked, seeking to build superior conditioning, stamina and toughness. But with football shut down for 57 days, the Eagles lost that edge. They enjoyed their vacation more than most teams and when they came back, they either couldn't or didn't care to make the sacrifices any more.

In Jaworski's eyes, everybody suffered. "It not only ruined a lot of careers—which I think it did for Dick Vermeil at that time, it ruined our ownership—Leonard Tose," Jaworski. "It ruined our football team. We were a playoff team that fell apart."

Writing for Sports Illustrated, Gary Smith described how the walls closed in on Vermeil:

*He tried to hurl himself into the same work schedule without the same illusions. It didn't work. He watched film at 2 a.m. and saw nothing. He began to cry during routine locker room speeches. His neck was so tense when he was driving, he could not turn it to see the left lane. At home, he was farther away than ever. "I'd say, 'Dick, I cut my arm off today, but I don't think it's too bad,'" says Carol, "and he wouldn't even blink."*

Vermeil became a zombie. Once, with the Eagles about to leave on a road trip, he just sat by himself in his car, paralyzed by his mental exhaustion. Could he go on? He didn't know. He just sat there, thinking about everything and nothing. Finally he was able to drag himself out of the car and get back to work.

"I was an emotional wreck," Vermeil said. "I'm an emotional guy, anyway, but I would find myself in tears thinking, 'What the hell's wrong with me?' Yeah, I'm having a very sincere conversation with somebody, but it shouldn't motivate tears. I still find myself in that state sometimes, but not all the time.

"I would come home on Friday night, especially toward the end of the season, eat and go back to work. Or fly home from an away game on a Sunday night and have Carol drive home from the airport at two o'clock, three o'clock in the morning, and I would go to the stadium. It became such a compulsion to find a better way, and I couldn't turn it off. I was so freakin' intense."

By the final game of the season, Vermeil knew in his heart that he was finished. He cried during the national anthem. The Eagles absorbed one more maddening defeat, 26-24 to the rival Giants, to finish this lost season 3-6. Tose wanted him to remain on his post, but deep down Vermeil knew it was over.

"Honey, I can't make a decision," he told Carol.

"Well," she said, "I've already made one."

She told him to quit denying the obvious. It was time to step back, before his physical and mental health got worse.

"He just ran out of gas," Carol said, "and he was not able to continue on this energetic path that he had cornered himself into without even noticing. Everything just became too much, and I think that he really didn't have any choice but to step away."

On January 9, the Sunday after the season ended, Vermeil went to Tose's home to tell the owner of his plans. He had three years and $600,000 left on his contract, but Tose gave him his release and selected defensive coordinator Marion Campbell as his replacement.

The next day Vermeil trudged down to Veterans Stadium to say goodbye. He saw Edwards in the locker room, gave him a hug and told him he was through. "It's going to be OK," Vermeil told him.

Edwards understood. "He was exhausted," Edwards said. "He had given every ounce of mental and physical energy, but our record was 3-6. As players, we were sad, but we were happy for Dick. He needed to get away."

Vermeil spoke to his other team leaders as word of his resignation spread through the team. Some Eagles were stunned that their coach resigned. Sure, he looked run down. But the thought of Vermeil backing down from any challenge was unthinkable. "We were shocked because we thought he was going to coach this game forever, he loved the game that much," Hairston said.

After saying his good-byes, Vermeil faced the media during the news conference to announce his resignation. With the cameras rolling, Vermeil became the poster boy for professional burnout. This was a relatively new area of psychological study and this tearful coach personified the condition.

"I had read a book on something called 'burnout,' by somebody named Feurdebenger, Freudenberger, something like that," Vermeil said. "Anyway, another coach gave it to me and said I better read it. The night before I announced my resignation, I was discussing with a friend how to explain my resignation."

The friend advised him to tell the world how he felt. But he couldn't. "Some of the words to describe it I could not use," Vermeil said. "Not politically correct, you know. I didn't want to use vulgarity. I did want to say how I didn't feel good about myself as a coach or a person, so I said 'emotional burnout.'"

Vermeil certainly appeared burned out. His body language screamed fatigue. Resignation was written all over his face.

"I'm physically and mentally drained," he said at the time. "I just have to get out of coaching for a while. It's as simple as that. This is the hardest thing I've ever had to do. I hope my coaches and players understand where I'm coming from. I mean that sincerely."

The more Walters reflected on Vermeil's decision, the more he realized how inevitable it was. The symptoms of a major problem had been glaring for some time. "I believe the questions raised three years ago —'Will he burn himself out, can he maintain the pace?'—were coming to light," Walters said. "He goes so hard that there comes a time when you can't take it any more unless you're an unbelievable human being."

Viewing from a safe distance, Charlie Johnson wasn't surprised the Eagles imploded in '82. The cracks in the foundation had been forming since the Super Bowl defeat. The obsessive Vermeil had run himself and his team into the ground. The strike only sped up the inevitable.

"I think Dick didn't want the organization to break down, but guys were losing faith in him," Johnson said. "The team was sagging. It was just too much for him to handle. I don't want to be the culprit to make him do what he did, but I was just telling him to slow it down a little. He's a fine football coach, but sometimes he overdoes it. He doesn't know when to slow down."

Initially, Vermeil blew off Johnson's assertion. He denied that the warning signs were in place the summer before, when Johnson demanded his trade.

"The defense was No. 1 in professional football for five years," Vermeil said. "It gave up fewer points than any team in football from 1977 to 1981. Whatever we were doing, it couldn't have been that far wrong. He just got tired of it. I respect that. What he said to me last summer had nothing to do with my decision to quit. His departure hurt our defense a little, in terms of leadership, but my decision was based on Dick Vermeil and what I had to do."

But as Vermeil reviewed what went wrong, he saw there was a lot of truth to what Johnson was trying to tell him. Vermeil needed to slow down and catch his breath. He should have allowed his players to do the same.

"I've made a lot of mistakes, but probably the most vivid was to set a tempo that may not be possible to keep through a 10-year pro contract," Vermeil said. "That's why I can say I'm just burned out. I know I pushed myself beyond the point. But with a break, I think I can regroup and regenerate the enthusiasm and the energy that it takes to do it my way. If I can't do it to my standards, I'm not going to do it."

As he retraced his demise in Philadelphia, he saw how the real trouble began after the Super Bowl defeat to Oakland. The disappointment of the defeat, compounded by the pressure to get back to the big game, tore him apart.

"The pressure became so intense, a whole lot of things caught up with me," he said. "They started eating away at me. I couldn't relax. I couldn't turn it off. It was either quit or wind up in the loony bin or the graveyard."

Though he had reached his wit's end, becoming so stressed out that he could hardly function, he continued to resist professional help. He had too much pride for that. He had always been so self-reliant, he figured he could find a way to tone down his obsessive behavior and learn how to handle defeat.

"I have to learn to handle my own drives, to stop trying to control so many variables. I don't need a therapist to tell me that," he said. "Cripes, I got more common sense in one hand than most of them have in their body."

He didn't relish the prospect of reviewing his childhood with a stranger, somebody looking to explore his relationship with Louie during those formative years in Calistoga. He didn't want to poke and prod at the emotional scarring left by his father's shrill criticism.

But as he began to unwind and recover from his coaching meltdown, he became more willing to explore his make-up. Why did his competitive drive push him over the edge? Why couldn't he let go of defeats? Why couldn't he truly enjoy success?

"It used to be with me that the thrill of winning did not last long," he said. "The agony of defeat, I never got over. It was always all my fault. If the guy fumbled, I felt it was my fault; I shouldn't have called the play. I wore myself out; I learned from that.

"I used to take everything personally and always blamed myself. I learned, no matter how had you work and coach, it's not always your fault. When you strive for perfection, all you're doing is striving to drive yourself out of coaching. I spent a couple of years with a psychologist who helped me understand myself better, my emotions and my intensity, where it all came from within my personality. I learned you don't manage stress. You manage yourself. That helped me."

Back in Calistoga, Sports Illustrated visited his parents early in his hiatus from coaching. Predictably Louie Vermeil figured that Dick's mistake was not cracking the whip even harder.

"Dick's a little too softhearted," Louie said. "I'd a chewed those players out in Philadelphia. There are three tough nuts in that league: (Don) Shula, (Bud) Grant and (Tom) Landry. I don't think that Dick could hold a candle to 'em."

Alice figured her son would jump back into coaching, and quickly. "I've got a bet with his father," she said. "Dick will be back coaching within a year. I know I'm right."

Deep down, Louie also knew his son would some day coach again.

After all, he was a chip off the block. A very hard block.

"He'll be back," Louie said. "It'd be like me leaving the garage. Yeah, he'll be back."

# CHAPTER SIX
# THOROUGHNESS

*"I was on CBS when John Madden started and I worked with Billy Packer. No one spent the amount of time and had the thoroughness of preparation that Dick did."*

-Brent Musberger, Vermeil's long-time broadcast partner

When Dick Vermeil quit coaching, he didn't quit working. He couldn't walk away from football, which had been his life since the 1950s. So he took his coaching acumen, his analytical mind and his communication skills and became the hardest working color commentator of his era.

Vermeil's first stop after coaching was CBS, where he spent five years analyzing NFL games. Just as he had in his coaching days, Vermeil absorbed and organized every last bit of information. He poured through media guides and sifted through newspaper clips before heading to the game site.

"I enjoyed the research," Vermeil said. "I enjoyed the study of the teams, what they were doing with the ball, how they were playing defense. I enjoyed evaluating the players. I enjoyed getting to know the kids and the coaches around the country, both in college and pro football."

He didn't work around the clock as he had as a coach, but he threw himself into his game preparation with the same zeal his assistant coaches in Philadelphia and UCLA saw. So what if it was overkill?

"He's not really great with leisure time," Carol observed. "He has this idea that if you're not doing something productive, you're wasting time. That's just the way he is. Dick loves to work. That's his favorite thing."

He arrived early at the game sites to meet with the coaches and players. He walked the sidelines observing practices and making mental notes. He sat in on film study. He huddled with the coaching staffs for the chalk talks. He devoured statistics and deciphered trends. In some cases, he even spoke to the team he was covering. He gave his coaching talk, stressing belief and commitment while drawing examples from his own teams over the years. He loved getting back in the middle of the action. He was a neutral observer, but a passionate one.

He would come to the game site on Thursday or Friday. "Why? Because I wanted to see how the great coaches did it," he said. "How do you get this done. How do you motivate your players? I watched Tom Landry do it. I've watched Don Shula, a general of all generals, do it on the practice field. I've watched Jim Mora do it. I've watched Mike Ditka, Marv Levy, Chuck Knox, Don Coryell.

"I don't think I was ever cut out of a football practice. I can remember going to watch Don Shula lead a practice when he would not allow any TV people on the practice field but me. I got to watch them practice, so when I was doing the ballgame, I could anticipate things, too. To watch other coaches coach, and sit in their locker rooms, and talk to their players and listen to players talk about what they like and what they don't like, I learned a lot about what's on a player's mind in relationship to the football program they are in. I guarantee they said things to me that they didn't say to their own coaches."

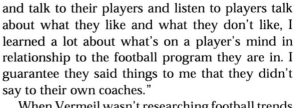

'I worked time to death, and it killed me.'

When Vermeil wasn't researching football trends to provide commentary on games, he would shift gears and use some of his old stump material to give corporate pep talks. Just as he never lost his love for football, he never lost his desire to motivate people. His visibility gave him entry to the business world. He discovered that running a big company was a lot like running a football team.

"When I go around to corporations and listen to what they're talking about and what they want me to talk about, there's an unbelievable correlation between being president of football operations and head football coach and being the CEO of a large corporation," Vermeil said. "They're having some of the same problems. And most problems are around people. Hiring the right people. Keeping them there. My greatest strength has always been a leadership role, bringing people together, collecting their energy, stimulating that energy and then focusing it in the direction that can best help us win."

He fired himself up for these gigs like he would to prepare for a big game, alternately drawing on his canned material and speaking from the heart. He became a star on the motivational circuit because he could captivate a room full of salesmen or managers the way he captivated his players.

"I enjoyed speaking to the corporations," Vermeil said. "I really did. I enjoyed it, especially with the real intense, high-energy groups that I was around in big corporations. I was excited over an hour and a half or 20-minute presentation or a 55-minute presentation because I had a team to coach. But the trouble is, two hours later, they're not your team and then there's a letdown that you can't fill until the next time you have a team to coach."

His insights on success weren't exactly groundbreaking, but he spoke from his heart and connected on a personal level with his audience. He won people over by opening himself up.

Sports Illustrated caught up with him in 1983 when he was working up some Kawasaki dealers with one of his stump speeches: "You got players who won't perform to their level, don't keep them on your roster," he urged the dealers. "Get them selling! Give them time to think your way, and at the end of the year, if they don't, cut 'em or waive 'em! There's not a man in this room who works as hard as his dad. Limits are self-imposed. There are no limits to human energy!

"My kids say to me, 'I'd never work as hard as you.' I'll tell you, one day there's going to be a wide-eyed awakening in this country, when young people see results. There are seven days a week and 24 hours in a day. If you're working a 40-hour week, you've got a helluva lot of hours at your Kawasaki dealership that you're wasting. I never gave a damn if it took 20 hours a day."

During such pep talks, he also infused some introspection. His flameout with the Eagles forced him to reflect on the perils of being overzealous. He admitted to the Kawasaki dealers that he had gone too far. "Instead of 17 to 19 hours, I should have moderated it," Vermeil said. "I should have kept it to 14. I worked time to death, and it killed me."

During that speech, Vermeil also implored the dealers to learn to handle setbacks. "People in management have got to learn to handle the negatives," he said. "People who interpret temporary setbacks as failure allow frustration to blind them. I've been guilty of this. You're looking at a failure. I licked 90 percent of the problems. The only problem I couldn't lick was myself."

After stepping back from coaching, Vermeil began learning how to harness his ambition with the help of therapists. He realized he could learn to how to handle frustration and defeat without diminishing his drive to succeed. He didn't have to run headfirst into walls.

Herbert Freudenberger, author of Burn Out, the book Vermeil cited when he quit coaching, invited him to New York for a chat.

Freudenberger was a pioneer in the study of occupational burn out, and Vermeil had unwittingly become Exhibit A of the problem.

Vermeil liked his first visit enough to drop by a few more times when CBS called him to New York for business meetings. His would talk with Freudenberger for about an hour each time—and he always came away amazed by how well this expert could read him.

"He told me things about myself that shocked me," Vermeil said.

After his first visit, in fact, Vermeil figured Carol had set him up. When he got home, he immediately broached this topic with his wife.

"Did you talk to Dr. Freudenberger?" Dick said.

"No, why," Carol said.

"He told me things about me that I know that I didn't think anybody else knew but you," Dick said.

As it turns out, he really was burned out. He was what the book said.

He also worked with therapist to get at the root of his short temper. He flew off the handle over relative minor issues and he sought to curb that habit. He continued those sessions for years, even after he got a handle on his perfectionism.

He took his own notes during the sessions, absorbing the material the way he soaked up football ideas at coaching clinics. Then he filed away the notes, giving himself personal checkpoints as reference points.

Vermeil liked his new self. "I learned to accept praise as a truth, not just to blow it off," he said. "There is such a stigma in this country about seeking help like that, but I can tell you it's one of the best things I've ever done."

The somewhat slower pace of commentating and speaking allowed Vermeil to get reacquainted with Carol, their three grown children and the growing supply of grandchildren. Dick and Carol had been together since high school and now they were really together, with no football to dominate their lives. They traveled. They planned vacations the way real people did.

This was Dick's time to make up for lost time with Carol, who had patiently played the role of the loyal coach's wife. "You spend half your time waiting," she said. "You spend a lot of time outside locker rooms, or in grandstands, or in stadiums, or breathing exhaust fumes from team buses.

"There have been times when I've thought, why am I here? But I never considered not being there."

Dick didn't have much play time with his own children when they were small, but now the next generation of Vermeils were being born. These were the kids he could take fishing. These were the kids who could hang out at his country home, a large log cabin structure built on a 110-acre spread beyond the suburban sprawl of Philadelphia. The grandkids rode on the tractor Leonard Tose gave him and helped him do some chores on the ranch.

But so much of Vermeil's lost time couldn't be regained. This was a sobering realization. "All of a sudden, I'm out of coaching, and the kids are all married and raising their own families," he said. "Carol was really the mother and the father to the kids because I slept in my office. I worked seven days a week, year round."

Vermeil enjoyed his freedom. He became an avid outdoorsman, hunting and fishing in some of the prime locations in the world. He applied his perfectionism to his newfound avocations. When former players like Bill Bergey went into the wilds with him, they found him to be as fiercely competitive as ever.

He loved to collect wine, to cook, to stage large barbecues at the Pennsylvania ranch for friends and relatives. He strove to improve in all his hobbies. Each time he tastes a new wine, for instance, he makes notations on the experience on a four-by-six-inch index card.

If a restaurant served him an exceptional meal, there was a good chance Vermeil would end up talking with the people responsible, perhaps back in the kitchen so he could see first-hand how the job was done. The owner of a restaurant chain later characterized Dick as the only man outside of the food industry that he could really discuss the Xs and Os of barbecue with.

Vermeil turned his analytical skills toward finance. Long after coaching, he maintained a number of commercial endorsement deals in the Philadelphia region. When he collected appearance checks for $2,500 or $5,000, he plowed the money into his stock portfolio, building stakes in growth companies like Wal-Mart and Home Depot Inc.

All in all, his life after coaching was pretty good. "This is such a nice way to make a living," Vermeil said during this stage of his career. "I never claimed to be a broadcaster. I'm a coach. I'm not an entertainer."

After getting released by CBS after five seasons, Vermeil moved on to ABC commentating on college football for the next nine years. He was pleasantly surprised by how advanced the coaching had become at the university level. He met some great offensive and defensive minds, men with cutting-edge ideas on schemes and tactics. He found out that all the best coaches in the country weren't in the NFL.

Vermeil always enjoyed the camaraderie of coaching, so his broadcasting career allowed him to renew and sustain friendships. Television also gave him a platform to weigh in on behalf of his colleagues.

When a coach he liked came under fire from boosters and the university's administration, Vermeil did what he could to help. He didn't want to name names, but at times he and Brent Musberger fabricated stories.

They would mention that a beleaguered coach was getting a contract extension from the school's president. This wasn't true, of course, but it backed off the dogs and gave the coach more room to operate.

"Got reprimanded for it," Vermeil said, "but it worked."

Musberger marveled at his colleague's rapport with the coaches. Football can be a nasty profession—with back-stabbing galore—but Vermeil seemed to click with everybody. Musberger had never been around a former coach with so many friends in the business. Part of that was his unwillingness to rip his colleagues or their players, which he attributed to his first-hand knowledge of all the variables.

Strong relationships with coaches like Gary Barnett, Bill Snyder and John Cooper prompted those men to share with Vermeil. They practically put him on staff during the weeks he worked their games. They exposed him to new strategies, new training techniques, new practice philosophies and new ways of relating to athletes. Rather than drifting away from football during his hiatus from coaching, he gained new perspectives on the sport.

When Vermeil sat down in the broadcast booth to call a game, he knew the game plans nearly as well as the assistant coaches working the headsets down the hall. From time to time, he saw a tactical adjustment that he had suggested while studying film with a college or pro staff. "He was the only analyst I ever worked with who could have coached either team on Saturday afternoon," Musberger said.

Carol would shake her head at her husband's thoroughness. Other analysts would just show up at games, watch the action unfold and wing it. But Dick couldn't operate that way. He would arrive at the microphone with exhaustive scouting reports. He understood the tendencies of each team. He knew their strengths and weaknesses. Musberger was right; Vermeil could have come down from the broadcast booth and coached one of the teams himself.

"He'd use all these different colored pens, which all meant something—red meant something, green meant something—all this information on every player, some of whom never got on the field," Carol said. "And he would use maybe 10 percent of the information that he had researched."

That's because the television networks wanted analysts to sprinkle some quick insights into the broadcast, not read a dissertation on the theory of football. The analyst job wasn't nearly as big as Vermeil made it out to be.

"I think sometimes I got so prepared that I got bogged down with information," he said. "I used to get really frustrated, especially early on, before I realized that, hell, this isn't a football clinic, it's a game.

"I was over-prepared. I couldn't use all the information if I did the team six weeks in a row. It didn't matter. I gained confidence by knowing. Whatever Brent threw at me, I had it. Whatever happened on the field, I had it."

Vermeil always dotted his Is and crossed his Ts. This is how he coached, so this is how he broadcast games. Vermeil had always gone over the top with his preparation during his career.

Trends fascinated him. Independent research intrigued him. He was always open to new information. Vermeil embraced computer-generated breakdowns while many of his peers were scoffing at the new technology.

"I was driven to learn, to be stimulated," he said. "I learned this in college because I was way behind academically, because I hadn't done anything. In a little, small high school, you didn't have to do anything. Go to class and you get a C. My graduating class had 29 kids in it. Of course, there were a bunch of brilliant kids, me not being one of them.

"I worked hard academically once I got going. I studied. I always felt so much more confident knowing that I invested a lot of time in preparation to take a test. All these things started spinning off into the more prepared you are, the more confident you are. I ended up graduating with department honors, I think it was. But I worked to catch up. I never cut a class in five years of college. And I don't know if you ever totally catch up."

He took the same zealous approach to learning the game of football. "I remember that every clinic I went to, I came back and I thought 'If I did this one thing, we're going to win them all, we're going to go undefeated.' Everybody's idea was a great idea. I was so green. As soon as I got home, I'd go to work on the notes, writing them up and studying them and plan them to my system that I was building as I was going along."

While he was at UCLA, a former semi-pro player named Joe Guardino gave Vermeil computerized scouting reports of Ohio State. The material analyzed every Buckeye play. Vermeil digested all the data and put it to good use while preparing his game plan.

"I gave Vermeil 10 pounds of computer reports on every conceivable Ohio State tendency," Guardino said. "Afterward, Dick said it was the easiest defensive game he ever played. He said it was never in doubt because he knew exactly what Ohio State was going to do."

Vermeil was willing to consider outside research while coaching the

When Vermeil sat down in the broadcast booth to call a game, he knew the game plans nearly as well as the assistant coaches working the headsets down the hall.

Eagles, too. He was among the first coaches to employ an independent scouting service run by Mike Giddings. "Some people use it as a back-up," Vermeil said at the time. "With us, his opinion gets tremendous weight in squad decisions. And sometimes I'll see a stat in his R&D book that'll just pop my eyes open. Like his draft stats. I remember one of his observations, that if you don't get a receiver in the first two rounds, you're as likely to get one in the last two who'll make your club as in the middle rounds."

Statistical probabilities fascinated Vermeil. Throughout his time away from the game, he continued his avid number crunching. He was like a doctoral candidate doing research, and he kept all the significant data that he came up with. He studied Super Bowl champions, profiling them statistically to determine the standards required in each phase of the game to win.

He developed a number of truisms, such as: "You lose three-quarters of the time in the National Football League when you have a punt returned against you for a touchdown."

From 1989 until 1996, Vermeil also analyzed preseason games for the Kansas City Chiefs on local television. He went to work for his old buddy Carl Peterson, who eventually landed in Kansas City after the demise the United States Football League and his Philadelphia and Baltimore Stars.

This assignment allowed Vermeil to stay current in the pro game. He attended training camp with the team and immersed himself in the squad's preparation, getting a feel for all the players and how they were progressing through the drills. He became an extra set of eyes and ears for Peterson, not to mention the team's best publicist during the franchise's dramatic upturn.

Vermeil also served as an ABC-TV commentator for World League of American Football games, working with Musberger in 1991 and 1992. He was able to keep abreast of the new trends in the pro game. He liked being up to speed, but it still wasn't coaching.

"There were moments over the 14 years that I would leave the TV booth and have an empty feeling," Vermeil said. "When the game was over, sometimes you would feel so insignificant. When you see the scoreboard, it tells you whether you did a good job or a bad job. You don't get that in broadcasting. It leaves you a little empty."

Within his role of a showman, he also felt a lot of frustration. He saw trends emerging on the field that the director or the cameramen failed to capture for the viewer.

"He worked as hard as he possibly could, but the outcome of the games, what people saw on TV, was out of his hands," Carol said. "I think it was frustrating to him to not be in the decision-making process. The replay would come up and he'd be prepared for so-and-so and to watch this tackle, and it would be somebody else. The truck would put up another play or something and it would just drive him nuts."

If he asked the director for a camera isolation on, say, the offensive line, and the camera failed to shoot with a wide enough angle to capture what he wanted, Vermeil would bristle. "It used to drive me crazy," he said. "I gradually learned to relax. It probably took me 10 years to relax and just be myself. Because that's just not my nature. I'd be so involved in the preparation and the preparation and so intense about it, that I probably wore people out.

"Eventually you develop a relationship with producers and directors and the people you work with, that you all work together and do a better job presenting what was actually going on," he said. "People basically want to show what the wide receiver, running back and maybe from time to time what the linebacker does. They don't want to show two key things that happened in the offensive line and the great play the defensive tackle made, or all these other things. Or the scheme that took away this thing. I felt it was my job as a coach and a broadcaster to educate as well, to really show what was going on, rather than just the glamour side of it."

He still took his craft seriously. Vermeil never wanted to join the other former coaches and become a studio analyst on one of the NFL pre-game shows. He didn't want to turn into a clown.

"Dick was courted by everybody to do a pre-game show, and he turned them all down," said Terry O'Neil, a former game-day producer at CBS and NBC. "And the reason why is because he said he spent 30 years trying to establish his credibility and then he goes on one of those pre-game shows and a 25-year-old producer wants him to blow that 30 years of credibility with one inane comment in 30 seconds."

But the more television work he did, the more he yearned to be back in football, where his analytical skills, his leadership and his thoroughness could be put to full use. He had way too much energy to be just a television analyst. Broadcasting was too easy for a worker like Vermeil.

"I was stealing for a living broadcasting games," he said with a laugh. "You work 18 to 20 weekends."

Carol found herself wrestling some of the same emotions after Dick left coaching. A broadcaster's wife felt less vital than a coach's wife. She had always lived and died with her husband's football teams.

"I thought, 'OK, we're going back and everything will settle in and we'll have a nice, quieter life without a lot of pressure,'" she said. "And then I missed it very much."

Dick stayed in touch with the old Eagles, who sensed his longing for the sideline. His former soldiers saw a comeback in the making. "He missed the involvement of being a coach," Herman Edwards said. "The more we would talk, I just kind of knew he would get back."

Inevitably, Vermeil began considering feelers from NFL teams. Atlanta approached him four years into his broadcasting career and got his juices flowing again. When Dick went back home to Calistoga around the time of Christmas 1986 to be with Louie, who was waging a losing battle with pancreatic cancer, Falcons executives made numerous phone calls.

But Vermeil, waist deep in family matters, never got together with team officials for face-to-face negotiations. "I got very serious for one week with the Falcons," Vermeil said. "I gave that serious consideration but never met with them. There were other times, but they didn't feel right personally."

He was afraid to visit Atlanta, in fact, because old friends like Marion Campbell were there. His loyalty would overcome him. "As soon as I saw Marion and Fred Bruney, that would be it, I'd take the job without thinking," he said.

Tampa Bay Buccaneers owner Hugh Culverhouse also called during that difficult period for the Vermeils.

"Dick, what's this you're going to take the job in Atlanta?" he said.

"Mr. Culverhouse," Dick said, "that's been a strong rumor all week, but I refused to go meet with them. I'm not going to do it."

"I have more money than I can spend in my lifetime and so does my family," Culverhouse said. "So you can write your own contract."

"I don't think so," Dick said before ending the call.

"Who was that?" Louie asked.

"That was Hugh Culverhouse," Dick said. He explained the gist of the call and the job offer.

"Do you need the aggravation?" Louie asked.

"No," Vermeil said.

"Then don't do it," Louie said.

Dick didn't. Peterson made his first overture on behalf of the Chiefs in 1989, but Vermeil still wasn't ready to jump back on the treadmill.

"He said he was enjoying television," Peterson said. "He said he was through with coaching. But I could see it in his eyes. He's a football coach. He's a fine television commentator, don't get me wrong. But he's a football coach. Television was something he did. Coaching is who he is."

Peterson had to be content to having him work his preseason games as an analyst. He chatted with Vermeil weekly during the rest of the year, touching on personal matters and also some football. Vermeil kept telling Peterson he wouldn't return to coaching, however, unless the situation was just right.

CHAPTER SIX: THOROUGHNESS 105

And it seemed perfect in Philadelphia in 1995, when Eagles owner Jeffrey Lurie came calling. His old team needed him after sliding to 8-8 and 7-9 finishes under coach Rich Kotite, who was as charismatic as woodwork. This was a chance to coach in the NFL and stay near his ranch. He was still extremely very popular in the area—he remained visible through numerous commercial endorsement deals—and a lot of his old players were around the franchise. Eagles fans still adored him, which was quite an honor in that hard-edged sports town. His face seemed to be everywhere on Blue Cross billboards.

"They know I respected them and spent a lot of time in the community," Vermeil said. "I really got out and got to know the community losing and winning. And it helped that I stayed in the community. Philadelphia is my home and the Philadelphia Eagles are my home team."

Vermeil's closest friends expected him to take this job. Many assumed it was a done deal. Philadelphia awaited the official announcement. Philadelphia was abuzz during this negotiation. His hiring would have been celebrated by a city that had seen a lot of bad football since his retirement.

When he had coached the Eagles from 1976 to 1982, Vermeil topped out at $200,000 in salary. His original asking price this time around was an unprecedented $10 million over five years, plus a five percent ownership stake. At the time, Miami Dolphins icon Don Shula was the highest paid NFL coach at $1.5 million a year. Vermeil also asked for total control of the football operation, despite his time away from coaching. He had worked very well with Tose and Jim Murray during his previous run with the Eagles, but he didn't know Lurie and demanded contractual protection from interference.

Lurie ultimately balked, stunning Vermeil. He had been prepared to round up much of his old gang and try to lead the Eagles back to glory.

"I think he was disappointed and somewhat bitter, bitter that we were unwilling to meet his requirements," Lurie said. "Maybe his life in broadcasting was so comfortable that it would take something out of the ordinary."

Vermeil knew how popular he was in Philadelphia and understood the impact he could have on the franchise. He wasn't just an up-and-coming coach hungry for an opportunity, like he was at UCLA when he took the job without discussing the salary involved.

"It seems almost impossible for an NFL coach to have the kind of popularity Dick has," Eagles play-by-play broadcaster Merrill Reese said at the time. "He really owned this city, and certainly when the prospect arose about the possibility of Dick coming back here as coach, this city was sky high. And it crashed when Dick and the Eagles did not agree to get together. "

Vermeil said his failure to connect in Philadelphia came down to power and not money. As George Allen had told him so many years earlier, he had to do it his way. That's why he expected Lurie to give him the control he needed. He was already assembling his staff when he learned he wouldn't get the job.

His disappointment was profound. He was finally ready to get back on the sidelines after all those years away . . . and he didn't have a team to coach. Now he was eager to get another offer.

"It finally got to the point where I felt better about myself and my own self control," Vermeil said. "The Eagles thing stimulated it. All of a sudden, it made me realize that, hey, there is still a fire there."

After the 1996 season, Rams president John Shaw called at the behest of owner Georgia Frontiere and new minority owner Stan Kroenke. They needed a savior, somebody to pull this once-proud franchise out of its decade-long tailspin.

A West Coast fixture for 30 years, the franchise moved to St. Louis in 1995 after failing to coax a state-of-the-art football stadium from skeptical officials in Orange County, California. Apathy enveloped the team in Anaheim during the early 1990s, largely because the Rams staggered to 5-11, 3-13, 6-10, 5-11 and 4-12 finishes.

Shaw traded superstar running back Eric Dickerson to Indianapolis during the 1987 season to avoid meeting his contract demands. In return for Dickerson, the Rams got six draft picks that ultimately brought little help. The franchise cornerstone was exchanged, in effect, for a sack of doughnuts. The seeds of disaster were planted. Shaw fired John Robinson after the 1991 season and tried to hire Vermeil. Dick said no, so Shaw brought venerable Chuck Knox back into the league.

Lacking a dominant running back to hand the ball to again and again and again, Knox failed to reverse the team's decline during his three seasons back on the job. On the way out of Anaheim, Shaw fired Knox and once again tried to hire Vermeil. When Dick took another pass, Shaw turned to Oregon State coach Rich Brooks, a former Rams assistant coach who had been out of the NFL for 18 years. Former Raiders and San Diego Chargers executive Steve Ortmayer gained control of the football operation as the team came to St. Louis.

Frontiere was one of the NFL's true eccentrics. The former showgirl inherited the team from her sixth husband, Carroll Rosenbloom, after he drowned under very murky circumstances in Florida in 1979. His death was ruled accidental, but persons close to the family couldn't help but suspect foul play, since he was a strong swimmer. Conspiracy theories have floated around the league for years.

Georgia quickly fired Carroll's son (her step-son), Steven, whom Carroll had groomed for the team's presidency. Georgia took control of the franchise and played her new job for all it was worth, posing for Sports Illustrated cover photographs for and yukking it up with Johnny Carson on The Tonight Show. Other NFL owners could only stand back and wince. The staid NFL preferred its owners—older businessmen, as the rule—to stay in the background.

She married her seventh husband, composer Dominic Frontiere, a little more than a year later. They divorced in 1988, two years after he was implicated in a Super Bowl ticket-scalping scandal that sent him to prison on tax evasion charges. Ever the trouper, Georgia soldiered on after this bit of unpleasantness. She sought a lower profile in the media but still enjoyed her team ownership immensely. She fawned over her players, hugging and kissing them on the sidelines and lavishing curious Christmas gifts on them, such as Cabbage Patch dolls.

She conducted her end of the team business at her Bel-Air estate, aided by a coterie of errand-running lackeys. Visitors often sat waiting for hours as she pulled herself together. It was not unusual for her to skip her own dinner parties without notice. The publication of the Rams media guide was often delayed while she fussed over her official photographic portrait. Frontiere counted among her friends a "B" list of Hollywood luminaries, including comedian Jonathan Winters, who performed 15 minutes of stand-up material at Rosenbloom's memorial service. Carroll's family was appalled.

A new male companion emerged in her life, pony-tailed musician Earl Weatherwax. Her most trusted aide remained Shaw, a shadowy accountant and attorney whose forte is hard-line negotiating. He navigated the franchise's enormously lucrative transfer to her hometown of St. Louis, playing that city off Baltimore, another jilted city, and Orange County.

The $350 million relocation deal enriched Frontiere beyond everybody's imagination. St. Louis had lost the football Cardinals to Arizona when owner Bill Bidwill failed to get the new football stadium he wanted. Aspiring expansion teams owners finally convinced the city, St. Louis County and the state of Missouri to build a new stadium, a downtown dome adjacent to the convention center. As construction began, St. Louis appeared to be the front-runner for an expansion team. But unseemly bickering among the would-be team owners torpedoed the expansion bid, and the NFL chose two fresh markets, Charlotte and Jacksonville, instead of St. Louis and Baltimore. This was Shaw's opportunity to make Georgia a lot of money. St. Louis business and governmental leaders were willing to take extreme measures to get a franchise and keep the $280 million dome from becoming a white elephant. The landmark deal they gave the Rams guaranteed the franchise annual profits exceeding $20 million in St. Louis. Fans were forced to pony up big money for "personal seat licenses" that earned them the right to buy tickets.

**The Rams were offering him an opportunity to correct the mistakes he had made with the Eagles.**

Kroenke, a billionaire real-estate developer and husband of a Wal-Mart heiress, bought into the franchise as a minority partner. The Rams got a spectacular training complex, dubbed Rams Park, built in the suburbs at no cost to them. This package became the standard that every NFL franchise to strive to achieve. Business was never better.

But the team itself…well, the Rams proved to be as inept as they had been in Anaheim. They started their inaugural St. Louis season with a giddy 5-1 spurt, playing before wildy enthusiastic crowds at Busch Stadium and then inside the new Trans World Dome. Georgia was seen all over town, smiling and waving and posing for photo opportunities. She spent most of her time in her new spread in Sedona, Arizona, but she flew to St. Louis during the season.

Rams fans didn't mind, since they finally had football again and the team was a lot of fun.

But reality hit. The Rams lost 18 of their next 26 games. Various crises arose, such as the series of career-threatening concussions suffered by quarterback Chris Miller. The hapless Ortmayer selected noodle-armed veteran Steve Walsh to succeed Miller, but the job landed in the unsteady hands of rookie Tony Banks in 1996 once it became obvious that Walsh would need a cell phone to reach his receivers. Banks had a remarkable arm, by contrast, but he was unpolished after jumping from minor league baseball to junior college football to Michigan State for two years. Brooks sent him in for his first NFL snap when the Rams were backed up to their own six-inch line against the powerful San Francisco 49ers.

Welcome to the NFL, kid! Banks threw one incompletion, then was called for intentional grounding and tagged for a safety. The Rams would lose that game 34-0. The jittery Banks would go on to set a league record with 21 fumbles that season and become a much-despised symbol of the franchise's futility.

Only at the end of his two-year tenure did Brooks regain his handle on

NFL coaching. Toward the end of the 1996 season, he finally learned how to make the halftime tactical adjustments needed for success. He finally cracked the whip on his unruly players and created some urgency to win. But it was too late to save him. After extracting a king's ransom from greater St. Louis to relocate, Shaw felt obligated to provide a decent product. He fired Brooks and aimed high for his next coach.

He courted former San Francisco 49ers coach George Seifert. He negotiated with 49ers aide Pete Carroll, who would end up in New England instead. Bobby Ross and Kevin Gilbride interviewed for the job, but they went to Detroit and San Diego respectively. Shaw looked at Eagles defensive coordinator Emmitt Thomas, too, but took a pass. He all but offered former New Orleans Saints coach Jim Mora the job, and then took one last stab at Vermeil.

This time, Vermeil agreed to take charge of the franchise. The Rams were willing to pay the elite salary that madeLurie balk, some $9 million over five years, and give him final say on all football matters. With those issues out of the way, Vermeil knew it was time to come back. His heart said so.

"I felt like I've awoken from a dream," Vermeil said.

The decision shocked Carol. The Vermeils were planning a vacation to the South of France at the time. She had been studying French in preparation for the journey, one they had always discussed but never found time to have. When Dick told her that he had agreed to coach the Rams, her response was equally abrupt.

"How do you say 'Screw you' in French?" she said.

Naturally, this hiring first elicited guffaws. Vermeil had been out of coaching since 1982. "The game has changed a lot in the last 15 years," sniffed Green Bay Packers offensive coordinator Sherm Lewis, who would have liked a shot at the job.

But as she saw her husband get back in high gear after taking the job, Carol realized he made the right decision. The Rams were offering him an opportunity to correct the mistakes he had made with the Eagles. The Rams were giving him the chance to coach the right way.

Vermeil was at a different point in his life. His kids were grown and had their own kids. His parents were gone; Louie had passed away in 1987, Alice in 1992. He and Carol had stepped back from the rat race and enjoyed a more normal existence for 14 years. Now could see the twilight on his horizon.

"I said, 'Christ, no one is going to offer me that opportunity again,'" he said. "I might as well do it."

The NFL was shocked by Vermeil's decision to return. Since he had been gone for so long, owners, general managers and rival coaches had

assumed he would never come back. When the Rams introduced him to
St. Louis at a news conference, much of the football industry tuned in as
well.

"I didn't like how I left," Vermeil explained. "I allowed the game to
consume me because I loved it so much. I had such a passion for it that it
blinded me to my own personal health and to everything else that was
going on around me, my wife, my kids. I just knew I needed a break, so
I took the break.

"I was 60 years old when the Rams asked me about this. All but one
year since I left I had people ask me (to coach), and I stayed away from
it. I felt if I didn't do it now, I'd never get the chance. I didn't want to be
65 and look back and say, 'I wish I would have.'

"I missed the leadership, the responsibility of feeling it's important. In
the booth sometimes, I didn't know what I had accomplished. It's fun to
be in a position where you can make a difference. I wasn't proud of what
kind of football coach I was when I left. I wanted the opportunity to come
back and try to do it right once more. I still have a passion for the game.
I've mellowed a lot. I think I have a lot better emotional stamina."

That's why the people who knew Vermeil best expected him to return
to coaching sooner than he did. They never figured out what he did with
all his energy during those 14 years.

"I never thought he would walk away, and when he did, I thought he'd
be back right away," said former Eagles linebacker John Bunting, who
joined Vermeil's Rams staff as an assistant coach. "I kept saying that in
year one, year two, year three. At about year 10, I started to give up. I was
shocked when he got back in."

Long-time San Francisco 49ers executive Bill Walsh also wondered
what took Vermeil so long. A switch from coaching to broadcasting had
become common in football, but most coaches quickly got the itch to
return. Nothing in life can duplicate the anticipation of a big game or the
thrill of a major victory.

"I wouldn't say he was wasting his time," Walsh said, "but he was
wasting his talents in broadcasting. He was a good broadcaster, but just
had way too much to offer to other people and to himself as a coach or
even in management in the NFL."

Edwards, a cornerstone defensive back on those Eagles teams,
cautioned Vermeil about the game he was getting back into. Edwards had
stayed in the game as an assistant coach and scout, building the creden-
tials to become a head coach himself. When he heard about Vermeil's
return, he gave him a call.

"Hey pal," Edwards said. " Are you sure you want to do this?" Vermeil
insisted he was ready.

"It never worried me that the game of football passed him by," Edwards said. "I just wondered how Vermeil might relate to today's athletes, who have evolved quite a bit since 1982."

Ron Jaworski, too, figured Vermeil would pick up the Xs and Os easily enough. After all, he had prepared like a maniac to broadcast those pro and college games. Vermeil talked strategy with some of the brightest minds in the business every season after leaving the sideline.

"My personal feeling when he took the St. Louis job, was he was more on the cutting edge than most coaches in the league," Jaworski said. "He got valid information and used the best parts of it. I found it amusing when people said the game had passed him by."

Although Vermeil's family enjoyed having him home on the Pennsylvania ranch, close to all the grandkids, everybody understood his need to pursue this ambition again. This was unfinished business. Had he never gone back, the unpleasant end with the Eagles would have nagged him to his grave.

"I think our children are cautiously optimistic," Carol said after Dick took the plunge. "They understand him, they know coaching is in his heart, it is something he wants to do. They're happy in that way. But none of them are as high-powered as Dick is and they think. 'Look at the great life you had.' When we moved from California to coach the Eagles, they all came to Philadelphia. Now they're all here, and we're leaving.

"They're happy for him, but I think they were satisfied and happy with the lifestyle we had prior this. They'll come to the games when they can, but it's a different situation now. They all have their own families. But they're all getting satellite dishes so they can watch Rams games."

Vermeil was more capable of maintaining perspective after years of introspection, but that didn't mean the passion was gone. Once he signed with the Rams, winning became the only thing once again.

"I say I'm not going to live and die with this team," he said before his first season, "But you know what? I know I will. For years, that's what was missing from my life. I wasn't on a team. I needed that. They don't have a transfusion where they can take it out of you. Once it's in your blood, it's in your blood. My wife saw it. There are 18 or 20 players who live in the Philadelphia area. Carol said whenever I was around them, I would just come alive.

"Well, I'm alive again."

# CHAPTER SEVEN
# PERSUASIVENESS

*"Coach, nothing's changed. All they have to do is look in your eyes, and they'll trust you."*

-Vince Papale, a former Philadelphia Eagles special teams standout, advising his old coach

St. Louis didn't exactly roll out the welcome mat for Dick Vermeil. Football fans had seen this sort of hire before, when well-meaning Cardinals owner Bill Bidwill inexplicably brought the legendary Bud Wilkinson out of a 15-year retirement from college football to coach his team. Predictably, that hiring turned out very badly. Perhaps that's why the St. Louis Post-Dispatch announced Vermeil's hiring with this headline: "Dick Vermeil?"

The new coach was unconcerned by such head scratching. "People are going to say Dick's a retread, a has-been, almost a never-was because I lost the Super Bowl, and possibly over the hill," he acknowledged.

But the snickering stopped when Vermeil stepped up to the podium at Rams Park for the first time to address St. Louis. Vermeil's commanding 31-minute introductory address dazzled the media, captivated Rams staffers and players and intrigued a large, local television audience. He squared his chin and delivered his words with great force. His eyes glistened with emotion. He believed he could transform this woeful franchise, and soon everybody in the room believed it, too.

"Ladies and gentlemen, you can't imagine how exciting it is to be here today," he gushed. "In terms of being a head coach again. I have never been, in my life, more confident or prepared. Each time I got a head-coaching job in the past, I was not prepared to do the job and should not have been given the job. This time, I'm fully prepared."

He made many proclamations, including these:

"The weight room ought to be a showcase. It is beautiful. But it isn't worth a damn if you don't have bodies in there working, sweating. That great big indoor facility, in the middle of the winter—it's not worth a damn unless there's a quarterback in there being driven.

"I have a saying, 'The main thing is the main thing.' As soon as a professional football franchise loses sight of the main thing, they're never going to get there. I have my No. 1 obligation defined. That's to provide talented athletes to a very talented coaching staff, athletes in the frame of mind to be coached. If they don't want to be coached and they don't want to be worked, they probably will not stay here.

"You can't control things like you used to because of the salary cap. You run a guy off and it can still cost you. You're still paying him after you run him off. You've got to be more intelligent. You've got to use good judgment and you've got to invest more time in the human mind. Because attitudes are nothing more than habitual ways of thinking. You're either the victim or the beneficiary of the way you think.

"I believe in building a football team, not buying a football team. It's tougher today than ever because of free agency, but it can be done.

"If you want to criticize me, hey, I don't give a damn. I've been criticized by the best of them.

"This is my last stop. It's an unbelievable opportunity. When you walk around these facilities, see what St. Louis has done for pro football, they have raised the level of what it's all about, of what class is all about in the National Football League. It's my job to make sure a player fits into that class."

And on and on he went, selling the Vermeil way. He left his audience slack-jawed.

"There's definitely an energy about him, no doubt about that," Rams tight end Aaron Laing said. "It's not the same old mundane speech."

Vermeil dove into his new job with 14 years of stored energy. He sought to build the most impressive staff ever assembled. He fired Steve Ortmayer, the head of football operations, and the bulk of Rich Brooks' coaching staff. He needed his own guys at the top. He pitched his dream to some of the most accomplished men in the business.

One of the first men he contacted was Jim Mora, his former Stanford and UCLA colleague. Vermeil offered him the role of defensive coordinator and assistant head coach. Disappointed that he didn't get the job himself, Mora passed and became a TV analyst instead.

Carl Peterson, Vermeil's former right-hand man, got a phone call from Vermeil at seven in the morning shortly after he agreed to coach the Rams.

"I'm taking the St. Louis job, and I want John Bunting, Carl Hairston and Lynn Stiles," Vermeil said.

"Dick, first of all, congratulations on the job," Peterson said. "But the rule is I can deny you permission to talk to those guys if they're under contract. So are you telling me or asking me?"

Vermeil mulled that over for a moment. "I'm telling you that I'm asking you," he said.

How could Peterson refuse his mentor? He freed those three to join Vermeil's new brain trust. "It was an opportunity to work with a guy that

I played for," Bunting said. "I told him, 'I've been waiting 14 years for you to come back.'"

Also joining Vermeil was offensive coordinator Jerry Rhome, who had played for Vermeil in 1971 as a back-up quarterback for the Rams. Old friend Mike White, most recently head coach of the Raiders, came aboard as assistant coach. There weren't many assistant coaching jobs that would have appealed to him, but Vermeil was like a brother.

"I came for that reason," White said. "Because of Dick Vermeil. His passion. His emotion, which we all see. His enthusiasm. His leadership. And then the other thing is a factor to a lot of these guys: we have a chance to win."

Dick Coury, 67, came to coach the receivers; he had been a member of Vermeil's first coaching staff in Philadelphia. Vermeil also called on some of the greatest coaches of his generation, including defensive guru Bud Carson, 65; offensive line coach Jim Hanifan, 63; and special teams expert Frank Gansz, 58. Coury and Carson weren't sure they wanted come out of retirement and step back into the meat grinder, but Vermeil insisted.

"I recruited, coaxed, pushed, called, leaned on and begged this group to be here," he said. "Because, No. 1, they're very fine teachers. No. 2, they're the kind of people that I want in our organization. They're extremely hard-working people. They're loyal. They're motivated to do the job. None of them will ever be afraid to stand up and assume responsibility for the performance of their players. None of them. They aren't excuse makers. Hey, if we don't get it done, it's going to be our fault. Not Georgia's fault, not Stan Kroenke's fault or John Shaw's fault. I'll tell you what, if this group can't get it done, it can't be done."

> 'I believe in building a football team, not buying a football team.'

The Rams figured this "Legends of Coaching" would try to turn things around in a hurry. "Of course, you get a bunch of 60-year-olds together and you'd expect them to feel some urgency," observed tackle Wayne Gandy. "They don't have a lot of time left."

Quarterback Tony Banks was even more blunt. "Why are they bringing the dinosaurs back?" he wondered.

During his first meeting with his players, Vermeil addressed their skepticism head on. "Trust me," he told the players. "I have surrounded myself with an experienced coaching staff that knows what it's doing, and we are going to win. I just can't tell you how long it's going to take. We're not here just to improve or get better. We are starting a crusade to win in St. Louis and eliminate the thought that this is a transplanted football team."

Vermeil had much catching up to do. Game tactics had evolved quite a bit during his absence. The business side of the sport was far more complicated. As the director of football operations, he had far-ranging responsibilities. Vermeil realized he would need a lot of help getting this program where he wanted it, so he gave his veteran assistants much latitude.

He realized a five-year program wouldn't do. Shaw didn't have the patience for that—and he suspected that St. Louis lacked such patience, too.

"It's an instant gratification business," Vermeil said. "They keep recycling football coaches so they can recycle season tickets and sky boxes. I'd been out of coaching for 14 years and I needed immediate experience. I needed a guy like Mike White, that I knew and could trust with my life. I needed Jim Hanifan, Jerry Rhome, guys that had been in the league."

At one of his first mini-camps, Vermeil admitted to being out of sorts. The notorious control freak felt like a mere observer. His assistant coaches were in the faces of the Rams, doing all the teaching. He mostly stood off to the side, supervising.

"I actually felt a little embarrassed," Vermeil said. "I had a feeling like, 'My god, what the hell am I out here for?' Everybody else was doing all the work. I'll make the critical game-day decisions. But this team is going to be run by a board of directors. I'm the chairman of the board."

One of those directors was Charley Armey, who arrived from the New England Patriots to clean up the pro scouting department. John Becker, one of Vermeil's assistant coaches from the Eagles days, got more responsibility, too. Stiles and White also had important input on personnel matters.

Vermeil set out to win over everybody at Rams Park, from the top administrators to the support staff. Everybody needed a new attitude to make the program work. Everybody had to have a hand in the change. Rather than clean house, he tried to give Rams employees at every level the opportunity to join the crusade. He took the time to seek them out, to get to know them, to make them feel important. Not only did he work his locker room every day, chatting it up the players, he worked the whole building at Rams Park.

The players were the toughest sell. He had lots of compelling Eagles stories, but they meant nothing to the guys playing in 1997. Most of the Rams were little kids when Vermeil took Philadelphia to the Super Bowl. Bill Bergey? Stan Walters? These names didn't mean much to these players. Ron Jaworski? He was that guy on ESPN, right?

These guys hadn't watched Bunting pile-drive the New York Giants back in the day. They hadn't seen running backs coach Wilbert Montgomery bowl through the Dallas Cowboys in his prime.

"I had to call my grandfather to try to study up on who Coach Vermeil was," Laing said. "I was 11 years old the last time he coached."

There was an astonishing amount of work to do. The Rams had grown accustomed to failure. Losing had jaded the veterans. Many of the younger Rams were unruly. They had lacked discipline under Brooks, who had missed an entire generation of NFL players while coaching college football. And Ortmayer hadn't placed a premium on character as he assembled a roster. The Raiders, after all, had adored outcasts.

Coming in from the perennially competitive Chiefs, Stiles was taken aback by what he saw and felt at Rams Park. A sense of doom hung in the hallways.

"The day we walked in there, there was a negative attitude," he said. "The two things the Rams could do very well in the '90s, they could hire coaches and they could fire coaches. They didn't know what to do in between. Dick Vermeil came into a very negative environment. He didn't create the problems, they were just there."

Vermeil resolved to win over the skeptics with his relentlessly positive outlook. During the final day of a mini-camp in May, he expressed his faith to about 9,000 fans during a public practice session in the Trans World Dome in downtown St. Louis.

"I don't know how many wins we're going to have this year," Vermeil told the crowd. "We've got a lot of outstanding football players, and if we do a good job coaching them, we'll see significant improvement. I wish I could tell you that we'll win 11 or 12 games, but I don't know. I do know this: They're going to be the kind of team you'll be proud of."

Then he rushed over to the fans to sign autographs, shake hands and pose for pictures. The enthusiastic response overwhelmed him.

"God darn, that was emotional," Vermeil later said. "My eyes were watering, and I've never had that before in a mini-camp."

During early addresses to the team, Vermeil challenged his players to challenge themselves. Day by day, step by step, he tried to raise expectations around Rams Park.

"Don't take anything for granted," he told them. "Nothing in life gets better by accident. It will take a degree of concentration you've never experienced as a Ram to succeed. Winning is not complicated. People complicate it. Consistent winning motivation comes from within."

Gansz became his Tony Robbins, giving stirring pep talks and writing inspirational messages on the grease boards in the meeting room. He was a history buff who punctuated his talks with, say, a fiery Genghis Khan tale. He became a frantic presence during mini-camps, training camp and regular-season practices, often donning his battery pack and portable amplification system so that EVERYBODY COULD HEAR HIM when he led drills on the field.

The staff would rebuild and reorient the Rams from the ground up. Reporters who assembled for Vermeil's first mini-camps were a bit surprised to see the coaches furiously teaching the Rams how to properly tackle ball carriers. This staff really was starting over from square one.

Vermeil also had to lay some groundwork regarding his relationships with the players. One by one, he would have to win them over. So he coached the only way he knew how, showing the players that he cared. The Rams were in for a surprise.

After the team signed veteran defensive end James Harris, Vermeil accompanied him to a Sunday service at Harris' place of worship, the Southern Mission Baptist Church in East St. Louis. When linebacker Mike Jones signed as a free agent, he didn't know what to make of his first encounter with the new coach.

Vermeil got up from behind his desk, walked over to Jones and extended his arms.

"I'm thinking, 'I know this guy doesn't want me to hug him,'" Jones said.

Oh, but he did. So Jones got up and hugged him.

"That was the first time I ever hugged one of my head coaches," Jones said.

Having come from the Raiders, Jones wasn't accustomed to sentimentality in the workplace. Raiders owner Al Davis didn't run a touchy-feely organization. Few franchises in the NFL did. But Vermeil kept his emotions on his sleeves. He would hug the Rams. He would cry in the presence of the Rams. And he would not apologize for behaving like this family's overly sentimental uncle.

"I've always been a very emotional person," Vermeil said. "It's embar-rassing sometimes. It's not so much that I'm crying, I get emotional and get tears in my eyes. I've prepared myself emotionally and mentally not to do it, and I still do it. I have a passion for this damn game. And I have a compassion for the people who coach it and the people who play it. I love my players. I've been made fun of because I say that. I'll tell you this, if I don't love them, I don't like to coach them."

He proved this by embracing troubled running back Lawrence Phillips, on whom the Rams had gambled a 1996 first-round draft pick. Phillips had enjoyed sporadic success during his rookie season for Brooks, but his off-field troubles mounted. Soon after Vermeil arrived, Phillips was charged with disorderly conduct when a party veered out of bounds at a motel in Omaha, Nebraska.

The summer before, the former University of Nebraska star had been arrested for drunk driving in Southern California. That misstep was deemed a probation violation on his earlier assault conviction for beating up his college girlfriend. Phillips got 23 days in jail.

Vermeil rallied behind him, dispatching Stiles to help shepherd Phillips through the legal process. He had the team give Phillips $100,000 of the $300,000 workout bonus he couldn't collect while incarcerated. When Phillips was released from jail, Vermeil traveled to Nebraska to escort him back to St. Louis. He viewed this as a valuable bonding opportunity with the player.

"You get to know a person better when they're under pressure," Vermeil explained. "I don't know how well we get to know people when everything is going well with their lives."

Vermeil saw vast athletic potential in Phillips and empathized with him as a person. A miserable childhood spent on the streets and detention centers of Los Angeles had left Phillips brooding, distrustful and volatile. He was capable of great charm, but his dark side always lurked.

"Every time I've been around him, I leave with a good feeling," Vermeil said early in his tenure with the Rams. "I've been around athletes all my life, and I've always prided myself in the ability to read whether a guy is conning me. But when a guy smiles easily and talks freely to you, just basic conversation, I felt relieved. I could be 100 percent wrong, but I'm going to give him the benefit of the doubt until he proves me wrong. That's what we're supposed to do in this society. I never used to think that way, but everything's changed."

These Rams would test Vermeil's will to coach again. Overcoming deep-rooted problems would prove to be an enormous task. Instilling a championship mindset would be difficult.

Fortunately, Vermeil came ready to work. His appetite for detail work was as ravenous as ever. Before the opening of Vermeil's first training camp, Sports Illustrated caught up with him on Independence Day, preparing for the weeks ahead in Macomb, Illinois. Back in Philadelphia

"I've always been a very emotional person," Vermeil said. "It's embarrassing sometimes."

21 years earlier, Vermeil had cursed the Bicentennial fireworks that disrupted his film study. On this Fourth of July, Vermeil put in a 14-hour day. He                                                                    was drawing up the play book and making plans for every practice during the pre-season and regular season down to the minute, before it even started. This was an entry for July 18: "4:02/4:07—Team-cadence/pursuit tackling."

Vermeil was brimming with confidence when he arrived at his first Rams training camp, at Western Illinois University in Macomb. But reality quickly smacked him upside the head.

Banks arrived at training camp with his six-month old Rottweiler puppy, Felony. He wanted the pooch by his side in his dormitory room. Perhaps they could take long walks together at night. Perhaps they could play a rousing game of fetch every morning. He could bring her scraps from the training table.

"She's like my daughter," Banks explained.

A horrified Vermeil told Tony that the dog must go, so a crestfallen Banks had to summon a couple of his cousins to drive up from St. Louis and take the dog back home.

"The dog is not going to stay in the dorm," Vermeil told reporters. "That's a first. I've never seen a player bring a dog to training camp."

This incident symbolized all that was wrong with the Rams. Years of losing had lowered team expectations and erased its work ethic. There was no urgency to improve. Banks, for instance, could have collected a $25,000 bonus for remaining in St. Louis to do his off-season conditioning at Rams Park. Instead, he chose to return to his home in San Diego so he could play basketball with his friends.

"Nobody's going to stop me from playing basketball," he said. "Nobody."

Phillips also had a miserable work ethic. He lacked physical toughness and was prone to nagging injuries. Vermeil did what he could to encourage him during their first training camp together. He tried to build Phillips up so he could become part of the team's foundation.

"Here's the man who's going to be one of the best running backs in the NFL this year!" Vermeil said to Phillips after the team's first camp session. "Good job out there today! How are you feeling?"

"Crampin' up, coach," Phillips said.

"Now Lawrence, you know that wouldn't have happened if you'd worked out as hard in the last month of the off-season as you did the rest of the time," Vermeil said.

"Had to take care of business, coach," Phillips said.

"The only business you have to take care of now is being the best football player you can be."

Skeptics stuck a "Father Flanagan" label on Vermeil for his willingness to embrace Phillips and other Rams with checkered pasts. But Vermeil insisted that this was nothing new, that he had addressed similar issues with the Eagles.

"We had players who drank too much, took cocaine, beat their wives," he said. "The world just didn't know about it. The NFL used to hide all that. I think problems with booze and drugs were greater then than now, when everything is tested."

Vermeil admitted that he had a more forgiving view of his players than he had during his first run through to the league. He tried to be more understanding of character flaws than he had been 15 or 20 years earlier. This new perspective was a byproduct of the self-exploration he had undergone during his time away from the sidelines.

"We've got a lot of guys on rosters now that are products of our society, and I didn't think about all that stuff before," he said. "I didn't take the time. The NFL doesn't come from a higher socio-economic bracket of society. They have all the same problems everybody else has. People assume just because they are gifted athletes, they have no problems."

That forgiving side of Vermeil didn't keep him from making extreme demands on his players. His regimen bordered on physical abuse. His first training camp mortified the Rams, who clearly hadn't been pushed hard enough by Brooks. Practices often lasted three and a half hours, complete with 30 "up-downs."

Many Rams couldn't remember the last time they did an "up-down"—an old-school drill that requires players to run in place, in full gear, then hit the deck, spring back up, run in place, hit the deck, spring back up . . . well, you get the picture. In 90-degree heat, it's no fun.

Vermeil put the players through six hours of full-pad work most days. Team meetings lasted until roughly 11 p.m. every night. Curfew was 11:30 p.m. Then the coaches kept going, meeting among themselves past midnight.

"He makes hard work automatic," Hairston said. "Dick's running the same practices he ran in Philadelphia." (For the record, the "up-downs" were Hairston's idea, learned from his days working for coach Buddy Ryan with the Eagles.)

Soon, Rams veterans were reeling. "Surprised isn't the word," defensive tackle D'Marco Farr said. "Try shocked. Horrified. I looked around at guys, and I said to myself, this one is dead. That one over there's dead. They'll never make it through camp."

Vermeil still had a volatile side after all these years. When he ordered his players to wear knee pads during a training camp drill and only a small percentage complied, he flipped out.

"This is nothing but an act of defiance!" he yelled. "Do what I tell you! Don't screw with me!"

He had laid down the law early in camp. He warned the players that they would have to find new levels of concentration to survive. Ultimately, nobody's job would be safe.

"As I build this team, I will eliminate those who aren't motivated enough to win on a weekly basis and replace them with people who have a deeper desire to excel, a desire that was implemented long before I ever came in contact with them," he told the team. "The true winner celebrates exhaustion as a measure of his complete effort. The players who do the most complaining are those who have invested the least amount of time preparing. Don't come complaining to me. I'll get you fired."

Vermeil started to reach some of his new players, the ones willing to do the work to end the losing. "I wouldn't care if Coach Vermeil didn't know a thing about football, I would do whatever he asked because he's a sincere man," center Mike Gruttadauria said. "I heard he was an emotional guy and I'm thinking, 'Yeah, sure, whatever.' But when he started talking, you can see the passion in his words and the passion in his face and how he gets choked up. It moves men. He just has that motivating aura about himself."

Second-year defensive end Kevin Carter was another player who became smitten with his new coach, who was a lot more personable than his college coach, Steve Spurrier.

"Coach has brought a level of closeness that is worlds apart from last year," Carter said. "We've got an edge. The goal is to turn the Rams into a polished, disciplined fighting organization, and you can see that happening."

Still, the new coach realized that the Rams weren't as good as he first thought they were. These players dazzled him with their athletic ability, but he soon found out that every other team had terrific athletes too. And those athletes actually knew how to win.

"The fundamentals of the game have not changed," Vermeil said. "The thing I'm struggling with the most is the difference in players today. The

> He laid down the law early in camp. He warned the players that they would have to find new levels of concentration to survive.

guys are so physically superior to even our Super Bowl team. They're so much better and faster and stronger, I'm having a hard time relating to just how good they really are and how good we are as a team."

Banks had a cannon arm. Receiver Eddie Kennison could run like an Olympian. The Rams had lots of physical ability, fueling Vermeil's optimism. Only when he watched the Rams play preseason games against similarly talented teams could really assess what he had.

Trouble, and lots of it.

Top draft pick Orlando Pace held out of training camp, hoping, in vain, to get a better contract. Star receiver Isaac Bruce popped a hamstring muscle. Fullback Craig "Ironhead" Heyward showed up 32 pounds overweight after collecting a $1.3 million signing bonus. Back-up quarterback Mark Rypien missed two weeks of camp to tend to his son, who was stricken with brain cancer. Veteran offensive lineman Gerald Perry arrived late.

Then during an offensive line meeting, Perry was criticized for a missed block. So he quietly got up and left.

"I thought he was going to the rest room or something like that," Gandy said. "He never came back."

Harris was dragged out of camp in handcuffs by Drug Enforcement Agency agents, who accused him of laundering drug money. (The charges were eventually dropped, but Harris never returned to the team.) And many problem players remained, just waiting to cause the new coach some grief.

"I know I will be let down," Vermeil said. "I know I will be disappointed. And I am exposing myself to a letdown and a criticism, which I don't mind. And there will be times I deserve it. But I think if I'm going to err, I'm going to make a mistake giving the guy the benefit of the doubt, giving him an opportunity to fail. And sometimes they don't fail."

When the Rams broke training camp for the first time under Vermeil, the coach got misty-eyed when he addressed the team. Despite all of the bizarre developments in camp, he believed he was bonding with the team.

"Everybody told me coming in that players have changed," he said. "Not you guys. Thanks for accepting the program and working."

But there was still so much work to do with these knuckleheads. Vermeil would needs lots of stamina for this job. He would need to remain on an even keel as much as possible, something he failed to do in Philadelphia. Years of therapy had given him a better handle on his emotions. He understood that he could not turn Rams Park into his perfect world. There were some things he would just have to accept.

Not only did psychotherapist Phil Towle help the team and the Rams coaches, but he helped Vermeil, too. Towle frequently sent Vermeil messages such as, "Burnout is not caused by stress. Burnout is caused by resisting opportunities that stress provides." Or this: "I embrace my fears because they contain my greatness within." Towle gave some Rams veterans the creeps, but the new Vermeil craved such reinforcement.

On the eve of the Rams' first regular season game for Vermeil, Gansz tried to work the troops into a lather. He brought some heavyweight inspirational material into the meeting room: a boxing video.

"Men, this game is going to be a 15-round fight," he said. "And you guys are Joe Frazier."

So the players wouldn't miss the point, Gansz played a video of the first Muhammad Ali-Joe Frazier fight, a 15-round slugfest that featured Frazier's late knockdown of Ali. Smokin' Joe had taken a terrible pounding, but he just kept coming at Ali. Finally, he tagged him.

"What a man!" Gansz gushed. "Most guys can't raise their arms in the 15th round. But Frazier had the power to knock down maybe the greatest boxer ever. That's what you have to be against the Saints, 15-round fighters."

Vermeil was also in top form as he addressed his team.

"We are fortunate to be here, men," he said. "This is going to be the best organization in football. It won't happen tomorrow, or in six weeks, but we're way ahead of where I thought we'd be. We're going to be a winning football team, but I can't guarantee it'll be this year. You want a guarantee? Join a union. Get tenure. There's no tenure in the NFL. Here you're challenged every day.

"You know, I just left the television business. In that business, some people who don't work very hard are stars. That's not for me. I had to come back to the most demanding way to make a living in America, in a business that forces us to be at our absolute best every single day.

"You will experience adversity tomorrow. But when something goes wrong, this is what you should think about guy across the way from you: 'I'm going to kick your ass the next play and on every play until the end of the game.'

"The finest coach who ever lived, John Wooden, once told his team that the only way to be great is to keep the pressure on your opponent every second you're out there. But be smart. We must play like winners before we become winners. Remember that."

His eyes welled up as he wound up his talk. "And I want to tell you guys I appreciate what you've done for me," he said. "I appreciate the acceptance."

# CHAPTER EIGHT
# PERSEVERENCE

*"What I learned as an assistant to George Allen was persistence. To think that nobody can beat you, and to surround yourself with people who think that."*

-Dick Vermeil

The new Rams regime began with much hoopla on August 31, 1997, against the New Orleans Saints and their comeback coach, Mike Ditka. With the sold-out Trans World Dome rocking, the pre-game introductions featured a laser light show and boxing announcer Michael Buffer uttering his trademark, "Let's get ready to ruuuummmmble!"

Vermeil raced through a cloud of smoke onto the field, through a reception line of cheerleaders waving pompoms. He pumped his fist and leaped into the waiting arms of tackle Fred Miller.

The Saints killed by immediately moving downfield for a 31-yard Doug Brien field goal and a 3-0 lead. But the Rams had plenty of life on this Sunday afternoon. Down 17-14 at the half, they stormed back for an exciting 38-24 victory. In third quarter, they out-gained the Saints by 201 yards.

Lawrence Phillips rewarded Vermeil's confidence by rushing for 125 yards and three touchdowns. Tony Banks bounced back from an early interception to throw a couple of touchdown passes.

"Like they say, sometimes real life's better than the movies," said tight end Ernie Conwell, who contributed a zig-zagging 46-yard touchdown reception. "And this was."

On the field afterward, he hugged old friend Brent Musberger and anybody else that got near him. He kissed Georgia Frontiere and shook hands with everybody who approached him. Then he ran back through the tunnel to lead the post-game celebration in the locker room.

"Pay attention," Vermeil told his players. "You couldn't ask for a better scenario. You came back, whipped their ass physically and they just wore down.

"Give me a football. Game ball goes to one man. I'm so proud of this guy. He's been through so much. I've been to jail with him, been behind closed doors with him and this is a good guy. We've talked about everything. Now his life's turning around. It's all looking up for him now. Lawrence Phillips."

Phillips mumbled a few words of thanks and sat back down. He seemed under-whelmed by the moment, in contrast to his ecstatic team-mates. On this day, their new coach made them believe.

"We know he's there late hours, he's disciplined, he's organized, and hopefully that was reflected on the field," Conwell said. "I really believe you saw some of his personality out there today, the don't-give-up attitude, the consistency."

The grueling summer in Macomb, Ill., seemed to pay off. "We had a long, hard training camp," Kevin Carter said. "Long hours. Meetings. Standing around. Getting to work early. It wasn't easy this week. We were on the field a lot. But when you work so hard on something, you really care about it, and you stand up for it. You fight for it."

Vermeil was flush with optimism after his team's powerful second-half showing. "Next week, I know you will take it to another level when we play the 49ers, the potential World Champions," he told the Rams.

Well, the Rams certainly did take it to another level against the 49ers. They went straight to the basement. The Rams fumbled five times and lost, 15-12, to a San Francisco team badly depleted by injuries. Hapless Jim Druckenmiller quarterbacked the Niners and still the Rams couldn't win. One more successful play or one less mishap and the Rams would have won this gruesome game, but the team seemed absolutely set on losing. Banks was especially dreadful, fumbling three times himself.

The next day, a crestfallen Vermeil left his office and wandered about the industrial park surrounding the Rams Park complex, struggling to gather his thoughts. This was the first time in 14 years the new Vermeil tasted real failure, and he didn't enjoy it a bit.

"I was feeling so emotionally drained, so overwhelmed, I had to get out," he said.

The Rams got waxed at Denver, 35-14, in Vermeil's third game, then bounced back to beat the New York Giants, 13-3, and square their record at 2-2. So far, so good, since the Rams had staggered to a 6-10 finish the season before.

Then the bottom fell out, with the Rams plunging into an eight-game losing streak. Receiver Isaac Bruce was hobbled by nagging hamstring strains and he spent a good bit of his time watching. Various injuries plagued Phillips as well. The Rams got beat up, physically and emotionally. But nobody suffered more than Vermeil.

The players were tired of losing, of course, but repeated failure had conditioned them to defeat. They could deal with it. Vermeil had no such defense mechanisms. The losses devastated him. Years of therapy had taught him better coping skills, but his competitiveness remained intact. He couldn't shrug off weekly humiliations.

He came back for this?

"I can see how he got burned out the first time," D'Marco Farr said. "I think you have to have a certain ability to let things go in this game, or you'll kill yourself."

Even the laid-back Banks could empathize with his coach. "It's been frustrating for him," Banks said. "When it comes to being a disciplinarian, he's probably as disciplined as it gets because he demands a lot out of us and pays attention to detail and expects the same out of us."

After a 17-9 loss to Seattle at home dropped the Rams' record to 2-5, Bruce offered one of his typically candid observations. "The offense is not playing hard right now," he said.

That was hardly a vicious rip, but Vermeil unloaded on the star receiver during his media briefing. He had already been at odds with Bruce, given the recurring injuries the player developed after spending so little time in the team's off-season conditioning program.

"There's no place in Isaac Bruce's contract that says he is a coach or a critic," Vermeil said. "He's paid to play, OK? That's what he gets paid to do. Now, he's missed most all of training camp and almost all the games. He's an intense competitor, and he loves to win, and he's tired of losing. Well, I guarantee you, there is not one guy on that football team not playing hard. Not one guy. It's my job to evaluate who plays hard. Not Isaac Bruce's."

Vermeil viewed Bruce's comments as disloyal to teammates, something he could not tolerate. While such comments could fire up the team, Vermeil said they shouldn't be delivered via the media.

"Stand up in a meeting, so you're looking them right in the eye," Vermeil said. "If I have a problem with you, I'm going to go right in your office. I'm going to talk to you about it. I'm not going to go to the guys on the television camera . . . that's not my way."

Bruce also noted that the Rams' game plan had been too simple against the Seahawks. This assessment irked Vermeil, too.

"He's getting paid a lot of money, and it has nothing to do with coaching," Vermeil said. "He's got, what, three years in the league? Four years? How many years does Jim Hanifan have in coaching? Do they compare anywhere close to Isaac Bruce's experience as a wide receiver?"

Ouch!

After calming down, Vermeil called Bruce in and explained why he was so upset—and why he needed his veterans to be more supportive during the rebuilding and reeducating. In turn, Bruce explained just how badly he wanted to win. "I need Isaac," Vermeil said. "He needs me. I think the problem was, I should have invested more time in Isaac. Sometimes you don't spend enough time with the good guys."

Early on, Vermeil clashed with other potential team leaders, including

Craig "Ironhead" Heyward and Leslie O'Neal. Meanwhile, he remained eerily patient with Phillips and the mistake-prone Banks. During the 1997 season, NBC commentator Cris Collinsworth, a former NFL receiving star, called Vermeil a "creampuff" for his perceived coddling of Phillips.

"I've been called a heck of a lot worse," Vermeil sniffed. "Cris is an expert. If being a creampuff is helping people achieve their talent, then I'm a creampuff."

Though he continued to screw up at every turn, Phillips appreciated Vermeil's efforts to help him turn around his life.

"He's genuine," Phillips said. "With Coach Vermeil, you can tell he cares about you as a person and not just a football player."

Vermeil also rallied behind Banks, who absorbed much public ridicule as the Rams' struggles worsened. Rams fans weren't comfortable with a quarterback who wore a do-rag on his head and sat off to one side of the Rams' bench after his ill-fated possessions, apparently sulking. Having that Rottweiler named Felony, named after a rapper in his native San Diego, didn't help his image, either.

"It's a matter of being proud of that cat, and it's a cool name for a Rottweiler," Banks said. "It ain't no poodle."

Banks' carefree approach also drove teammates and the club's management crazy, but Vermeil remained supportive. He realized that Banks had been rushed into action without the requisite two or three years of training. He also saw that Banks was confident, tough and resilient. The young quarterback shouldered much of the blame for the Rams failure—that responsibility comes with the position—and he never hid from reporters and made excuses in defeat.

The more fans booed and the media ripped him, the more resolutely protective of Banks Vermeil became. As he said time and again, he had traveled the same road with another raw, strong-armed youngster, Ron Jaworski.

"What we have to do is play better offensively," Vermeil said. "That's frustrating. Everybody is screaming at me to bench Banks, but these are our guys. We're married to them. We can't divorce them when they lose and remarry them when they win."

After a 28-20 loss to the Chiefs dropped the Rams to 2-6, Vermeil was again at wit's end. Again, he found himself wandering around the Earth City industrial park, struggling to compose himself. The Rams didn't seem to be responding. He wrestled with self-doubt. Could he really lead today's players? Had the game really changed that much?

He wondered if the Rams would be better off without him. He rattled this thought around, then talked himself off the emotional ledge. He cleared his mind and got back to work. Ultimately, he was too stubborn and too competitive to give in. He dove back into his job with the fiery resolve the Eagles saw in the 1970s and '80s.

The players, sensing his angst, threw him a little birthday party on the practice field on October 30. Vermeil was given birthday cakes and a No. 61 jersey, honoring his 61st birthday. The players sang "Happy Birthday" to him. Carol joined the get-together and Vermeil's eyes welled up again.

"There's no place I'd rather be than right here with you guys," Vermeil told his team.

"We really stand behind our coach because he's been here for us from Day One," linebacker Roman Phifer said. "It's not just a business to him. He gets to know a person. He cares for us."

Still, he frequently became exasperated with this group. Farr said it was easy to tell when Vermeil was about to blow.

"He paces back and forth real fast in practice like he doesn't know which way to go," Farr said. "He has like four things he wants to say, but he can't really say them all at the same time."

The players of '97 were a tougher bunch to coach than even the first group of Eagles he inherited in Philadelphia. Instilling group pride and a sense of team was harder. Pro football had become an enormous industry and the players, as a whole, were a more mercenary bunch. Players were constantly on the phone with their agents, who had become an intrusive third party in this sport.

The job of coaching was a lot different, too. The responsibilities were much broader. Vermeil got caught up in some issues he never imagined. The Rams' move to St. Louis had been a contentious one—the NFL resisted it, hoping to maintain franchise stability—and the Rams filed an antitrust suit against the league. Though Vermeil wasn't working for the Rams during this period, he still got dragged into court to provide information. He had to set aside his mid-week game preparations to field questions in the courtroom.

"In Philadelphia, if you had told me I'd have testify in court for something on a Tuesday, I wouldn't have done it," he said. "But I don't fight things I can't beat anymore. I think I know myself better."

The biggest one was about to occur. On November 16, the Rams lost to Atlanta 27-21 to fall to 2-9. Phillips was shelved by "flu symptoms." In fact, he had spent Saturday night drinking himself into a stupor. He was so hung over the next morning that he required I.V. treatments to fight dehydration. He had already been fined at least 20 times for team infractions, and team president John Shaw had seen enough. He urged Vermeil to cut Phillips loose. By Wednesday, Vermeil was getting ready to concede defeat on the troubled running back. He called Lawrence and told him his job was in peril.

"When you go to practice today," Vermeil told Phillips, "you'll go out as Jerald Moore's back-up."

Phillips was unapologetic about his behavior. Nor did he promise to do better if he got another chance. His response, or lack of it, exasperated Vermeil.

"Lawrence, tell me something," Vermeil asked. "What would you do if you were me?"

"Coach," Phillips said, "I'd cut me."

When Phillips subsequently stormed out of Rams Park and skipped a team meeting, he was finished. The next day, Vermeil called him into his office to give him the pink slip. Ever the father figure, Vermeil gave the running back some words to live by as he sent him out the door.

"Lawrence, playing in the National Football League is a privilege," Vermeil said. "You haven't made the most of that privilege, and we're going to have to let you go. But please, wherever you go, you have to learn one thing. You have to learn to listen."

Though Phillips lost $2.25 million by getting cut (his salary wasn't guaranteed and he got no signing bonus from the team, given his well-chronicled instability) he showed no emotion when Vermeil let him go.

"Bless his heart, Coach Vermeil tried to do whatever he could for him," safety Toby Wright said. "If Lawrence doesn't have ability, I don't know where he would be."

While explaining the dismissal to the media, Vermeil got choked up. "I think as he matures and totally understands what he has to give, and what it takes to be a top-quality NFL football player, we'll end up playing against him in playoff games, and he'll end up being in Pro Bowls," he said. "I'm very disappointed it came to this. Extremely disappointed."

It would take Vermeil a while to recover from this episode. Phillips had let him down, yet he still worried about him, for good reason. Vermeil allowed himself to get too close to the young man. He got too wrapped up in trying to save him. "This will eat at me for a long time," he said.

The season took a heavy toll on the coaching staff. Defensive coordinator Bud Carson had some teeth knocked out during a practice collision, then needed gall stone surgery. Wilbert Montgomery needed 25 stitches in the head after running back Ron Moore crashed into him during a practice drill. Dick Coury suffered a broken leg when he got run over in a training camp drill, then he suffered a concussion when he got crushed along the sideline during a game. The coaches literally couldn't get out of their own way.

Confusion reigned on offense, where Jerry Rhome's scheme failed in the unsteady hands of Banks. Still, Vermeil decided against micro-management. He often withheld his opinions during meetings to allow his assistants work out the problems.

He didn't want to assert himself on offensive game planning until he got a better handle on the system and how it fit into the modern NFL. Also, he didn't want to undermine his coaches so early in the program. Vermeil hoped that his contribution would be made on bigger issues, such as whipping the entire organization into the right frame of mind. The whole franchise had sunk into a malaise. Raising spirits and building confidence was a full-time job around Rams Park.

"The No. 1 thing we need here is leadership," he said. "A foundation has to be formed here, and we're forming it. Whenever there's a catastrophe, a crisis, a player with some sort of problem, if you handle it properly you can grow. I'll you this, we're going to have a foundation. And it's going to be based on more than Xs and Os."

Much of that foundation was based on work ethic, but the Rams' veterans began rebelling during the season. They weren't accustomed to spending so much time on the practice field. O'Neal complained that the Rams were leaving their game at Rams Park during the week.

"Wednesday is not a game," O'Neal said. "Thursday is not a game. We should be building up to a game, not playing two during the week."

The players rolled their eyes at much of what they saw. With the team reeling, Gansz's motivational attempts fell flat. He continued writing pithy quotes on the meeting room grease board, citing figures as diverse as Nietzsche and Walt Disney. Perhaps this explained some of the special teams' sloppiness: maybe the coverage team was too deep in thought to make tackles.

By winning three of their last four games, the Rams made the season less slightly less depressing. The late surge started with a 23-20 victory at Washington and continued with a 34-27 victory at New Orleans. Before morale got too good, however, they lost a nationally televised Sunday night game to the dreadful Chicago Bears, 13-10.

This loss at home featured astonishingly incompetent play, even by the Rams' well-established standards. The team earned nine penalties to set a new team record. Banks got sacked five times and turned the ball over five times, including a late interception in the end zone that ended the Rams' comeback bid. He couldn't blame the fans for booing so mercilessly as this debacle ended.

"I don't know who's going to want to check us out again," Banks said. "We couldn't have a nightmare playing any worse than that."

Perhaps it was fitting that Banks missed the Rams' final full practice of the regular season because Felony got hit by a car. Vermeil excused him from practice to tend to the dog, which survived the accident but suffered a broken hip.

"I love my dog," Banks explained. "Even if he wouldn't have given me permission, I would have left anyway because that's my girl. And some people aren't going to understand that."

No, they wouldn't, but a relieved Banks led the Rams to a season-ending 30-18 victory at Carolina and finished the season with 3,254 yards passing. During his hot stretches, Banks threw the ball around the field as well as any quarterback in the league. His arm strength was nearly unmatched.

Alas, this finale did little to raise the organization's spirits. The 5-11 season had been an unmitigated disaster.

"My goal was to win seven games, one more than the year before," Vermeil said. "We haven't done that. Coaches always have the responsibility for losing, so I have not done a good enough job and my assistants haven't done good enough."

The team's failure left him with mixed emotions about his return to coaching. The Rams not only lost, they invented new ways of losing that Vermeil had never imagined. The Rams raised incompetence to an art form. Their games became theater of the absurd. He came out of semi-retirement for this?

"I'm not sorry I did it," he said. "But I'm not sure I'd do it again. What it's done to my wife—she's not happy—has been tough."

Carol still took the losses hard, just as she had in Philadelphia. That early-season collapse left her in tears after several games. But the Vermeils had been through this before and come out on the other side.

"I'm happy," Vermeil said. "I needed this fulfillment in my life, and I really like my chances to turn this thing around. We've been asked to put some Band-Aids on some cancers, but I'm very confident we'll win. I'm excited, really excited."

He dismissed player complaints about his grueling training camp and the exhaustive game preparations. He vowed to push the Rams just as hard in the 1998 camp, despite speculation that his intense regimen would cause free agents to flee and potential free-agent recruits to sign elsewhere.

"I've always been accused of working players too hard, and I probably do work them harder than some people," Vermeil said. "But the end result has always been pretty good. At UCLA we won. At Philadelphia, we won. The Rams have been losing all through the '90s, and with our roster set, the only way I see these people getting better is to work them."

What about all the rumblings of player discontent, the speculation that many Rams wanted out?

"We lost one free agent in Bill Johnson, who looked me directly in the eyes and said he wanted to stay," Vermeil said. "But we couldn't pay him, and then later there's talk he couldn't play for me. I worked 30 pounds off his big fat ass last year and he played pretty good for us.

"Look, they had been so lousy for so long, when I got here, I felt I had to change to physical and mental toughness and do some weeding out. The only way you can make it easier on someone is to make it tough on them in first place so they can appreciate the difference."

Vermeil kept grinding in the off-season. Bud Carson retired as defensive coordinator, so John Bunting was elevated to co-coordinator with Peter Giunta. Mistakes from the Steve Ortmayer era, unhappy or unproductive veterans like feckless linebacker Robert Jones, dirigible-sized guard Dwayne White and the grumpy O'Neal, were weeded out. The draft yielded energetic defensive end Grant Wistrom, hard-working running back Robert Holcombe and speedy linebacker Leonard Little.

Most veterans embraced Vermeil's off-season conditioning program. Even Banks passed up playing basketball back home in San Diego to participate faithfully. Looking to get Banks on track, Vermeil asked trusted aide Mike White to take over as the quarterbacks coach. Stiles, his other key lieutenant, replaced White as the tight ends coach.

Vermeil entered his second season still striving to instill the same pride his Eagles developed. Unfortunately, he still faced resistance. Heyward, who battled weight problems during his one season under Vermeil, didn't even bother reporting for Year Two after failing to get down to the mandated weight of 260 pounds.

"I don't want to play or work for that man again," Heyward said. "Let's just part ways. You go your way, I'll go mine. Let me go, please."

Vermeil angered Heyward by suggesting he "should cut the teeth off his fork" to control his chronic weight problems.

"He just needs to shut his mouth," Ironhead said. "Last year, the way things were going, the only time we got a break was on game day. Guys are either tough or not tough coming out of college. You can't make them tougher on the practice field."

"That's why he shouldn't come back," Vermeil countered. "At 289 pounds, practices are really tough. It's the National Football League. It's not his right to play in it. It's a privilege. There are standards to be met by everybody on the field. All he had to do was meet them." So Heyward was history.

Vermeil's second training camp was just as brutal as his first, and the results were not favorable. Veteran guard Ed Simmons abruptly retired, citing knee troubles. The offense sputtered so badly in the preseason that Vermeil started calling all the plays from the sideline. His rationale was simple: Sometimes head coaches are more willing to take risks than assistant coaches.

Harmony didn't reign on the coaching staff. Holcombe had a fine preseason, but Rhome wanted to cut him. Rhome didn't want to keep Kurt Warner as the third quarterback, preferring the immortal Will Furrer, but he got overruled. Veteran running back Greg Hill also excelled in the preseason, but Vermeil didn't even dress him for the opener. Moore got the start, although Holcombe (100 yards, 19 carries) and Hill (89 yards, 23 carries) clearly outplayed him during exhibition play.

The Rams opened their season by falling behind the mediocre New Orleans Saints, 24-0, in the first half, then falling short with a second-half rally. Moore fumbled three times and Rams fans were in an uproar. Vermeil continued micro-managing the offense, calling the plays with various aides chiming in. The result was chaos; it was all the Rams could do to get a play in to Banks on time.

One disgusted fan, Jeff Roberts, mailed Vermeil an angry letter and enclosed his season tickets, saying he could take no more abuse. Vermeil had Carol track down the fan and invite him to the team's meeting the night before their game with Minnesota. Roberts came with his six-year old son, Murphy, watched the presentation of the game plan and then gulped when Vermeil referred to the angry letter in his pep talk to the team.

Suddenly Jeff Roberts sensed everybody was looking at him.

"I know you guys work your butts off day in and day out, so I thought I would give Jeff and Murphy a chance to come in and see what you guys are all about," Vermeil told the team.

Vermeil also had the Roberts in for a private chat. Jeff asked him why he started Moore in the opener ahead of Hill. Vermeil explained that Moore had a better feel for the offense, including the pass protection blocking. Hill was still learning the scheme as the preseason ended. At the end of the night, Vermeil handed Roberts' season tickets back to him. "I think these belong to you," Vermeil said. "Are you willing to take them back?"

Roberts did, and saw improvement the next day when the Rams engaged Minnesota in a wild shootout. Hill started in place for Moore and rushed for 82 yards and two touchdowns. But the Rams lost, 38-31, when Banks, scrambling, was tackled a yard short of the end zone as time expired.

The offensive excitement generated in this game did not prevent the team's morale from continuing to sink. The difficult training camp and exhausting regular season practices had left the team drained just two games into the season. The players seemed ready to storm the castle.

"Yes, there was going to be a mutiny, I thought so, anyway," recalled Steve Bono, a back-up quarterback on that team. "But we dealt with it and did the best we could."

On September 14, the players presented their concerns to their coach. They argued that the endless practices and interminable meetings left them sluggish at the start of games. In turn, their fatigue led to sloppy practices and even sloppier games.

Vermeil was at least willing to listen. "I understand you guys want to cut down on practices," he told the players. "We can do that. We can figure out a way where we can work together and get a better result."

The coaching staff went back to the drawing board and condensed the team's schedule, looking for ways to get the players off the field more quickly during the week. By agreeing to make some changes, Vermeil finally made a connection with many of the veterans.

"That was the first time the players really started to understand Coach Vermeil," linebacker Mike Jones recalled. "Even though it was a strange situation, that was the first time we were able to go to him and say, 'We want this changed, and we want that changed.' That might have been the turning point as far as relationship with players. That year, he started trusting a lot more players."

And some of the players began trusting him. They could understand why his guard was up after that disastrous 1997 season. Vermeil had inherited lots of problem players who, predictably, caused problems.

Vermeil cut back the length of practices and the Rams finally showed some life. Banks rallied them to a thrilling 34-33 victory at Buffalo. But this triumph was a hollow one. Hill suffered a season-ending broken leg while rushing for 158 yards in the victory.

The Rams returned home to lose to the dreadful Arizona Cardinals, 20-17. It was a typical Rams fiasco; with the game tied at 17 with 5:30 to play, Rams cornerback Dexter McCleon earned a disastrous pass interference call on a hopelessly overthrown third-down pass.

This was the eighth straight home loss for the Rams and their ninth in 11 games at the Trans World Dome. The honeymoon was officially over. A month into the season, Vermeil was drawing the wrath of fans, newspaper columnists and radio call-in show hosts. The losses continued taking a toll on the players, who struggled to keep their spirits up. The practices began to drag again, with Vermeil inching back toward his original schedule.

Though some players were starting to accept Vermeil's approach, the team continued to play hideous football. Though the initial revolt had been quelled, the grousing continued. Warner described the worsening morale in his book, *All Things Possible:*

*I couldn't believe how much complaining and moaning was going on around me. It created this mental lag that, in my mind, we never really over - came. The negativity kept snowballing into the season to the point where it was almost like we were defeated before we even took the field. It was a self-perpetuating process: we were losing, and everybody was trying to find a reason for it. Instead of coming together as a unit, everybody was pointing fingers, and it was like 'Us against the coaches.' It was different than anything I had ever been a part of, and it created an incredible amount of tension. The players wanted some relief, and the coaches weren't about to change.*

Although he returned the play-calling duties to Rhome, Vermeil continued to alter calls on the fly. Hanifan advised him on running plays. Vermeil's most trusted aides, White and Stiles, often weighed in, too. As a result, the Rams continued to have trouble just getting the plays in. And producing a coherent offensive script was nearly impossible with this play-calling by committee.

The Rams' hopes were briefly raised by a 30-10 whipping of the New York Jets, but then they got nothing done during a 14-0 loss at Miami. Afterward, Banks wandered off the team bus and elected to stay in South Florida rather than fly home with the team. He also skipped the team meetings and video review the next day. Vermeil fined him, but didn't suspend him.

On Wednesday, Banks straggled into work and issued a half-hearted apology for his actions. St. Louis was in an uproar over his behavior. So, on Thursday afternoon, owner Georgia Frontiere took the extraordinary step of walking onto the field after practice to give the young quarterback a talking to. She told Banks that he needed to do a better job explaining his emotions to reporters so that fans could see that he cared.

"I know he didn't mean it the way it came out," she said. "Sometimes we hide our feelings. He's been close to tears. But men don't cry. We all have to grow up. Sometimes we do it sooner, sometimes we do it later. If you relax, then you can do it well, as we've seen him do it."

A sheepish Banks then addressed the media. "By no means was I trying to say that I don't care, because I think maybe my biggest thing is that I care too much," he said. "I've got a lot of weight on my shoulders. I'm representing a big business. People think this is just a game, but it's not. I enjoyed it when we beat the Jets and I was able to go out downtown and the fans were supporting us. This past week against Miami, I didn't feel like I wanted to support the fans, I didn't want to face my teammates, because I didn't play well enough for us to get that win after we had a good week of practice. I was really high going into the game. And I didn't play well. That's my biggest negative attribute right now. You ask any of my teammates, they know I care deeply. If we lose, I'm one of the toughest guys to deal with."

The Rams had more grave issues to deal with in the wake of the loss to Miami. Teammates talked Little into joining them for drinks at a downtown St. Louis club for his birthday. Little normally eschewed the party life, but this time he agreed to come.

After leaving the gathering, he crashed his sports utility vehicle into a car driven by a St. Louis woman, Susan Gutweiler, killing her. Little would be convicted of involuntary manslaughter, sentenced to 90 days in jail and suspended by the league for eight games the following season.

Vermeil rallied around him. "Leonard Little is a non-drinker, OK?" Vermeil later said. "I have had him over to my house, offered him a glass of wine, he does not drink. Teammates take him out for his birthday, 'Oh, you have to have a beer with us.' He goes along with them, and he commits a terrible mistake. He will live with that mistake the rest of his life. But he is not a problem person. He is just the opposite."

On the field, the collapse was complete. The Rams fell to San Francisco, 28-10, and then got steam-rolled at Atlanta, 37-15. That was all assistant coach Wilbert Montgomery could take. Speaking on a Chicago radio station, Montgomery said, "On our team, we have a lot of guys that don't have a lot of heart. You look at your own guys and you say, 'How many of my guys on my squad are willing to give the extra and not complain?' You can sit back and count them, and you've only got a handful of those guys willing to go the distance."

According to Montgomery, only 10 or 12 players on the roster of 53 had "football smarts."

Thus chastised, the Rams responded with a 20-12 victory over the Bears. But the good feelings quickly subsided and the carnage continued: a 24-3 loss at New Orleans; an astonishing 24-20 loss to Carolina at home (after Rams linebacker Roman Phifer fumbled just short of the end zone trying to score the winning touchdown); and a 21-10 loss to Atlanta.

On December 3, 1998, Vermeil returned to Philadelphia for a game against the floundering Eagles. The Rams stumbled into the nationally telecast game with a three-game losing streak. If ever the players were going to win a game for their coach, it would be in this game—back in Vermeil's old haunt, Veterans Stadium, against a pathetic 2-10 Eagles team with a national ESPN audience watching.

Vermeil received a hero's welcome. He held a news conference in the team's hotel to satisfy the myriad interview requests. An army of former Eagles got field passes to the game and greeted him when the Rams came onto the field for warm-ups. Former Eagles owner Leonard Tose walked the Rams sideline at Vermeil's invitation.

And then the Rams stunk up the joint, losing 17-14 to fall to 3-10. "I went there," Vermeil said, "and got my rear end handed to me. I was embarrassed."

This game summed up all that went wrong for Vermeil during his first two seasons in St. Louis. Banks threw an early interception that led to an Eagles touchdown. The Rams mustered just 82 yards on the ground against a Philadelphia defense ranked 27th against the run and missing three starting defensive linemen. The Rams' receivers dropped passes and ran incorrect routes. Kicker Jeff Wilkins missed a potential game-tying field goal.

Oh, the humanity! A sense of resignation pervaded the team.

"When we start off slow," Banks said, "I think there's some people on this team that can't help but get the feeling, 'Oh, no, here we go again.'"

On the other side of the ball, the Rams' defense got torched by third-string Eagles quarterback Koy Detmer, 900-year-old receiver Irving Fryar (playing on a broken foot) and running back Duce Staley, who rushed for 99 yards despite playing with a slight hernia. And so on and so forth. This game was a horror show. But Vermeil refused to throw in the towel. He denied that his players tanked the game and insisted he still saw redeeming value in his team.

"I can show you any clip you want to look at, any snap you want to see," Vermeil told reporters the next day. "Those guys are busting their butts, playing like hell, trying to get to the football. So for me to browbeat them, or call them losers, or dogs, of whatever the fans might like me to do to show I'm more upset, is poor leadership."

Through all of this, the coach's overall approach remained eerily upbeat, even in the face of some catastrophic football.

"I can't do it Bill Parcells' way," Vermeil explained. "I believe strongly that there is a better way to motivate than through intimidation. If you can help a person feel he's responsible for changing the fortunes of a football team, that can bring a stronger commitment than if you're standing over him, screaming."

As the losses mounted, the grumbling worsened. Veteran defensive tackle Joe Phillips wondered aloud if the Rams were leaving their game on the practice field during the long afternoons of preparations. Vermeil rebuked Phillips and vowed to stay the course. Once again, reporters wondered if this ongoing controversy would hurt the Rams' ability to attract players for future seasons.

Out of desperation, the Rams opened a home game against the New England Patriots in their two-minute offense. Only 48,946 fans showed up at the Trans World Dome, about 16,000 below capacity. Banks finally found his rhythm and got the Rams rolling toward a 32-18 victory before suffering a season-ending leg injury. A 20-13 loss to Carolina dropped the team to 4-11, precluding the possibility that the Rams would improve on their 1997 showing.

Carl Peterson called Vermeil every Friday during each of these two long, miserable seasons. He knew the defeats were beating Vermeil up. But Vermeil was determined to battle on.

Not even that Lawrence Phillips debacle could jade Vermeil. "I like dealing with people like Lawrence Phillips and trying to help them be what they can be," he says. "That's what fun about coaching. Some of them don't make it. But when they do, that's real coaching."

As the losses piled up, fans and the media were calling for Vermeil's head. But in the face of the most fervent criticism he had drawn in his entire professional life, Vermeil was at least outwardly stoical. Yes, he admitted, it's quite possible that he could get fired. But that possibility didn't scare him.

"If it bothered me, I wouldn't have come back," he said.

The rest of Vermeil's family couldn't take the criticism in stride. "It's not easy for the wife and the children and your grandchildren and your friends to take the abuse because the press has the final word," Carol said. "A lot of times, it's great when you're on a roll. But it's not great when you're not."

The Rams ended their 1998 season with a loud thud! They absorbed another beating from the 49ers, 38-19. The only notable aspect of the loss was Warner's NFL debut mopping up for the over-matched Bono. Some of the Rams' coaches lobbied to get Warner the start, but Vermeil tried to play the game straight and go with his veteran.

The severity of this beating left the Rams with little hope heading into the off-season. The Rams ranked 27th in the NFL in total offense and 24th in scoring offense for the 1998 season. They scored fewer than 20 points 10 times. A fringe player named June Henley led the team in rushing with 313 yards. Three hundred and thirteen yards! When the season finally ended, several disheartened players skipped the final team meeting and fled the disaster scene.

One of those absentees was veteran cornerback Todd Lyght, who headed back to Southern California disillusioned. "I'm upset that I've played eight years without an opportunity to win," he told friends. "The team we've got right now isn't going to get it done."

Vermeil took the boycott by the veteran players personally. A terrible 1998 season ended on a suitably sour note. His assistant coaches wouldn't have been surprised if they showed up at Rams Park one day after the season to see the place surrounded by yellow police tape.

"It was probably as low as I've ever been in my entire sports career," Bunting said. "Morale was low in all aspects of our organization. To be quite frank, I don't know that I would have given us another chance if I were the owner. I say that with due respect for a man I love, honor and hold in high regard. But it was out of control. The direction wasn't clear cut. It was due partly to losing. Losing breeds that. And it was partly to the fact we had no leaders."

When he gained some distance on the debacle, Vermeil admitted that he suffered considerably the first two years at the Rams helm. Yes, he often had second thoughts about coming back. But at no point did he seriously consider quitting.

"There have been times when I've been down," he said. "There have been times when both Carol and I know that if we had the decision to make over again, I wouldn't do it. There have been times, sure, when I wondered if I had made a mistake coming back. I'm thinking I could be on my ranch with my kids and grandkids. It's hunting season. It's trout season and all that kind of stuff. But there was never a time that I said I shouldn't have done it."

And his perseverance was about to be rewarded in ways even he couldn't have imagined.

# CHAPTER NINE
# ADAPTABILITY

*"Once he felt the players were buying into his program, he kind of backed away from some of the things he had been doing. He knows more about Dick Vermeil than he once did."*
— Kansas City Chiefs executive Lynn Stiles, on Vermeil's revised program for 1999

Rams president John Shaw called Vermeil onto the carpet after the 1998 season. He didn't want to fire Vermeil after just two seasons for three reasons: Vermeil was honorable and likable; the Rams would owe him millions; and he had canned his last coach, Rich Brooks, after just two seasons. Shaw hoped to slow the revolving door and establish some credibility in the industry.

But he couldn't endure any more of the nonsense he saw in '98. The Rams offense had to be overhauled. Much-vilified quarterback Tony Banks had to be banished for everybody's sake. Vermeil's grueling regimen, which seemed to suck the life out of the team in each of his two seasons, needed toning down. The coach also would have to yield some say on personnel matters. Enough was enough.

Vermeil went into the five-hour summit meeting in Los Angeles with an open mind. He still had a stubborn side, for sure, but he had also proven himself adaptable during his time in Philadephia. After all, he brought in passing guru Sid Gillman and changed the face of the Eagles' offense. Armed with a more dangerous passing game, the Eagles won a National Football Conference title.

So Vermeil agreed that sweeping changes were in order. Heads would roll. Tactics would change. The offense would become much more exciting. Business was business. The St. Louis market was beginning to shun the Rams. The team was about to begin its renewal campaign for the luxury suites, so the money side of the Rams operation was getting edgy.

Jay Zygmunt, Shaw and Rams vice president Bob Wallace joined Vermeil in the meeting room for a marketing summit. Consultants had a presentation to make. They showed videotaped interviews with focus group members assembled to assess the team.

The fans prattled on about what was wrong with the Rams, Vermeil and his coaching style. When the videotapes were over, it was time to discuss the insights gleaned from these interviews.

"Dick, what do you think?" Shaw asked Vermeil.

"John, I don't know how much you paid to have all this research done," Vermeil said, "but if you had just listened to my radio show on Monday night you would have gotten the same information free."

The whole episode summed up what today's coaches are up against.

"People have absolutely no clue what it takes to win National Football League games, what it is to build an organization, what it is to motivate an organization and what it is to handle criticism, or what it is to handle all the complex things it takes . . . and we're spending a lot of money with the marketing plan," Vermeil said. "The only thing that really markets a football team is winning."

Vermeil was anxious to win again after two humiliating seasons. His pride had been pummeled. He kept hearing that he was washed up, that the game had passed him by. He knew that his job was on the line, that his 9-23 record was ugly enough to get him canned in the frantic NFL.

He had plausible explanations for much of went wrong, but nobody wanted to hear them. "If you don't win, no matter what else, you are an idiot," Vermeil acknowledged. "That's just the way it is."

So he understood why Shaw was vexed. Repeated failure had sapped his patience. Ranking among the biggest losers in the league was no fun. Vermeil wasn't fighting two years of losing; he was fighting the last eight years of losing.

"I understood that," Vermeil said. "First off, I knew where their heart was. I knew what they wanted badly to do, win. So if they're mad at Dick Vermeil because they're losing, I understand. I'm mad at Dick Vermeil. My wife is mad at Dick Vermeil. My kids are mad at Dick Vermeil. 'Dad, why don't you yell on the sideline like you used to.' My daughter told me that. As if I wasn't coaching."

Before the L.A. summit, Vermeil had already dismissed Jerry Rhome as his offensive coordinator. Receivers coach Dick Coury chose to retire again and move back to the West Coast. So the wheels were already turning.

Who could he find to revive the offense? Vermeil settled on Washington Redskins assistant coach Mike Martz, a former Rams receivers coach who was well-schooled in the Don Coryell system. Among Martz's plusses was his positive relationship with Bruce, one player Vermeil still couldn't reach. The relentlessly upbeat Al Saunders was later hired on as Coury's replacement, further changing the offensive environment.

Underachieving receiver Eddie Kennison was jettisoned to New Orleans. Marshmallow-soft guard Zach Wiegert and inconsistent tackle Wayne Gandy were allowed to exit as well. Vermeil tried to make a case for Banks, but Martz gave a thumbs-down evaluation. A Banks makeover could take a couple of years, time this franchise clearly didn't have. Martz also campaigned for free-agent quarterback Trent Green, a native St. Louisan who was reluctant to jump from the Redskins to the Rams if Banks was still on the team.

So, grudgingly, Vermeil eventually agreed to a deal that sent Banks to Baltimore to clear room for Green. "I had to be pushed," Vermeil admitted. "I don't mind listening to the top people that I have around me. I surround myself with good people. And I think from the ownership to the management, to my coaching staff, it was a unanimous decision. We have to make a move."

The Rams were very busy in free agency. Besides luring Green, the front office was able to sign veteran guard Adam Timmerman from Green Bay to anchor the offensive line. The Rams grabbed explosive receiver Torry Holt with their first-round draft pick and Shaw was able to engineer a remarkable trade that brought all-pro Indianapolis Colts running back Marshall Faulk for a couple of draft picks.

Voila! The Rams had a whole new offense.

Martz was ecstatic with the high-skilled players Shaw, Vermeil and Charley Armey gave him. He was thrilled with the latitude that Vermeil offered him. The offensive play book was now his. He could write the play script and orchestrate the game from the press box. He took the old Coryell offense, as Norv Turner had adapted it in Washington, and began adding his own touches to exploit his dazzling personnel.

"I couldn't ask for anything better in a head coach," Martz said. "I happened to be in the right place at the right time. It's like winning the lotto."

Besides Green, Faulk, Holt and Bruce, Martz also inherited lightning-quick slot receiver Az Zahir-Hakim, rangy tight end Roland Williams, speedy kick returner/receiver Tony Horne and sure-handed possession receiver Ricky Proehl, one of the few stars from the previous season. There was so much talent that running back Amp Lee, a third-down specialist who caught 64 passes the year before, could hardly find a role. And he had been the team's best offensive weapon in 1998.

After the mini-camps, Martz realized he could spread his weapons across the field and throw like crazy. Green knew the offense inside and out, so the Rams could be aggressive. Vermeil was a bit taken aback when Martz asked for the freedom to pass the ball aggressively on first down. The two coaches talked it over during an early June morning, then the ever-thorough Vermeil called the Elias Sports Bureau to get a pass-frequency printout.

"We looked at every team in the NFL," Vermeil said, "and we found that the best offenses in the league last year, Denver and Minnesota, actually threw the ball more in the first quarter than they ran." So Vermeil endorsed the philosophical shift that created an historic offense.

Vermeil also agreed that the Rams would spend fewer hours on the practice field in the third year of his regime. Many of his more troublesome players were gone and those who had survived the first two seasons had proven their toughness. Perhaps Shaw was right about easing off the troops in camp so they could start the season fresher.

**Privately, Rams executives were prepared to cashier him if he ever got three games under .500.**

When the Rams lured him back into coaching, Vermeil realized he would have to delegate more responsibility than he did with the Eagles. The Rams' travails during his first two seasons underscored that. His attempt to call the plays for a portion of the 1998 season was a fiasco. He needed to remain in the CEO role and make certain the whole operation was moving forward. He needed to give Martz and defensive co-coordinators Bunting and Peter Giunta even more room to lead their units.

In Philadelphia, Vermeil had run his own offense and coached the quarterbacks before he brought Gillman in. He designed most of the offensive game plan himself.

"Now, it's impossible to maintain concentration long enough during the week to zero in on one phase of anything . . . all of a sudden, there's something happening on Tuesday, and the whole day of game day you're involved in this, and Tony Banks doesn't get onto a flight, or Leonard Little gets into an accident," Vermeil said. "And you're calling the plays? Who are you kidding?"

Over time, the Eagles built a legion of blue-collar players who could relate to their tireless coach. After taking some chances on players that proved unworthy, the Rams needed to get some self-starters. Armey found undersized-but-energetic middle linebacker London Fletcher at Division III John Carroll University and signed him as an undrafted free agent.

Quarterback Kurt Warner, an Arena Football League refugee, was promoted to second string. He was a classic battler, a player that refused to quit after the Green Bay Packers gave him just a cursory training camp look coming out of Northern Iowa. Before latching on with the AFL, he stocked grocery store shelves by night so he could work out in the day.

Even the last two first-round picks—Grant Wistrom, an undersized defensive end, and Holt, a wide receiver—brought unusually strong commitment to the game. Holt had even done some hard time making Whoppers at a Burger King, so he was not above doing thankless work.

Vermeil realized, belatedly, that he never had the players who could be whipped into championship form. He had been far too optimistic about certain individuals. He was more than ready to shake up the roster. He admitted he compromised his values to fill team holes with veterans who just didn't buy in. These guys bristled at the two-a-day training camp workouts in full pads. They rebelled against the three-hour regular season practices. So a greater emphasis was put on player character.

There was no more time to do social work. "They don't give you time to save everybody," Vermeil said. "I invested a lot of time in Lawrence Phillips. I like Lawrence Phillips, to this day. But his problems were deeper than I could solve in the amount of time I had—especially with only a five-year contract."

Heading into the 1999 season, Vermeil realized his coaching career hung in the balance. He earned one more season by making sweeping changes, but insisted the prospect of getting fired didn't worry him. He wasn't going to coach scared. He was 63 years old, his family obligations were covered and he had lots of money in the bank.

"I don't know how many times I can say this: I'd done it before and I knew how it had to be done. I was going to do it as planned, with the people I had, and gradually get it done," Vermeil said. "If I didn't get it done in three years, then someone else would continue."

Privately, Rams executives were prepared to cashier him if he even got three games under .500. Offensive line coach Jim Hanifan, they had decided, would finish out the season as an interim coach. The Rams veterans figured out that their head coach was on a short leash, given the nature of reprieve. Should Vermeil relapse into his raging drill sergeant persona, the veterans knew he could be easily toppled in a coup.

Though he agreed to ease off the troops, Vermeil still made hard labor the theme of his third training camp at Macomb. A wheelbarrow became a fixture on the corner of the practice fields. Billy Long, a Southern University strength coach who assisted the Rams during training camp, developed a "Gotta Go to Work" chant that began ringing in the ears of the players.

Finally, the Rams had the mix of players that could actually embrace that theme. Finally, they began to embrace their coach. "What he did with the Rams is what he did with the Eagles," former Philadelphia linebacker Bill Bergey said. "He's a very tough coach, but that's his way of doing things. We were all his children. You kiss your children and you spank your children. It took a while, but we all came to understand that."

Vermeil's third training camp was demanding, for sure, but not punitive. Small, common-sense concessions were made at every turn. "There is just a huge turnaround," D'Marco Farr said. "You didn't expect it out of him. It's a welcome change."

He listened to his players and respected their input. Perhaps Shaw's mandate spurred some change, but now Vermeil was forging a better relationship with the players. Those players unworthy of his trust were gone. The survivors and the hard-working newcomers responded to his leadership.

After the team played quite well during a Saturday afternoon scrimmage against Indianapolis at Champaign, Ill., some of the Rams convinced linebacker Mike Jones to ask Vermeil for the next day off.

"They know who to send when they want something, don't they?" said Vermeil, who granted the wish.

The season before, he would have dragged the team back up to Macomb for a full Sunday of work. The season before, there would have been lots of grumbling and groaning by angry veterans. Receiver Isaac Bruce, who had been openly critical of his coach during their first two seasons together, applauded Vermeil's new approach.

The Rams were working smarter. In Isaac's case, Saunders developed a specific work plan that kept Bruce busy but didn't overtax his hamstring muscles. Saunders created a balance that spared Bruce's legs while letting him do his share of work. More care was taken with the other veterans as well.

"I don't think we could win with the first two training camps we had," Bruce said. "Other teams like the Broncos were winning Super Bowls and not having camps like us. We would be too tired coming out to win. Same with cutting back with practices. It's something he should have sensed without being told. His eyes were wide-open shut, I guess. But you can't kill players on the practice field because they are going to try to kill themselves on Sunday."

Lynn Stiles knew that his boss' first inclination was to outwork his problems. But in the third year of this regime, Stiles watched Vermeil adopt a more deft management style. "All the quirks are still there," Stiles said. "But he's not digging ditches like he used to do. He can stand and look at the horizon. He's developed a great chemistry, and it's not just the athletes. It transcends the whole organization. And he's letting the lieutenants make the decisions.''

The Rams offense blossomed immediately under Green. Martz brought a Redskins-like attack to St. Louis and Green began running it to perfection. He had been tremendously productive in that scheme the season before in Washington, when he stepped up from the No. 3 quarterback slot to help salvage the 1998 Redskins season.

Faulk's presence brought a great deal of confidence to the organization, too, though he missed the start of training camp while negotiating a new deal. He wasn't on hand to see the Rams score three touchdowns in their first controlled scrimmage, against his old team, the Colts. Even without Faulk, the Rams moved the ball at will.

In his preseason debut, against Oakland, Green threw all eight of his passes on the money. Seven were caught, one was dropped. The first-unit offense just glided up and down the field. "And it's not a mirage, because when we've gone 11-against-11 on our practice field, Trent Green and associates have done the same thing," Vermeil said. "When we went 11-on-11 against Indianapolis, they did the same thing."

The Rams continued to blitz their preseason foes, although Martz revealed only part of his play book. Green completed 28 of 32 preseason passes for 406 yards and two touchdowns. Under his leadership, the first offensive unit was utterly unstoppable . . . and then San Diego Chargers safety Rodney Harrison dove into the side of Green's knees after a pass attempt in an exhibition game. The needless hit disabled Green for the season with a knee injury. As its quarterback was wheeled off the field in agony, the organization wept.

Bruce dropped to his knees and pounded the turf with both hands. He was angry that this could happen to Green and upset that the team's cycle of misfortune was continuing.

"Disbelief," is how Zygmunt remembered the scene. "This is the worst I've ever felt."

Vermeil seconded that emotion. "When Trent went down," he said, "I felt like I was stabbed in the heart."

Many of the players felt the same way. Vermeil looked up and down his bench and saw sadness, anger, frustration and shock. Just when it seemed the Rams were onto something, disaster struck again.

The new Vermeil handled Green's shocking demise well, immediately rallying behind Warner. The old Vermeil might have plunged into despair after suffering such a setback. But his coping skills were much better at this point in his life. "If something leaps up and hits me in the face, I no longer say, 'Ah, shoot,'" he said. "I say, 'Sure, I expected something."

Vermeil's composure was critical here. All the changes he made with his staff, with his personnel and his own approach to coaching would have meant nothing had Warner not been able to pick up for Green. Vermeil was determined to make him a success.

"It hurts," Vermeil said, fighting back tears after Green went down. "We will rally around Kurt Warner, and we'll play good football. Some of the guys that have been playing good will play better. But that doesn't mean that it doesn't hurt."

At the Rams' next team meeting, Vermeil made a point of stepping behind Warner to reassure the players.

"You're the guy," he said. "I expect you to play well."

Fortunately, Vermeil had already bonded with Warner. Vermeil had always been supportive of him, even while Martz berated Warner in camp, dogging him about every misstep, booting him in the rump to get him up to speed for his new offense. "None of us realized what we had in Kurt Warner," Vermeil says. "But I did believe he could play."

Warner was different brand of quarterback from Green. He could throw the deep ball with touch, but his footwork was clunky. The stuff Green could do really well—throwing off a counter-spin move, making deft shovel passes, throwing off of nifty little rollouts—Warner struggled with. Despite his success in the rapid-fire action of arena football, Kurt just wasn't nimble. In basketball terms, Green was a point guard and Warner was a shooting guard.

Martz didn't back off Warner until the team broke training camp in Macomb, and returned to St. Louis. Had Vermeil not stood behind Warner, he might have been rattled by the constant criticism he absorbed from the new offensive coordinator. Warner was just starting to gain a comfort level with Martz and the offense when fate abruptly erased Green from the picture.

Suddenly Warner had the keys to this high-powered offense. Vermeil asked Armey to locate a veteran quarterback to support him, settling on Paul Justin, but he was firm about giving Kurt a fair shot. Warner appreciated the trust. "He was one of those guys, those upbeat guys, that made me feel confident in what I was doing," Warner said. "He never let there be a lull. He never worried about what I did on the football field. It was always a positive, always building me up."

Even during Warner's season as a No. 3 quarterback, doing "service work" on the scout team, Vermeil made him feel important. "He said numerous things to me during that time that let me know that he was confident in my abilities," Warner said. "And it came true when I became the starter. I never had a doubt that he believed in me.

"Whether he did or not, I'm not sure."

Warner took charge immediately, marching the Rams to a 17-0 lead in the first half of their preseason finale at Detroit to help the entire organization relax. Until he stepped into the No. 1 role, Warner had been unimpressive in camp. The front office braced itself for an unmitigated disaster. This game helped restore a normal pulse rate around Rams Park. Vermeil gave Warner the game ball.

"Who else would get it but Kurt Warner?" he told his team in the locker room after the game. The Rams whooped it up. Vermeil misted up, hugged Warner and told him he loved him.

Before the season opener against Baltimore, Vermeil threw another bouquet at Warner. "Kurt is going to play better than any of the No. 1 draft picks at quarterback this year," he told reporters. Rams fans weren't so sure. Their season opener, at home against the Baltimore Ravens, didn't even sell out. The television station KMOV had to step in to buy the remaining tickets to get the local blackout lifted.

Warner was simply brilliant, throwing for 309 yards and three touchdowns, and the Rams won easily, 27-10. But was that a fluke, a one-game burst of adrenaline? This team had shown promise its first two seasons under Vermeil, then took turns for the worse. Their next opponent, defending NFC champion Atlanta, would tell more about this team.

This game came after a bye week, a break that could have sapped the team of its momentum. Skepticism still surrounded this team. Would Cinderella's carriage turn into a pumpkin? "When we won the opener against Baltimore, in the locker room after the ball game, I told them that we were going to beat the Atlanta Falcons," Vermeil said. "If they were a Super Bowl team, then it was time for us to play at that level."

They did, slapping around the Falcons 35-7. Warner made quarterbacking look easy again, calmly completing 17 of 25 passes for 275 yards and three more touchdowns. Martz tailored the offense to his strengths, downplaying those plays that asked the quarterback to move around. Warner had a quick mind, not quick feet, so Martz settled him in the pocket and got him in a quick-pass rhythm with his dangerous receivers.

And since Warner could throw the deep ball with ease, Martz put more emphasis on the vertical passing game, too. Not only were the Rams receivers able to convert little slant-rout passes into big plays, they were able get behind defenses on deep posts and fly patterns as well. As the touchdowns mounted, the Rams receivers unveiled their "Bob 'N Weave" end zone celebration—gleaned, in part, from all that Muhammad Ali footage that assistant coach Frank Gansz had shown the team to fire it up. Suddenly the long-dreadful Rams were cocky. Suddenly they could toy with defenses.

Martz kept calling four-receiver sets, often in running down-and-distance situations. Opponents couldn't cover Bruce, Holt, Hakim and Proehl, plus Faulk coming out of the backfield. The Falcons had outstanding cornerbacks, but still they had no answer for the Air Martz offense. The Rams emerged from this rout a brand-new team.

"I think that added confidence to them and started it going. I think it started them saying, 'Hey, the coach told us we can beat these guys and we did it.' Then it just exploded from that time on," Vermeil says. "They started getting in the wheelbarrow, they started believing in themselves and the guys they lined up with, and the coaching staff."

Vermeil honored Shaw with a game ball after the Falcons game. This recognized the good that their summit meeting had wrought. "John Shaw, like Dick Vermeil, has had his rear end chewed and criticized and told how stupid he is for the state of the Rams for the last 10 years," Vermeil explained. "I think when an organization starts to appear that it's getting better, that some of the people who have taken the biggest criticism ought to get some of the biggest rewards."

With Hakim scoring four touchdowns, the Rams continued their romp by whipping the Bengals 33-10 in Cincinnati. So much for the theory that the Rams were just a dome phenomenon that would struggle outdoors. Their confidence rose another notch as they neared the pivotal game of the season.

"Guys, this next week we're at home in our dome against the San Francisco 49ers," Vermeil told his team afterward. "They've beaten us 17 times in a row. Enough is enough. When they come into our dome, we're going to beat the living hell out of them."

Before that titanic 49ers game, Vermeil reiterated the message. He assured his players they were through losing. This franchise had been abused by their old West Coast rival. Enough was enough.

"You guys have been flying around all week and you're ready to play," he told them during his pre-game team address. "This is our time—it's our time to beat the 49ers and get things moving in our direction. Somebody has to step up; why not the Rams?"

Like many previous meetings, this game wasn't much of a contest. Only this time the Rams administered the punishment, winning 42-20 behind Warner's five touchdown passes. This was a shocking spectacle, since the 49ers defenders were literally helpless. Rams ran free all afternoon.

Warner just sat back in the pocket, playing pitch and catch with his streaking receivers. He could have thrown 10 touchdown passes if he needed them. This performance made him a national phenomenon. A guy from nowhere was making a mockery of the sport.

The gift he had—reading defenses and making correct decisions under fire—could not be discovered in auditions or practice. It could only emerge in games. He played spectacularly in his one season as a starter at Northern Iowa, then he starred in the Arena Football League and NFL Europe. But what could he do in the NFL? Nobody would know until he got a real chance.

With Warner rolling. Martz just kept expanding his list of targets. Long-snapper/tight end Jeff Robinson, a former defensive end, became a viable option in the end zone. So did Ryan Tucker, the subject of a special tackle-eligible play around the goal line. In all, 10 different Rams would catch touchdown passes as this offensive juggernaut steamed on.

Vermeil fought back tears after Fletcher announced that the team had given its coach the game ball for the 49ers victory. The bond between the players and their coach was now complete.

"Thank you very much," Vermeil told the players. "I appreciate that, guys. I can't tell you much I appreciate that. We put a lot of work into this thing and you guys do all the physical work and our coaches work very hard, unselfishly, just like you guys do. This is very, very meaningful thing to me."

San Francisco executive Bill Walsh ducked his head into Vermeil's news conference to congratulate him.

"You're going all the way, baby," Walsh said.

"Don't say that," a misty-eyed Vermeil said.

Walsh turned to the reporters. "I'm not supposed to smile," he said, "but what a wonderful victory."

The Rams and their coach knew something extraordinary was happening this season. Before games, Vermeil often told Warner "I love you." And Warner, a man secure with his ability to feel and express what he feels, would respond, "I love you, too."

Such exchanges are unheard of in professional sports, especially football. The media had a great deal of fun lampooning Vermeil, the crying coach. The players came to appreciate the caring side of their coach. As Vermeil let down his guard, so did they.

"At first, there might have been a little joking going on about it —'This guy can cry at the drop of a hat,'" Warner said. "But you realize it's because he cares so much about his players. When he talks about a guy he has to cut, a guy who's accomplished something that he feels strongly about, you realize we've come together as a family. He's the father of that family. He cares about us just like he cares about his children. To us, it's something that's really special."

So, no, the Rams were not embarrassed by their coach's behavior. In fact, a lot of Rams players found themselves misting up during their miraculous season. They were secure enough in their manhood to just let their emotions flow. Veteran defensive tackle Ray Agnew, one of the spiritual leaders of the '99 Rams, credits Vermeil for fostering the closeness that served the team so well on their championship run. His loyalty to the players, somewhat misguided at first, was paying dividends now.

"It starts at the top," Agnew said. "He's the first coach I've been around that has said he cares about his players—and has really proven it. Every incident that I've seen around here, Vermeil has been right there for the players. And that trickles down to the players. When the head coach cares about the players, you care about each other. We have a good thing going. People can say that nice guys finish last, but I don't think so."

As the season unfolded, Vermeil was good to his word to the players. He instituted "Victory Monday," giving his players a day off after wins. Vermeil spoke less in the locker room, deferring to veteran players more often. He was willing to address player concerns as they arose.

"When you're a new coach, you have to be strict and be on top of everything," cornerback Todd Lyght said. "Sometimes you stress the wrong things, but I think he's more relaxed. We don't wear pads all the time like we used to. You can't beat each other up during the course of the week and then go out and win games. We would practice in full pads until Friday. We had team meetings late every night. The night before a home game, we would stay in a hotel and have team meetings until midnight or so. It wore us down."

Vermeil trusted that the Rams would show up in excellent shape for their games, without him having to check up on them. The problem makers, like Phillips, were long gone. "He beat us up for two years, and his whole idea was to weed out the people who weren't strong mentally," Jones said. "He sacrificed two respectable seasons to turn in one great season. Now we have guys here who you can trust and count on."

So the Rams no longer had to spend the night before each home game in the team hotel. Vermeil challenged his players to behave and gave them the opportunity to spend the evening with their families. The players appreciated his trust. They enjoyed being treated like winners for a change. They welcomed the responsibility and accountability.

Vermeil realized he could maintain command of the group without strict scheduling and lots of rules. Even when the team suffered a hiccup— like Tony Horne's four-game NFL suspension for substance abuse—he didn't waver from his more trusting approach.

Montgomery admitted that his boss' transition didn't come as easily as it appeared to outsiders. Some of the changes went counter to Vermeil's nature. At heart, he was still an old-school coach. He still believed that what worked for Bill Bergey and Stan Walters should work for Mike Jones and Orlando Pace. He admitted that loosening the regimen was difficult. He warned his assistant coaches that he would revert to his old ways if the team began to drift.

"You could see this was a really stubborn guy," safety Keith Lyle said. "He didn't want to buy into the notion that today's players were different. We could see how hard it was for him to change. But he did, and I really respect him for it. It became our duty to respond by giving him everything we had. We had to show him that he didn't have to break us down to get what he wanted out of us."

As the Rams' tide turned, Vermeil's ever-positive approach helped fuel their confidence. Now all those supportive statements he came up with made sense. Even the wheelbarrow made sense. Well, sort of.

"Coach Vermeil, back in the first mini-camps, he would always say, 'Look at the people we have around us. Why not the Rams? Why not us?'" cornerback Dexter McCleon said. "I mean, he would say that every day, 'Why can't it be our year?'"

The Falcons vowed that their second game with the Rams would be much, much different. And it was—the Rams gave them a more severe thrashing, 41-13, with Faulk running wild for 181 yards. Another highlight was defensive end Grant Wistrom sprinting 91 yards with an interception, outrunning Falcons receiver Chris Calloway. Wistrom credited fresh legs for his ability to win that race. "Coming out of camp last year, I felt like I'd already played a season," Wistrom said. "Now I still feel terrific."

With the peerless Faulk totaling 200 offensive yards by himself the next week, leading the Rams to a 34-3 victory over the expansion Cleveland Browns. The team had a 6-0 record.

"What's our next test?" Vermeil told his players after the game. "Our next test is playing a team that has lost only one football game, and a damn good one, on the road. That's our next test, guys. The Tennessee Titans. Let's get ready to play."

The Rams finally took a misstep, in part due to an overly pragmatic team address the night before the game in Nashville. Vermeil anticipated trouble in this game and expressed those concerns in his Saturday night speech. The fact he angered Rams veterans with his too-candid remarks was testimony to how far the team had come. In his book, *All Things Possible*, Warner described the scene:

*"The night before the game, Coach Vermeil, as he always does, addressed us during our team meeting. He started out by saying, 'Now, if we lose tomorrow, I just want you to know we're in good shape.' Guys looked around the room at one another, wondering why he would have chosen those words. Then a couple of minutes later, he did it again: 'If we lose, we're still at the top of our conference and in a great position for the rest of the season.' And then he said it again. All around the room, guys were mumbling to one another, 'What's he talking about? Is he doubting us?' No one could figure out why he was talking this way. Usually Coach Vermeil is so upbeat; even when we were lousy, he thought we could beat anybody we played. Now it sounded like he was preparing us for the disappointment of defeat.*

*"The fourth time Dick said, 'If we lose,' Isaac Bruce, who's a bit of a renegade, actually muttered, 'We ain't going to lose!' A few minutes later, Dick awarded a game ball in advance to Kevin Warren, our vice-president of player programs. Amazingly, he said it again. 'If we don't win this game, this ball can be for next season's victory.' Kevin stood up and made a point of saying, 'Now tomorrow, when we win, I'll be proud to accept this game ball.' Guys were really angry; I know I was. Coach Vermeil's speech was all anybody could talk about when we walked out of the meeting, and Isaac was practically in a frenzy. As he said later, 'I thought it was (Titans coach) Jeff Fisher standing up there.'*

*"To me, it was great we were so irate. The year before we had gone into games anticipating defeat; our goal had been to keep it close and hope for the best. Now, after six games, we were already at the point where we expected to win every week. Losing wasn't even in our vocabulary, and when Coach Vermeil brought it up, guys were offended."*

Dazed, the Rams fell behind 21-0 in the first quarter. Then the Rams awoke and controlled the last three quarters, battling back to nearly force overtime. But when Jeff Wilkins missed a 38-yard field goal with seven seconds left, the Rams lost 24-21.

Their resolve, however, was established. Vermeil would never again doubt his team, even after a late-game mishap caused them to lose at Detroit 31-27. Their splendid comeback was wasted when they allowed an inexplicable fourth-and-26 completion to Germane Crowell in the waning seconds. Oops!

By drubbing the Carolina Panthers at home 35-10, the Rams got back on their championship track. They followed that with another victory over the 49ers, 23-7 at San Francisco. This was a sloppy success, but it brought a reaffirmation.

"We haven't gotten respect from them since I've been here," Farr said. "So to have guys like Jerry Rice come up and tell us how good we are, and tell us that they hope we go all the way, that means a lot. That other team knows about us. It's awesome to be validated like that by the 49ers."

Then the Rams blasted New Orleans 43-12 and handled Carolina 34-21 to clinch the NFC West title. Before that Panthers game, Vermeil served up an inspirational message first coined by one of his mentors, George Allen: "The street to obscurity is paved with athletes who performed great feats before friendly crowds. Greatness in major league sports is the ability to win in a stadium of people pulling for you to lose."

After the game, Agnew led a team prayer, then Vermeil spoke to his players. His voice cracked. Tears flowed. He called his players champions. Long-suffering Rams veterans were pinching themselves. They were winners at last. For veterans like Lyght, who had been through the bad times in Anaheim, this ascension was nearly unthinkable. They were giddy as they passed around NFC West Champion ball caps. "It feels great to be able to put on the hat and be champions of our division," Lyght said. "There have been so many times we've been on the bottom. All those times when you read those preseason magazines, and everyone is making fun of us, picking us to finish last. To finally rise up and be a champion, it's an incredible feeling. It's just so exuberant in here. All smiles and hugs."

Vermeil was not a washed-up old fool after all. "It's an unbelievable feeling," he said. "I thought that with the right kind of people around me, I could do it again. I don't like to use the word 'I.' But I thought we could do it again.

*The year before we had gone into games anticipating defeat... Now, after six games, we were already to the point where we expected to win every week.*

"It's not Dick Vermeil magic or anything. There's a deep philosophy and a deep belief. It's worked for before and I didn't see any reason to change. And this group of kids ... my wife, Carol, says this, and she's fed them all, and she knows ... she says this is as fine a group as we've ever had. And they're willing to make a commitment."

During the post-game news conference, he cried or started to cry five times. "I know the fans were really disappointed when Bill (Bidwill) left," he said. "I know they were disappointed when they lost the St. Louis Cardinals. But they've got a hell of a lot better organization in the St. Louis Rams. People can take that any way they want. I think most people in St. Louis will learn to appreciate Georgia and Stan and John Shaw and Jay Zygmunt. We've got people here in the organization who care about St. Louis."

The Rams banked another victory over the Saints, 30-14, to complete their 8-0 run through the NFC West. The season before, they had gone 0-8 in the division. Such complete reversals just don't happen in the NFL. In the locker room, a beaming Vermeil honored Frontiere.

"Georgia's birthday was last week, guys, and she was sick and couldn't make the trip," he told the team. "So Georgia, for your birthday, we give you your first winning season in 10 years. Happy birthday."

Vermeil continued to impress his players with his flexibility. By beating the New York Giants at home, the Rams could lock up the home-field advantage through the playoffs. Normally, such stakes would have left Vermeil frenzied. But when Jones came with a request from the team—to practice in the indoor facility at Rams Park four days before the game—Vermeil granted it.

"A year ago, I would have had them in pads, and there would have been contact, and we'd be outside," Vermeil said. "But last year, I was still trying to turn this into a team. And the only way to make them into players is to put on the pads and have them hit."

Such adjustments continued paying off. The Rams beat the Giants 31-10 in a very rugged game, then squashed the Chicago Bears 34-12 as Faulk crossed the 1,000-yard mark in both rushing and receiving.

Despite pulling their offensive starters early from a season-ending defeat at Philadelphia, the Rams made the biggest offensive improvement in NFL history. They jumped from 27th to first. Their 526 points were the third most in league history. They scored 30 or more points 12 times. Warner became just the second NFL quarterback to throw at least 40 touchdown passes in a season. Faulk set league record with 2,429 yards from scrimmage.

Faulk, Bruce, Warner, and Orlando Pace were chosen for the Pro Bowl, along with Kevin Carter and Lyght. Warner edged Faulk for the league Most Valuable Player award. "I don't think anyone could have seen this coming," Lyght said. "Someone said we had been touched by a magic wand. Maybe they were right."

The Rams outgunned Minnesota 49-37 in their first playoff game, with Warner throwing for 391 yards and five touchdowns. They trailed 17-14 at the half, but made a few adjustments and blew up the Vikings in the third period. Horne opened the half by returning the kickoff 95 yards for a touchdown and the Rams were off to the races. They scored 35 unanswered points.

What did Vermeil tell his team at the half?

"We're down three but we've taken their best shots," he said. "The only people who stopped us is ourselves. There was no whooping or hollering. These guys expected to win the football game."

Sensing that his coaching redemption was at hand—and mindful that Martz would become a prime head-coaching candidate after this season—Vermeil agreed to anoint the offensive coordinator as his official successor. The announcement came before the Rams played the Tampa Bay Buccaneers in the NFC Championship Game.

Martz became a head coach in waiting, earning a significant salary raise that would make the wait more pleasant. Vermeil entertained the thought of retiring if the Rams won it all. If they didn't, perhaps he would coach another year. Either way, he had proven his point—that he could win after being off the field for 14 years, and that he could win without beating the crap out of himself.

Vermeil's colleagues honored him by electing him The Sporting News NFL Coach of the Year. Voting for that award is done by the other head coaches in the league. "I won it 20 years ago, almost to the day, in 1979," he said. "It's in my office and I take great pride in it because it is selected by our peers. I appreciate it very much."

Former Eagles quarterback Ron Jaworski, now a commentator for ESPN, said a personally evolved Vermeil won the award the second time around. This was a coach comfortable with his staff and secure enough to delegate responsibility. This was a far cry from the coach that burned out in Philadelphia. He noticed the difference each time he came to St. Louis as a reporter. Jaworski came by Vermeil's townhouse the night before a game and found his old coach in the kitchen cooking salmon.

Jaworski couldn't believe how calm Vermeil was on a Saturday night. "Coach," he said, "I remember when John Sciarra's wife was having a baby on Saturday night and you wouldn't let him leave the hotel."

The Rams reached the Super Bowl by slugging out an 11-6 victory over the physical Buccaneers. Reading a one-on-one opportunity in the secondary, Warner lofted the decisive 30-yard touchdown pass to Ricky Proehl on a gutsy third-and-four call up the left sideline.

On this play, "Flex Left Smoke Right 585 H-Choice," the pass was supposed to go to Faulk coming out of the backfield to force a mismatch in the right flat. But Warner sensed a blitz coming and in the huddle he told Proehl to take off on a fade route if free safety Damien Robinson came on the rush.

Robinson did blitz and Proehl got half a step on cornerback Brian Kelly. Warner parachuted the ball in and Proehl made the catch of his life, cradling the ball with one arm while getting feet down in the end zone with 4 minutes, 44 seconds left to play. That was his first touchdown catch of the season; he was in the game because the speedier Holt and Hakim left with injuries.

After going 7-9, 6-10, 5-11 and 4-12 during their first four seasons in St. Louis, the Rams reigned as NFC Champions.

"We won four games last year," Lyle said. "Trent Green gets hurt. I said, 'Oh, man, not this.' If a psychic would have told me we were going to the Super Bowl in Atlanta, I would have asked for my money back."

Vermeil was vindicated. Given time, he COULD turn this franchise around. True, Shaw forced him to make some significant changes. But he still held his players to high standards. He still goaded them while caring for them. He instilled a terrific work ethic and a collective sense of pride.

Being a Ram meant something special again. "Dick had a blueprint; he had a dream," Bunting said. "They've changed that blueprint some, but the dream is there. The players believe in him, and they believe in us."

The difference a year made was nearly unfathomable. One of the worst teams in the history of the league became one of the very best ever. "It was the greatest example of adaptation by an NFL coach in the last three decades," Carter gushed as the team moved on toward the Super Bowl.

# CHAPTER TEN
# POISE

*"I'm enjoying it more. I'm not nearly as uptight. I'm a different person. I'm older. I'm a grandfather with 11 grandchildren. Hopefully, I'm more aware of things, not quite as blind. I've invested a lot more time thinking about the leadership role, rather than the quarterback's first read when they go into a double zone."*

-Dick Vermeil

When Vermeil flew to New Orleans with the Eagles to face Oakland in his first Super Bowl, he felt like his stomach was tied in knots. That feeling never really went away and, well, you know the rest of the story.

A different Vermeil reached the Super Bowl this time around. This coach was utterly at ease. Some of the Rams might have been jittery or uptight, but their coach was the picture of confidence. Vermeil remained all smiles as the media swarmed him in the days leading to Super Bowl XXXIV. He appeared relaxed and self-assured as the biggest game of his life neared.

Ron Jaworski, who covered that Super Bowl as part of the ESPN reporting team, knew the cauldron was still boiling inside his coach. But now, nearly two decades later, he was more capable of handing the heat. "He's the same intense person he's always been, he's just channeled it a little differently," Jaworski said. "I know deep down inside of his belly that flame is just blazing for success."

His decision to delegate responsibility paid dividends during this week, since he had the time and energy to shepherd the team through the hoopla. Vermeil was able to keep his team on a confident, business-as-normal track.

"When I did it last time, I coached my own offense," he said. "I called my own plays. I ran all my own quarterback meetings, plus I was head football coach, plus we were preparing to play the Super Bowl. So there was a lot more pressure on every second of the day. Now I have other people doing these other things and I make suggestions and observations and provide the leadership and hopefully some motivation for the game."

To make certain his Super Bowl week would pass smoothly, Vermeil got his plan together well in advance. Before the playoffs started, he dispatched Mike White to Atlanta to examine the NFC hotel and evaluate the potential logistics. Vermeil didn't want to be scrambling if the Rams reached the big game. "He came back and prepared a schedule from Monday to kickoff," Vermeil said. "Every detail. What time we practiced, the buses, meal times, free time, meeting times."

When the Rams indeed reached the Super Bowl, Vermeil led the team to Atlanta and left his assistant coaches behind at Rams Park so they could prepare the game plan on Monday and Tuesday. The staff flew in on private jets late Tuesday night to join the circus.

Vermeil set an even-tempered tempo for the whole football operation. "My whole theme when we got to Atlanta was, 'We've got to play like we've been here before. We have to visualize in our minds the picture we have played in the Super Bowl. We've got to play like an experienced Super Bowl team'. If we don't, we're liable to end up being seduced by the extravaganza of the whole event," he said.

What did Vermeil tell his team before it left for the game? Here was Warner's recollection of it:

"There's going to be a lot of craziness—a million things to do, people pulling and tugging at you, and media attention unlike anything you've experienced before. Just try to enjoy it. Don't get caught up in everything that you have to do, because the more you fight it, the tougher it's going to be. Just take everything in stride, enjoy the fact you've gotten to this point, and try to concentrate on football."

Vermeil didn't clutch up with the stakes raised. Trusting his players to the end, he didn't set a curfew. Unlike his Eagles, the Rams were free to enjoy some of the extracurricular activity. Vermeil remained poised. This time, coaching in the biggest stage in sports wouldn't eat him up.

"No curfew? Who cares," defensive end Kevin Carter said. "If he said, 'Kevin, in order to play in the Super Bowl, you have to drink a big glass of milk, eat some cookies, say your prayers and go to bed at 8 o'clock every night this week.' I'd do it. You kidding me? It's the Super Bowl."

Vermeil discussed his team's success in a matter-of-fact fashion with reporters. He accepted the role as the favorite with good cheer. "We expected to win," he recalled. "That's not being cocky, that's not arrogance. We felt they couldn't cover our receivers so we thought we could beat them. And that's what takes some of the edge off it."

Ever the football historian, Vermeil compared these Rams with the other great NFL teams. "I follow the game statistically as much anybody in football, and I've got profiles of Super Bowl teams over the last 15 years and we match the profile, in statistical information," Vermeil said. "We really do."

The Rams' first practice in Atlanta, on the Wednesday before the game, was not pretty. The entire coaching staff was edgy, perhaps because they were operating on minimal sleep after arriving on very late-night flights. Instead of the letting hyperactive Frank Gansz do all the barking, the entire staff yelled its way through the workout. The players were making lots of noise, too.

"Before you knew it," linebacker Mike Jones said, "it was chaos out there because everybody was yelling and screaming."

As the defense tried to go through its reads and calls against the scout team offense, signals kept getting crossed. The players couldn't hear each other and they couldn't hear themselves think. Finally, Carter had heard enough. "Shuuuuut uuuuuuup!" he yelled.

The practice grew quiet. And then it got a lot better, as the coaches and players got back to the task at hand. From that point on, the Rams kept it together.

"I haven't pushed them or driven them," Vermeil said as the game neared. "I have allowed them to, more or less, go at their own tempo. Our Wednesday practice in the cold wasn't very good and I told them it wasn't very good because I have said all along that if you are going to win on Sunday, you have to win the battle of preparation. You have to win the battle of handling the distractions.

"We have stayed with the exact same practice routine that we used in the league opener against the Baltimore Ravens, the same exact routine. The next 48 hours is critical but I don't want them all tied up. I want them to relax and have fun. I think they will play better that way."

Friday night, Dick and Carol took a little time out to celebrate their 44th wedding anniversary. On this trip to the Super Bowl, he wasn't too distracted to spend some quality time with his wife. Many players spent the Friday night with their families as well.

An ice storm hit Atlanta Friday night, leaving the roads too treacherous for bus travel Saturday. Vermeil was told his team could not go to their practice field for the traditional "walk through" session. The new Vermeil did not flip out after his carefully prepared plans were ruined. "They become a security blanket," he said, "and I have learned as I have gotten older to listen to advice and change when you feel change is needed. I think I grew a lot, not getting hung up on so many little things."

Vermeil's comfort was rooted in his belief in this team. Finally, Vermeil had a group that meshed as wonderfully as his NFC championship team in Philadelphia. "From 1 to 53, this is best group I've ever been around," he said. "No question they're bigger, faster and smarter. And they all make more money. But in terms of quality people, this is an outstanding group."

As the game neared, Vermeil reminded the Rams that all they had to do was to play their best. If they did, they would win.

"We don't have to be anything different than what we are now," he told them. "We are capable of winning this football game. We are here because of what we are and what we've done. What we've overcome the last three years is a heck of a lot bigger challenge than the one we're going to face on the field today."

Vermeil didn't overdo his pep talk the night before the game. "He went over the whole season," Jones recalled. "He told us what got us here and what would win the Super Bowl for us. He reminded us of what we did against Tennessee the last time we played them, how we dug ourselves in a hole but fought our way back. But he reminded us we were on a neutral field now; and how we played them pretty much to a standstill at their place. He said, 'If we don't turn the ball over, we're going to win the game.'"

Vermeil summoned former UCLA player Randy Cross to add a few words to the pep talk. "We don't know who's going to make the play Sunday," Cross said. "Who's going to make the play that decides the Super Bowl?'"

When Sunday arrived, Vermeil was as cool as could be. Carl Peterson was surprised when his friend phoned to gab. "He's calling me to see how I'm doing," Peterson recalled. "And we wanted to be sure we got together after the game. I just found that unbelievable. Just before the Super Bowl, he's calling me. That totally shocked me. I turned to my wife and said, 'Dick Vermeil has changed.'"

The Rams were calm and relaxed too. The locker room was more quiet than usual. Everybody was doing their own things, listening to their own music on headphones or whatever, but each player appeared focused. There was no nervous chatter. Instead, the Rams seemed silently determined. This time, Vermeil would bring a confident and poised team into the Super Bowl. There was no need to dig into a motivational bag of tricks.

"The only thing I have talked to the squad about is something I deeply believe in," Vermeil said. "They can never catch me in B.S. They can't catch me in that. I tell them exactly how I feel and what's on my mind. Sometimes they don't want to hear it. Hey, but that's how it is. Sometimes I'm a little too impulsive, a little too emotional sometimes."

He told Martz to unleash his weapons, right from the start of the game. "You're doing a hell of a job," Vermeil told Martz on the field during warm-ups. "Just relax, have fun."

"I've never been more relaxed in my whole life, honest to God I am," Martz said.

Facing the biggest game of his career, Vermeil seemed loose. He sang along with Ray Charles' version of "America the Beautiful." He chatted with an official along the sidelines. "I first saw him in 1959," Vermeil said. "It was my first coaching job, at Del Mar High School. We drove to San Francisco to hear Ray Charles sing. Long time ago.

"With Ray Charles singing, things are going our way, guys."

The Rams won the coin toss, elected to receive and immediately embarked on a five and a half-minute drive should have ended in a Jeff Wilkins field goal. But holder Mike Horan bobbled the snap and the Rams couldn't establish the early advantage they sought.

"Five blitzes in the first series," Vermeil told Warner when he came to the sidelines. "They're blitzing us a lot. If they're going to do that, we're going to get some single coverage out there."

The Rams got that single coverage and converted pass after pass. "He's really throwing the ball downfield," Vermeil barked through his headset. "Everybody is singled up. Every single guy is singled up. Whoa! It's stealing!"

They could have blown the Titans off the field—since they drove inside the Tennessee 20 five times—but they just missed some key plays. Kicking woes continued hurting the Rams, too, since Wilkins also missed a 34-yard field goal.

Toward the end of the half, Warner appeared to be wearing down from the beatings the Titans pass rushers administered. Vermeil grew impatient with the play of his offensive line after the quarterback got leveled again.

"How did he get hit like that?" Vermeil asked Jim Hanifan. "How did he get hit? He got his ass knocked off!"

Vermeil also pulled Warner aside on the bench and put the prod to him. "What's happening is you're getting hit a little bit now," Vermeil told him. "You're throwing off your back foot a little bit. Just set up there. With the batted balls, you might be dropping your arm down to throw it a little quicker."

"I'm having trouble seeing," Warner said. "I'm getting guys in my face. I'm trying to move to find guys."

"Make sure you're doing your part and getting your good drops," Vermeil said.

The advice didn't help. Warner continued to move the ball downfield and then miss his big throws. "The red zone is killing us," Vermeil told Martz through the headsets. "We have not punted the football today. They cannot cover our two wide receivers out there."

True, but the Rams didn't take full advantage of their opportunity. Warner overthrew Ricky Proehl in the waning seconds of the first half and the Rams had to settle for a 9-0 halftime lead on Wilkins' third field goal. They had out-gained Tennessee 294 yards to 89 but allowed the Titans to stay in the game. They dominated the Titans, but failed to put them away.

Vermeil spent halftime reminding his players that they controlled their fate in this game. "Keep the pressure on them, wear their ass out, and guys, play smart, play smart, play smart," he told his players. "They cannot stop us unless we stop ourselves by not executing. Pass protection is critical. They are going to play us man to man and blitz us. They can't cover us. They have to change their coverage. All we have to do is keep protecting him."

> There's no freakin' way they can stop us. All we have to do is keep protecting (Warner).

Bruce and Vermeil talked before the start of the second half, plotting a big play downfield. "They haven't changed their coverage, Ike," Vermeil said. "There is no freakin' way they can stop us. All we have to do is keep protecting (Warner)."

Victory seemed in hand when the Rams struck first in the second half, on Warner's nine-yard touchdown pass to Torry Holt. They led 16-0 and enjoyed complete territorial control. Still, Vermeil and Bruce wanted more.

"The post is there," Vermeil said.

"He's got to throw it," Bruce said.

"We told him," Vermeil said. "There is another way to get it, No. 748 out of the blitz, because the 'four' will take the guy away and eat up the safety even better. We'll come back to it."

But then the Titans mounted a comeback. Getting back to their power ground game, Tennessee gave the football to bulldozing running back Eddie George again and again and again. The game turned. George scored one touchdown, then another as the Titans pounded through the middle of the Rams defense and controlled the ball.

With 2 minutes, 12 seconds left, Titans kicker Al Del Greco tied the game with a 43-yard field goal. Now the game was 16-16 and Tennessee had all the momentum. "This is what world championships are all about guys, let's go," Vermeil told his team on the sidelines. "Now we battle. Let's go. One good drive, one good drive, one good drive."

Over the headset, he told Martz: "Keep your poise, Michael."

On the sideline, he, Bruce and the assistant coaches talked about exploiting the single coverage Bruce was getting from the Titans. Tennessee was mostly covering man-to-man with its cornerbacks and both starting Titans safeties had been wiped out by injuries. Now,

Vermeil resolved, was the time to take the shot.

"We've got to go throw the ball to the outside receiver one-on-one," Vermeil told assistant coach Wilbert Montgomery.

The moment had arrived. "If you're going to take a shot," Martz told Vermeil from the press box, "put the ball in Isaac's hands."

Vermeil turned to Warner. "We couldn't ask for a better script," the coach said. "Let's go win it right now."

Martz called the fateful play: 999 H-Balloon. "Mike said, 'Hey, let's take a shot, then if we don't get it, we will use two downs for the first down, then get the drive going that way," Vermeil said.

Holt lined up wide left and three Rams lined up right; Proehl, Az-Zahir Hakim and Bruce. From the inside, Proehl ran a post pattern route. Both Hakim, in the slot, and Bruce, the wide out, ran "go" patterns up the field. Bruce drew single coverage from cornerback Denard Walker, which is what the Rams were looking for.

"Look at Isaac out here," Vermeil said as the ball was snapped.

By this point in the battle, Warner was in a great deal of pain. He had taken a pounding from the Titans and his ribs were a mess. Still, he was prepared to take one more shot. He dropped back from the Rams 27-yard line and heaved the football down the right sideline as Titans defensive end Jevon Kearse crashed into those aching ribs. "I was thinking, I hope Ike comes back for it, because it's not far enough," Warner said later.

The ball was indeed short, but Bruce eased up to make the catch as Walker overran it. "He never saw it," Bruce said. "He fell on his face and by the grace of God I made the play." Bruce hit his accelerator, blew by Anthony Dorsett and Samari Rolle and finished off the 73-yard scoring play.

"The guy covered him well," Vermeil says. "Earlier, Isaac had beaten him deep."

But the Titans had time to come back. Mobile quarterback Steve McNair wasn't an accomplished downfield passer, but he had a knack for creating big plays with his scrambling ability. "A minute and 54 seconds! A minute and 54 seconds! A minute . . . the only way they can beat us is to throw and his ass scrambling," Vermeil yelled at his defense. "Get after him!"

To Vermeil's horror, McNair marched the Titans downfield into scoring position. The key play was his 16-yard third down pass to Kevin Dyson, which came after he somehow scrambled away from Carter and fellow defensive end Jay Williams in the backfield and unloaded the ball while rolling to the right sideline in desperation.

Vermeil was getting tight on the sidelines. "Kevin Carter, tackle him!"

Vermeil screamed. "They just stood there and looked at him, seemed like it anyway. They're exhausted."

Carter was astonished that McNair got away. "I had a firm grip on his jersey," Carter said after the game. "I had a strap and I guess his jersey was wet, it came right out of my grip. I thought he was going down."

The Titans called their final time out. There were six seconds left. Tennessee had one play to score from the Rams 10. With a touchdown and point-after conversion, the Titans could force the exhausted Rams' defense into overtime. The championship would be in their hands.

"I can tell you one thing, we did not want to go into overtime," Jones said.

Tennessee was streaking again, so the Super Bowl essentially came down to one play, 10 yards out, everything at stake. "All right, guys, last play of the game," Vermeil said, as hundreds of millions of people waited to see what would happen next.

The Rams called a basic red zone pass defense, "Nickel, 4-3 Blast, 77 Cover." This was the defense Tennessee expected. The Titans called a play that lined tight end Frank Wycheck up to the far right and ran him into the end zone, hoping to attract a crowd. This was a no-brainer; Wycheck had caught the winning pass in the AFC Championship Game and had been their go-to guy in these situations all season.

Dyson lined up to the right, then went into motion to the left, then came back to the right. He was to slant underneath the coverage, catch the pass and knife over the goal line. McNair took the snap and dropped back. He saw that Jones was covering Wycheck, as he hoped. McNair fired the ball to Dyson and was confident that he would score.

But Jones sensed the ball was going to Dyson. Jones was looking through Wycheck to Dyson and the receiver's body language said the ball was coming to him. "It seemed like slow motion," Jones said. "I couldn't see McNair throw the ball, but I could feel it."

Dyson caught the ball in full stride at the five and appeared certain to score. Jones did not appear to have the tackling angle to bring him down. But Jones somehow lunged over and pulled him down just short of the goal line as time expired.

When the final whistle blew, the Rams were strewn about the field. They were more relieved that ecstatic. Confetti rained from the Georgia Dome ceiling, creating a surreal battle scene. The Titans were stunned. The Rams were stunned. Vermeil didn't jump around at the game's conclusion, he merely raised both arms and yelled: "That's it! We won it! Whoa! That's the game! It's over! We won! We're World Champions!"

Rams linebacker Lorenzo Styles ran up to Jones screaming "We won the Super Bowl!"

Jones stared back at Styles with a blank look. "Are you all right?" Styles asked.

"Yeah. I'm all right," Jones said.

"Are you sure you're all right?" Styles asked again.

It took a while, but the Rams defense joined the celebration. Vermeil was hugging everybody and, yes, his eyes were watery when he reached Carol for the championship embrace. He grabbed some grandkids and carried them onto the field. He was beaming, clearly at peace with the world.

The Rams, pitiful 4-12 losers the year before, were champions of the world. The Rams had won Super Bowl XXIV 23-16. The former stock boy, Warner, won the MVP honors with his astonishing 414-yard passing day. Vermeil would finally get to clutch the Lombardi Trophy.

"I'm humbled in the presence of so many outstanding people," he said after the game. "I want all the organization to touch that trophy. It's just as meaningful to everybody in that organization, from our janitors or our equipment guys to the guys who take care of the field."

And the Super Bowl champions truly were a group. "I take pride in saying this, and I can't prove it, but I really believe that through the games we lined up and played, no team played as close to their ability, as consistently, as we did," Vermeil said. "And to get teams to do that today, I think it takes kids who care about each other, mutual give and take, communication, caring back and forth for the whole organization rather than just on Sunday. It shows in how we play."

By engineering this remarkable Rams turnaround, Vermeil knew his coaching career was finally complete. "This was a journey," he said. "Fourteen years of thought and three years of hard work went into this."

After he stepped down from the news conference podium, he embraced Peterson. "Good things happen to good people," Peterson said, "and you're the best."

At the team's victory party back at the hotel, Vermeil partied like it was 1999. Yes, that was Dick dancing with the Roland Williams' grandmother, to the strains of "Soul Man." The coach's stoicism had melted. Everybody in the room was unhinged. "I didn't do it," he said. "We did it. What makes this special is sharing it. I love sharing. Just love it. Look at how happy everyone in here is. You can imagine how happy the people in St. Louis must be."

This was the best part of winning. "Where my satisfaction comes is sharing experiences with other people," he said. "I think the people who know me know that's true. The expressions on people's faces Sunday after that ballgame and at our party were worth all the three years of work just to see how much joy it brought to them."

Who could sleep after a night like this? Not Vermeil. He did lie down, but he could not shut down. "I was so overwhelmed about it," he said. "Even when I was asleep, I wasn't asleep. My mind was just running. And Carol was even more excited than I was. My mind was cluttered with a lot of grateful thoughts, grateful to players and people that helped us get this done."

The next morning, his eyes welled up when he recalled conversations with his family after the triumph. "The only time I shed tears was when my brother said that our mother—excuse me—said, 'You would go back and coach a Super Bowl-winning team before you quit," Vermeil told reporters. "God, she was right. I didn't think she was. But she was."

The Rams' victory was, in Vermeil's mind, an accomplishment that all coaches could draw from. "When you believe in yourself and believe in the people you surround yourself with, and you believe in your players, they will believe in you," he said. "More often than not, you end up winning something big. Maybe not this big, but something big."

Sure, he made some key adjustments during his third season as Rams coach. But he refused to dismiss his first two Rams seasons as a complete fiasco. "Anyone who thinks this happened overnight is wrong," he said. "This is the result of 1997 and 1998. They had to learn how to win. They had always been losers, and the organization was a loser; it was shattered. There is now a work ethic ingrained that we didn't have before. I knew what I was doing. I was working their asses off and getting rid of the guys who didn't fit. There are only nine players left from when I got here, but they are the core of the team, the leaders. I told people we would be better this season, but they were too busy calling me an old geezer and saying the game had passed me by. I was too old when we lost; now I am wise. Go figure."

Deciding he had done all he could do in coaching, he elected to go out on top and retire. He had been coy about his plans immediately after the game and during his news conference the morning after the Super Bowl. After watching his team suffer some near-disastrous breakdowns in this classic game, he sounded ready to take his team back onto the practice field to fix it.

"I think we need to be a little tougher in training camp," Vermeil said during the next-day news conference. "We are such a finesse team that I think we lost a little edge in the trenches. You can't just turn that switch back on. We dropped a snap on a field goal attempt in the Super Bowl, we missed a field goal and we didn't convert in the red zone very well. We need to rebuild that edge of toughness."

But in his heart, he knew he wanted to quit again. Earlier in the play-offs, after that exciting victory against Minnesota, he and Carol discussed retirement. "Dick, what else do you have to prove to yourself," Carol asked. "You got them back into the playoffs. Maybe it's time."

Vermeil came into the Super Bowl expecting to quit. "I was exhausted," he said, "not from one season, but from three years. And I have 11 grandkids and three siblings and their families. That meant a lot to me. I knew they wanted me to come home."

After he got back to St. Louis and took his bow during the celebratory parade, his feelings were the same. "After that parade, we got home and talked about it a little bit," Vermeil said. "What can we possibly do to top that?"

The Vermeils discussed it some more the morning after the parade, then Dick officially called his cab. "We talked about the time being right to do it," he said. "And that was it."

He figured there was no more to do. "I came back for two reasons: one, to clear the guilt I had within my personality about how I left, to get that flushed out of me so I could live and feel better about myself, and two, so I could once again share their relationships . . . I'll miss that part," Vermeil said.

What would have happened had Jones not made that saving tackle on Dyson? What if the Titans had forced overtime and won the Super Bowl? "I'd have stayed," Vermeil said. "Because a championship was coming. It was going to happen. I could feel it in my second year there. You couldn't measure it on the scoreboard, but I could see a lot of things happening. Young players were getting better, chemistry, depth, all the things you need. People forget we were the second-youngest team in football. They're not going to go away. Oh, no, They could be right back there this year. This is a talented, talented group."

In the months that followed, there was considerable speculation that Vermeil had been forced out of his job, that the Rams had already told him that the 1999 season would be his last. Vermeil insisted such talk was hogwash. "I created the situation myself," he said. "I didn't have to resign, they didn't ask me to. It was something I thought was the best thing to do at the time. I made an impulse decision that it was time to go."

That decision, he said, "was the worst mistake I made in my life, to leave the Rams. I was emotional; I was drained and I made a decision that the best thing for me to do was leave a world champion."

Before Vermeil left, assistant coach Al Saunders had a chance to pick his brain. "The game changed a little bit and he changed his ways a little bit," Saunders said. "The main consistency was always his organization, his discipline. I asked him after he won the Super Bowl what is it, in his philosophy, that allows him to be successful everywhere he's been, high school, junior college, college, National Football League.

"No. 1, he has a plan. He has an unbelievable plan. He is so detailed in what he does. Second thing is, you hire good people. Third thing, is you show them that he cares and the fourth thing is you work hard. He does all of those things. Everybody in this organization, he makes an effort to know everybody on a different level. He really cares about these players, these coaches and the people that work for him as individuals. It motivates you to perform at a high level for him, rather than just for yourself."

Vermeil again found himself in demand as a corporate speaker. He went to Newport Beach, California, to speak to 200 Lincoln-Mercury dealers about dramatic turnarounds. Lincoln-Mercury mired in single-digit growth in California. Among those eager to hear him talk was Jim Splendore, a Lincoln-Mercury marketing executive.

"Vermeil did a hell of a job with a team that had no expectations of winning," Splendore said. "Maybe he can get our dealers to stretch."

The coach told them his career story, about growing up as the son of an auto mechanic, about working in his dad's garage on all-night projects. He talks about his stint as a Cadillac pitchman in Philadelphia.

"Your problems are greater than any problems I had trying to build a football team," Vermeil said. "You have to worry about imports. I didn't."

The dealers laughed. Then Vermeil talked about his highly personal managing style, a hugging, crying style that many have ridiculed.

"If you care, they'll care," he said. "If you believe, they'll believe. If you cry, they'll cry."

He also made more charitable appearances, such as speaking to an assembly at St. Charles (Mo.) West High School. He told the students of his own story, of being a marginal student who became motivated to do better because he dreamed of becoming a coach some day.

"Anything you want bad enough, you can do," he told the students. "The greatest thing you have to learn is to listen. And don't be limited by your test scores or what someone else tells you can't do. Don't be limited.

"If the Rams can do it," he said, "you can do it."

Vermeil hoped to parlay his Super Bowl triumph into a nice television deal. As always, he set his sights high, aiming for a spot on the "Monday Night Football" crew. Alas, ABC preferred to hire a comedian, Dennis Miller, rather than an old coach.

"I would have liked to have a shot at 'Monday Night,' but they don't want a football person and I didn't really want to be a studio guy," Vermeil said. "I'm not being critical of them, but I listen to those guys, and . . . if you don't have a shtick, you can't last," he said. "Instead of having someone inform the viewer, the networks would prefer to have someone go on and be critical, get after players, get after coaches, say how stupid that was and what a bad call that was. That's because they don't have enough knowledge to be analytical. They have street smarts in regards to it, but that's about it. Some can do it, but they still have to have a shtick . . . and they make things up as they go.

"I have too much knowledge to be critical. I could be analytical. But the biggest critics of the game are people who don't have enough knowledge to analyze it properly. I don't want to ever put myself in that category."

He was disappointed not to receive an NFL broadcast offer for the 2000 season. He expected the networks to come to him with open arms, since he took such pride in his analyst work.

"I'd like to do it," he said at the time. "I'm too young to totally retire, and the only thing I know anything about is football. I'd like to stay around it in that capacity because it's fun. I really enjoy it. I really loved working with Brent Musberger. I don't know what the future holds, but if it's good, I'll do it. I'm not talking money-wise. If it's a good job, I'll do it. I don't want to go back into a frustrating experience where it's not taken seriously.

"I'd rather do games. In the studio, you're paid to B.S. I'm not a story-teller. I'd like to present football. I would do it if they wanted me to, but they give you 30 seconds to tell everything you know. They want you to be funny, they want you to be critical, they want you to be analytical in 20 seconds. I don't know if I can do that."

ABC offered him an analyst job on college games, but he declined. "I would do it if it were pro football, but it's not," he said.

Though out of coaching AND broadcasting, Vermeil couldn't sit still. He made a number of personal appearances, attended dinners and gave motivational talks to business groups.

"I think it was easier being in football," his personal assistant Suzette Cox noted at the time. "It's been quite a run and he hasn't come down yet, I don't think. I don't know where he gets the energy. He even finds things to stick in between what we have on his schedule. The trouble with Dick is he really has a hard time saying, 'No, I'm sorry, I can't,' especially to a friend or someone he knows can use his help."

He did turn down a chance to speak at the Republican National Convention in Philadelphia. "I was intimidated by it," Vermeil said. "My first thought was, what the hell am I going to talk about?"

Vermeil became a partner in a $200 million venture capital fund, SGS Capital, to help women and minorities wanting to get into the high-tech industry. His son David was involved in this group, as was former Eagle Reggie Wilkes. Dick's job was to recruit investors and help evaluate candidates for funding. "He's always had that gift of being able to get a good read on people and make accurate judgments on people," David Vermeil said. "I think he'll be very successful."

The new challenge excited Dick. "It'll be a neat, new experience, a learning experience for me," he said. "I could have gone back into college broadcasting, but I decided not to, because I couldn't do that and the SGS Capital work. If I was going to do them both, I might as well stay in coaching.

"I'm really excited about this. Less than five percent of the venture capital funds allotted in the U.S. go to minorities and woman-run organizations, so there's a huge market out there, and very, very talented people. Our society now recognizes that it's an area that's been neglected. There's a gap to bridge, and we hope to initiate a lot of things throughout the country with this fund."

Unfortunately, this was not the time to get into the venture capital or the dot-com world. The market for both crashed in 2000, so Vermeil shifted his business focus to Wilmington Trust Corp., a multi-bank holding company that provides tax shelters for major corporations and manages stocks for rich families. The company, which also hired David, rolled out its "Dick Vermeil Super (Bowl) Investing Program" that featured Vermeil speaking to prospective clients at exclusive clubs.

"He can work a room," noted Bob Christian, Wilmington's Chief Investment officer. "If he were to run for office, he'd be governor in no time."

Still, he was getting restless. He stilled made lists every day, but one day this was his list:

Grease the tractor.

Power-wash the barn.

Go trap-shooting.

Scope out the start of duck-hunting season.

"It was a joke," Vermeil later recalled. "I wrote it down and looked at it and was embarrassed to read it back to myself. There was nothing meaningful and I didn't feel like I was accomplishing anything."

Maybe, just maybe, Vermeil wasn't ready to retire from football after all.

# CHAPTER ELEVEN
# LOYALTY

*"If you work hard for him, he'll do anything for you, it's that simple. We all got into this thing a long time ago. We'll be loyal till the day we die. That's the way it was with Dick Vermeil in Philly, and I'm sure that's the way it was for him in St. Louis."*

— New York Jets coach Herman Edwards, a former Eagle

It was inevitable that Dick Vermeil and Carl Peterson would ride again. They shared so much history. Though their career paths diverged, they remained in close contact. Vermeil stayed loyal to his former right-hand man and Peterson continued garnering advice from his mentor.

After the demise of the USFL and his return to the NFL as general manager of the Chiefs, Peterson made various overtures to lure Vermeil back into coaching. Dick always declined, so Carl settled for having him around during the preseason, commentating on the televised exhibition games and watching a portion of training camp.

When Vermeil came out of retirement with the Rams, he raided the Chiefs to assemble his cabinet. He hired old friend Lynn Stiles from the front office to serve as one of his right-hand men. He also hired Chiefs assistant coaches Carl Hairston and John Bunting for his staff.

Once back in the game, Vermeil maintained a steady dialogue with Peterson on various NFL issues. Since the franchises operated in different conferences, they could speak freely on football matters. They were as tight as ever.

During Vermeil's second "retirement" from the NHL, the Chiefs scuffled through a difficult 2000 season under second-year coach Gunther Cunningham. After starting the season 5-3—clobbering Mike Martz's Rams 54-34 in the process—the Chiefs wobbled into a tailspin and lost five games in a row.

Peterson began realizing that his franchise needed fresh leadership, a more commanding coach that could provide instant credibility. He needed somebody that could overhaul a football operation. As the Chiefs limped toward a 7-9 finish, Peterson had to consider Vermeil again. Was his friend really and truly retired?

Vermeil came to Kansas City to speak at a charity dinner for the National Paralysis Association preceding the Chiefs Dec. 10 game against

Carolina. He accepted Peterson's invitation to stay over and watch the game. Over dinner, they chatted some more.

Carl asked Dick if he missed coaching. Carol cut in and answered for him. "She said he missed it badly," Peterson recalled. "He missed being on the field, he missed the practices, he even missed the stress.

"Dick didn't disagree. I really didn't have anything made up in my mind, but that was good to know."

A year removed from his Super Bowl run, Vermeil hadn't settled into retirement mode. He was not whiling away his days in a rocking chair on the porch of his Pennsylvania ranch. He didn't have any time-killing hobbies. He didn't whittle. At the age of 64, he had lots of energy and nothing outside of football could consume him as coaching did. The business world couldn't satisfy him, regardless of how grand the new ventures were. He still had a passion for the game and the men that played it.

After the Christmas holiday, Peterson resolved to make a coaching change. The gung ho Cunningham, a former Chiefs defensive coordinator, had gone 16-16 in two seasons after replacing Marty Schottenheimer after the 1998 season. Schottenheimer "retired" after going 7-9 in '98, so the Chiefs were 23-25 during a disappointing three-year span. This wasn't going to do, not for franchise that won 10 or more games six times on Peterson's watch.

Peterson regarded Vermeil as the perfect replacement for Cunningham, but he didn't know if he could coax his friend back. He didn't need a long-term commitment; Peterson just wanted him to help shove the franchise back on track and groom a head coach for the future. Peterson convinced Chiefs' owner Lamar Hunt that Vermeil was the man they needed.

But would Dick coach again? Thanks to the Washington Redskins, he got to make his pitch. One day after the season ended, Vermeil called Peterson from his ranch. Pepper Rodgers, his predecessor at UCLA, was now a Redskins consultant. He had convinced Vermeil to chat with mercurial Redskins owner Daniel Snyder about that team's coaching job. Vermeil agreed, but only to evaluate other potential candidates for the opening.

"Guess who just left my house?" Vermeil said.

"Who?" Peterson asked.

"Pepper Rodgers and Dan Snyder," Vermeil said. "They wanted me to help them look at candidates for the Redskins' job."

"You mean they don't want you to coach?" Peterson asked.

"Of course they did," Vermeil said. "But I really have no interest in going there."

an extremely difficult thing to do, especially after the financial beating he took with the dot-com venture.

"Hopefully we're worth it," he said. "In the football world, you have to be successful on the field to sell tickets, to get air time, all the marketing things. If you don't win, you don't make money."

Shaw was stunned when he learned Vermeil was making another comeback. The Rams were still paying Vermeil $500,000 a year to serve as a "consultant," but he gave the Rams no hint that he might get back into the coaching—even when he called to secure some Super Bowl tickets shortly before joining the Chiefs. Once Shaw's shock subsided, his bargaining instincts took over. He held out for a first-round pick as compensation.

The Rams insisted the club still had Vermeil under contract. The Chiefs insisted he was a free agent whose consultant gig was merely a going-away present. The franchises finally reached a settlement without the help of commissioner Paul Tagliabue, who had threatened to intervene. The Rams got a second- and a third-round draft picks for releasing their old coach.

> The Chiefs offered Vermeil one more ride, this time doing it his way with his people.

This bickering between teams left Vermeil with a sour taste. Other coaches might have shrugged off the controversy, but not Vermeil. He treasured his relationships with both Peterson and Shaw. "People have a way of saying, well, that's just the business side of the business," he said. "I hadn't coached one minute as the business side of it. It bothers me. I don't carry a grudge, but it bothered me."

He noted that Shaw also stepped back after the Super Bowl season, handing much of his daily duties to Zygmunt so he could spend more time in Southern California. "John was leaving when I left, but it was legal for him to change his mind," Vermeil said. "Don't think that didn't impact me a little bit. I resented it, but I can live with it. When they try to block you from coaching because you changed your mind, maybe that goes a little beyond. If the shoe were on the other foot, I'd never put them through the same process. No way."

Vermeil denied he was being disloyal to the Rams. That's not the way he operated. "What happened on January 2 was the same thing John Shaw did to me after being away for 14 years," Vermeil said. "I said 'no' to John Shaw a few times, and finally, I said, 'All right, I'll talk to you.' And when I talked to him, I was convinced he was sincere. I was convinced he thought I was the guy to do it . . . So I made the decision to do it."

Peterson and Stiles took the same tact with Vermeil and won him over. They knew him inside and out. They knew what button to push. "Look at Stiles, he ought to feel guilty," Vermeil told reporters after taking the job. "Carol could not, nor could I, contradict anything they were saying. Because they told me how I feel, they told me what I missed. They told me what I am. And the only thing I could say is yes. The only thing they couldn't do was bring my family with me."

Vermeil's old friend Jim Mora wasn't surprised when he took the job. Mora knew that Vermeil's motor is always running. Giving motivational speeches and developing new businesses wouldn't be enough to satisfy his friend.

"Some people like the stress," Mora said. "You like the competition. You like the challenges. Those are the things that make living exciting. And you've been doing it all your life, so it's hard to give it up. I guess once you get a taste of this, it's hard to give it up. Sometimes when you're out of it for a while, you forget about the bad stuff. The hardest part of this business is losing and you forget about how that hurts and you remember all the good things."

Vermeil, like Mora, had enjoyed considerable coaching success in his 60s. So Dick dismissed age as an issue. His three years in St. Louis had brought him up to speed with the new NFL.

"In our society, if we were really concerned about guys 60 and older, a lot of the major leaders of a lot of corporations, a lot of our political leaders, wouldn't be working," Vermeil said. "I don't think there is anything more valuable than experience."

The old gang could be reassembled. Vermeil convinced close friend Mike White to join him as assistant head coach. Stiles would be his personnel man. He hired Carl Hairston back from the Rams to direct his defensive line. He hired Al Saunders, the receivers coach on the explosive Rams teams, as the offensive coordinator and ordered him to enliven the Chiefs' offense. If all went well, Saunders would be groomed as Vermeil's successor.

He couldn't get Frank Gansz to run his special teams, but he got Frank Gansz, Jr. Even Billy Long, the Southern University strength coach who helped in Rams camp, was summoned to join the cause. Long had led the "Gotta go to work" chants during the '99 Rams camp, the chants that served as the championship rallying cry. He joined the Chiefs staff as an assistant strength coach.

Vermeil's Kansas City adventure followed his life-long pattern of looking out for people he cared for. "What you remember is that he was the most loyal person you could ever meet," said long-time Arizona football coach Dick Tomey, a member of Vermeil's staff at UCLA.

He never forgot the people he broke in with, maintaining regular contact with colleagues from Hillsdale High School and every other stop on his journey. When he jumped from UCLA to the Eagles, he not only took Peterson and Stiles with him, he would call on several former Bruins players as well during his first few seasons there— including quarterback John Sciarra and receiver Wally Henry.

During the 1978 he signed his nephew Louie Giammona, Laura's son. The pint-sized Giammona had followed in the footsteps of his Uncle Al to play at Utah State. "I'm very proud of Louie as a player and as a nephew, and anybody who wants to say it's nepotism can forget it," Dick said at the time. "He's a football player and he gets the job done."

With the Eagles, he formed lifetime bonds with many of his key players, such as future New York Jets coach Herman Edwards. Vermeil wasn't one to turn his back on players, even if they got in trouble. He cut running back Mike Hogan in 1979 after he was arrested on drug charges, then he brought Hogan back in 1980 after those charges were dropped. "I told Mike when I released him, if he didn't have a job within a year, I would give him a job," Vermeil explained. "He was out of work and I need some help here. He's been acquitted of his charges. I'm not upset with him."

Vermeil also looked after his staff. He gave Peterson an opportunity to move into management in Philadelphia. When the USFL formed, the Philadelphia Stars franchise offered Peterson its general manager's post. As valuable as Carl was to the Eagles, Vermeil wouldn't stop him from pursuing the opportunity.

"The Stars called and asked for permission to talk to him, and I said, 'You can only talk to him if you start negotiating at $300,000 a year," Vermeil said. "If you're not going to pay him $300,000 a year, you can't talk to him. He was too valuable to me to let him go for a regular salary."

Peterson's defection didn't strain his friendship with Vermeil. "He was a kid, just establishing himself as a fine administrator in the National Football League when he left me in 1982," Vermeil said. "But we maintained a good relationship since that time. I pretty much know how he thinks and he knows and understands me. I think that's an advantage in our relationship."

As the disastrous 1982 season wound down for the Eagles, Vermeil continued working around the clock. He was trying to salvage something, anything, from this dismal campaign. His daughter Nancy was graduating from Penn State University and he just couldn't get to the ceremony. The Eagles had a game the next day.

So he called on Peterson to stand in for him. The USFL was a spring league, so Peterson, in his off-season, pulled free from work and attended Nancy's graduation. Uncle Carl was glad to help.

During his first hiatus from coaching, Vermeil remained friendly with Eagles owner Leonard Tose after almost everybody else bailed on him. A compulsive gambler, Tose played himself into bankruptcy by running up $40 million in debt. He had to sell the Eagles in disgrace in 1984 to pay off his debts to the Atlantic City casinos. The big-living Tose, who had counted celebrities like Frank Sinatra among his pals during the high times, was left with nothing.

"If you beat the Cowboys, there'd be a case of Dom Perignon on your front step when you got home," Vermeil said. "Then he started to giving cases of Dom Perignon for each grandchild born. When you have 11 grandkids, you're living pretty good."

Vermeil couldn't forget these good times when Tose went broke. So he sent Tose some money from time to time to keep him going. "He's my good friend," Vermeil said. "I consider him one of the key people in my life. When he needs something, I'm there for him, that's all. He'd do the same for me. He's always been loyal to me. He always cared. It's sad what happened. But I think he's handling life pretty good."

As a broadcaster, Vermeil called on old friends as he toured the country working NFL and then NCAAfootball games. Homer Zugelder, his former coaching colleague back at Hillsdale High, recalls getting a phone call from Vermeil each time he passed through the San Francisco airport en route to a West Coast game. Former players and colleagues cherished the supportive notes Vermeil sent them over the years, each written with Vermeil's famously flawless strokes.

Loyalty played a part in Vermeil's return to the NFL after 14 years. When the Rams came calling in 1997, he was willing to listen to Shaw because of his two earlier stints with the franchise as an assistant coach.

"I said, 'Gee, the Los Angeles Rams are sort of my roots in the NFL. I might as well talk to them,'" Vermeil said.

Ironically, the Rams were prepared to give the job to Mora, one of Vermeil's closest friends in the business. Vermeil was on John Ralston's staff at Stanford when Mora hired on. Later, Mora coached the Philadelphia and Baltimore Stars of the UCLA under Peterson.

After the Rams hired Vermeil, Mora followed Vermeil's path into broadcasting. Not surprisingly, Vermeil tried to help him with the transition. "He sent me a bunch of notes, what to do, what not to do," Mora said. "He was a big help."

Later, Mora became head coach of the Indianapolis Colts and he spoke frequently with Vermeil to exchange ideas. "In this profession, you need somebody you can lean on from time to time, someone who understands what you're going through," Vermeil said.

Vermeil hired former star Eagles running back Wilbert Montgomery to his Rams coaching staff, though he had no coaching experience. This hiring was a payback for Montgomery's heroic play in Philadelphia.

"People in my position owe people certain things," Vermeil said. "Wilbert is one of those people. This is my way of paying my debt." Montgomery repaid Vermeil by becoming an outstanding assistant coach.

Vermeil tried to develop the same bond with the Rams that he had with the Eagles. And even when these players faltered, Vermeil remained amazingly faithful to them.

Lawrence Phillips? After Vermeil cut him, he tried to land him work in Green Bay. He calls Packers coach Mike Holmgren to pitch him. "Mike, he's so close!" he said during a phone call to Green Bay. "So close! If you get him there with the leadership of Reggie White to help him, I think he can really help."

The Packers took a pass, but the Miami Dolphins took a flyer on him. After the Dolphins let him go, he tried to get Phillips another shot in St. Louis. "If it wouldn't be a distraction," he said, "I'd like to bring him back."

Vermeil got pounded for that admission. "What would you have liked me to say, 'Hell no, that jerk doesn't belong here?'" Vermeil asked. "I understand it created a little news thing around the country. I'm sorry I did that. I'm going to have to start not answering questions honestly when someone asks me something. Because it just creates problems. I get ridiculed."

That plea fell flat, predictably, but he prevailed on old friend Bill Walsh to give him one last chance. Phillips paid some early dividends for the 49ers, but eventually fell out of favor with the coaching staff and got cut.

Tony Banks? He argued to keep the embattled quarterback, then put him in a favorable spot with the Baltimore Ravens. The Rams took a lesser offer from the Ravens to give him another opportunity to start. When Banks got married during an off-season in Baltimore, Vermeil was there at the wedding. Later, he offered him the back-up quarterback spot in Kansas City before Banks signed with the Cowboys.

And when the Cowboys whacked him, Vermeil gave him a ringing endorsement with Schottenheimer. Marty's son Brian, who joined his father on the Redskins staff, had worked for Vermeil and with Banks as a Rams aide in 1996. Also, Vermeil had talked up the Redskins coaching job with Schottenheimer after turning it down, at the behest of his old boss Rodgers. Marty was in his loop now, so Dick offered an unsolicited endorsement of Banks.

"I just wanted Marty to know I believed in the kid, and I think he's got a lot of potential," Vermeil said. "He's a strong-minded guy. He's tough as hell. He's got a strong arm. At the time I had him, he was a little bit immature. Just handling all that pressure properly was tough for him, which is not unique for any young quarterback."

Leonard Little? The Rams took him back during the 1999 season, after he had been convicted of manslaughter for a drunk-driving accident that killed a St. Louis woman. Vermeil remained supportive of Little as the player served his jail time, then his eight-game NFL suspension after his conviction.

*Vermeil rounded up some of his old Rams players to make him feel at home – including Trent Green.*

"He'll never be able to right the wrong," Vermeil said. "He could be my son or anybody's son. He's a tremendous young man. It's a burden he's going to have to carry. But he's a Ram and he's part of our family. It's just as if he worked at General Electric or anyplace else. He deserves the right to go back to work."

At every turn over the years, people returned Vermeil's loyalty. When the Rams visited Philadelphia during his second season, Vermeil got the hero's welcome from Eagles fans. Just as he hadn't forgotten the folks who made his tenure there special, the people hadn't forgotten him.

Few coaches develop this sort of bond with a community. "It's a great city; it really is," Vermeil said. "The people always over-react one way or another here and I'm glad they over-reacted to me in a positive way. It's a special relationship. It was nice to get the reception I got. And not just from the former players. Even an old groundskeeper here, an old Polish guy who I think they called Spanky, waited an hour and a half just to see me. When I coached here, he had homemade wine and we would share a glass beneath the bleachers from time to time."

After the Rams won Super Bowl XXXIV, Vermeil was swarmed by all sorts of old friends. Everybody there meant something to him. "Oh my God!" he yelled, embracing an older gentleman. "My buddy! He's my waiter from an Italian restaurant in Delaware! A great man!"

During his one-year hiatus from coaching, Vermeil hooked up with many of his old friends. He and his old high school football coach at Calistoga, Bill Wood, went on a South American fishing adventure that was taped for ESPN. Vermeil had remained close to Wood over the years, checking in with him and sending him game balls.

He lent his old Rams players a hand when he good. He and Carol drove two hours to spend a Saturday night at a charity event organized by receiver Ricky Proehl. "Whenever a player asks me to do something, I'll do it if I have the time," he said. "It's always the first thing I mark on my calendar."

Once somebody got close to Vermeil, they were always close to him. "I think what players today who play for Dick Vermeil now are going to realize 10 years from now is the same thing we realized when we played with him," Ron Jaworski said. "He cared about us. Yeah, he pushed and demanded as a coach, but he also cared about us as people. And that kept going on after they were football players."

He sought to create this same atmosphere in Kansas City. The Chiefs had become a dysfunctional family in the preceding years. The roster was full of suspect characters and the coaches and managers were not always on the same page. Vermeil's first challenge as coach was to change all that. He did little things, like having televisions installed in the Chiefs locker room so the players could watch Game 3 of the NBA Finals together after doing some of their off-season work.

He capped a mini-camp by hosting a team barbecue. "Team unity is important," Pro Bowl tight end Tony Gonzalez said. "When I talk to friends on Super Bowl teams, they always say they like coming to work. That's the sign of a winner."

Vermeil created unity in Philadelphia and St. Louis and he set out to do the same in Kansas City. "There's so much pressure, there's such a swing in emotion in the profession, that if they are the right kind of people, you become closer. I've had a ton of players tell me, 'Hey, coach, I love you,'" Vermeil said. "Now, I know they don't love me like they love their wife, or their father, or their children.

"When Tim Grunhard announced his retirement during our first mini-camp, he came down on the field for practice. The team came together and Will Shields talked about Grunhard. Do you remember what he said at the end? He said, 'Tim Grunhard, we loved you.'

Vermeil rounded up some of his old Rams players to make him feel at home—including quarterback Trent Green, who cost the team a first-round draft pick. (The Rams did throw back the third-round pick they got as compensation for Vermeil's signing.)

For years, Green had clung to work as a No. 3 quarterback in the league. When the Redskins finally gave him a shot in 1998, he flourished. He suffered a catastrophic knee injury in 1999 with the Rams, leading to Kurt Warner's remarkable emergence during the Super Bowl run, but he bounced back to record a 101.8 quarterback rating during the 2000 season in St. Louis. Green was Vermeil's kind of player, the sort of character player a team could rebuild around.

"I love the guys who don't give up," Vermeil said. "They're the ones you look at them and ask, 'What keeps you going?' All those years, Trent refused to pack it in. He wanted it that badly. That's what you need to see in your quarterback. Trent Green will build camaraderie, an esprit de corps that we need. I've seen him do that with a team before. He's a charismatic guy but he also comes across as humble and honest."

Lesser former Rams acquired included Tony Horne, defensive tackle Nate Hobgood-Chittick, receiver Chris Thomas, tackle Willie Jones, cornerback Taje Allen and, at the end of the preseason, quarterback Joe Germaine. They would help the Chiefs understand where their new coach was coming from.

Another Vermeil challenge was to rebuild unity in the front office. His arrival put Peterson at ease, since Vermeil and Stiles had worked so well together in the past. White could fit into the group easily, too, since he clicked with Vermeil and Stiles in St. Louis.

Since he couldn't bring his entire Rams staff down the highway to Kansas City, he had to find coaches capable of building relationships with his players. New defensive coordinator Greg Robinson, hired from the Denver Broncos, was among those that fit the bill.

"The first thing I always want to know is can they establish good relationships with the players?" Vermeil said. "Will the players know they care about them?"

Vermeil has a gift for getting an entire football staff on the same page, all the assistant coaches and all the personnel guys. When he brought in new coaches for Year Three of his Rams tenure, he put them in a position to flourish. "He listens to other people," Peterson said. "That's a rare thing. Here's a man who has done it all. Won it all. And yet, he will say, 'What do you think?' And he really listens, whether it's the offensive line coach or the general manager or the team trainer. He listens."

Peterson felt rejuvenated as the Chiefs flew from Kansas City to Minneapolis for the first training camp in River Falls, Wisconsin, under Vermeil. As the jet took off, Peterson shook hands with his old friend.

"Let's do it again," Peterson said. "Let's have some fun. "It took me 13 years, but I'm glad you're here."

Vermeil found working with Peterson to be as rewarding as he expected it to be. He wouldn't be butting heads with his boss on this job. He respected the work Peterson had done in Kansas City, building a consistently competitive football team. He knew they could pick up where they left off in Philadelphia. Both men had grown a great deal since that time, but their bond remained strong.

"It's very good because you know how he thinks, although he's older, more mature guy than the last time we worked together," Vermeil said. It's been very smooth. Having Lynn Stiles and Mike White here has been a tremendous asset because we've worked together. Lynn and I, in all three programs I've been involved in, have been together. He understands me, I understand him, I make him mad, he makes me mad, you know, and we go on."

By the time the Chiefs traveled to St. Louis for a preseason game, whatever ill will Vermeil felt toward the Rams had evaporated. He realized the reunion with his former players and bosses would be an emotional one. He would remain loyal to that group for the rest of his life. Their final year together was magical. Most of the key Rams were still there.

He realized that St. Louisans appreciated what he and his Rams did for their community. He attended the annual Baseball Writers Award Dinner in St. Louis shortly after taking the Chiefs' job and he still got a nice hand.

"I think they understand I thought I was doing the right thing when I left," Vermeil said. "It was nothing personal (against St. Louis). It was personal for me and my family. As I look back on it now, it wasn't the best thing for me. If I had known I was going to come back and coach again, I never would have left. That doesn't make good sense. But I left there with good intentions of staying out of coaching. Here I am, back. I think they respect that. I think most of those people that will be there have changed their mind from time to time in their lifetime."

St. Louis threw out the welcome mat for his return to the Trans World Dome. Vermeil's smiling face was on the cover of the game program. He and Martz chatted amiably on the field before the game, as various Rams players stopped by to welcome their old coach.

After the game, many Rams hugged Vermeil on the field and the Rams fans assembled around the Chiefs' field entrance gave him a nice ovation. Several Rams players also stopped by the Chiefs locker room to say hello. Defensive end Grant Wistrom sought out Carol and gave her a big hug in the hallway outside the room.

This preseason game felt like a family reunion to many involved. "The people in the organization are my friends, people that I admire and respect," he said. "John Shaw and Jay (Zygmunt) and Georgia (Frontiere), I'm very close to those people. Without them, we would not have been able to do what we did. Without them, I would not have gone back into coaching, because John Shaw is the guy who convinced me to do it. I'm in debt to those people. It's very meaningful.

"There are so many great memories there, standing in that tunnel with those guys. They're no longer players that I coach, but they are all people I have very good relationships with and feel close to. The coaches that are left there, they are not my coaches, but they are my friends."

# CHAPTER TWELVE
# ACCOUNTABILITY

*"We've got to do a better job of coaching as we go along. I'm not hiding behind a lack of talent or anything like that."*

-Dick Vermeil

The new Chiefs era dawned with great optimism at their training camp in bucolic River Falls. As Vermeil prodded his troops through their paces in his inaugural session, there was spring in everybody's step. Carl Peterson, Lynn Stiles, Mike White, Carl Hairston, Al Saunders . . . the familiar members of Vermeil's cabinet were all smiles as they supervised the unveiling of their new program.

But the Chiefs' offense performed horribly. The addition of new quarterback Trent Green, replacing the talented but exasperating Elvis Grbac, did not magically transform this team. As the first practice wound down, the muffed snaps, botched hand-offs, missed blocks, dropped passes, downfield fumbles and errant throws added up.

Where was the talent? Where was the execution? Clearly, these Chiefs weren't going to resemble Vermeil's Rams squad any time soon. Vermeil dipped into his coaching manual while discussing the first session, giving reporters a glimpse of his data-crammed world. This morning session did not compute.

"Defense was plus-four in takeaways," he said after the debacle. "You're going to win over 90 percent of the time when that happens. Of course, minus-four, offensively, we're going to lose. We've got to be smarter. Last year, they were plus-three in turnovers and we'd like to be more than that. The good teams are always plus-13, plus-16 in takeaway-giveaway ratio. Marty Schottenheimer did such a great job establishing that in years past. We want to get back to where that's part of our profile."

Not only was the Chiefs' offense spastic, it also carried the weight of greater expectations. In St. Louis, Vermeil presided over one of the most explosive attacks in modern NFL history. He vowed to apply some of those principles in Kansas City, with Saunders, a former Rams assistant coach, drawing up the Xs and Os and calling the plays.

"We're going to be an attacking-mentality football team," Saunders promised Kansas City. "If you're afraid, don't show up, because it's going to be fun. It's going to be fun to play and it's going to be fun to watch. We're going to throw the ball long, we're going to throw it short, we're going to throw it sideways, we're going to throw it up the field. We're going to run it laterally, we're going to run it vertically, we're going to run draws, we're going to run screens, we're going to run traps, we're going to run a power game."

Those were big promises in a town unaccustomed to such fireworks. Chiefs fans were more used to Martyball, the plodding run and-defend system favored by former coach Marty Schottenheimer. Kansas City fans were used to territorial struggles, not high-scoring shootouts. Saunders' promises sure sounded good.

But flash and dash alone wouldn't make this team better. The Chiefs also needed to regain their playoff-caliber work ethic. They would get it back the only way possible, by grinding it out on the practice field. Many of these players received quite a jolt.

They would come to dread their new regimen just as the Rams did. Vermeil had to discover which players were truly committed. He couldn't punish the Chiefs the way he punished the Eagles, but the former Rams at River Falls would certainly suffer some flashbacks to their days in Macomb, Ill.

"I promise it won't be a country club," Vermeil said. "It won't be a marine boot camp. We're coaching different kids than the day of the Marine, but you have to have a little of that kind of discipline, that kind of toughness, that kind of regimentation because that's how the game is played on Sunday. As closely as you can duplicate that environment and yet not drive them crazy and drain 'em—because I've been guilty of doing that—but prepare them to be mentally and physically tough, the better your training camp."

Vermeil had to convince the Chiefs that his plan was the right plan for this proud franchise. Having some former Rams coaches and players in the mix was a plus, too. They knew the plan and could help implement it. Plus they all had Super Bowl rings to show off.

The Chiefs weren't as bad off as the Rams when he got there, but they weren't great either. When he took the job, the team was a whopping $31 million over the salary cap. Grbac fled as a free agent. This team was perilously thin at wide receiver, since Sylvester Morris suffered a season-eradicating knee injury during the off-season. The team's talent base took an off-season hit with the exit of five former Pro Bowlers. Due to the cap problems, the Chiefs had to find some kids and journeymen to fill out the ranks. Their depth was suspect.

Vermeil brought 45 new faces to training camp. He was prepared, once again, to battle through the growing pains with a team that had to start over. On the eve of his first Chiefs training camp, he gave one of his famous pep talks to set a positive tone for the summer's preparations.

Peterson had heard similar speeches in the past, but, as always, the coach added some new twists and turns.

"He has a philosophy he has adhered to from the very beginning," Peterson said. "He's refined it and fine-tuned it and so forth, but there are three aspects—I'm not going to give away Dick's secrets—that he thinks are important for the success of a football team. He can do it statistically, he can do it philosophically. He has such a wealth and depth of background and experience that I think the players know he is right."

Saunders believes Vermeil's motivational skills override all his other strengths. He has a knack for spurring players, giving them confidence and inspiring them to give more. He creates a positive atmosphere, where every last detail is designed to help the team succeed. He forms a world where the players can concentrate on making the needed improvements.

"He creates a great environment to work in, where the only goal is to win a championship," Saunders said. "I don't know how long it will take, when we're going to it, but we will do it. It took him five years to get to the Super Bowl in Philadelphia, it took him three years in St. Louis and he made the statement that he wanted to do it faster here. Everything he does is directed toward winning a world championship, whether it's player acquisitions, whether it's practice environment, whether it's meetings, whatever it is."

Vermeil and his staff swarmed the players during their first training camp together, correcting them and encouraging them during every drill. Their approach was to be swift and direct. The best time to teach was right after a player screwed up. "The mistake is still fresh in his mind," Saunders said. "We can tell him, 'OK, this is why you made the mistake,' and he will listen. And that's what we want. We aren't here to yell. We are like teachers who want everyone to get an 'A.' We don't want to fail anybody. We want them to play the best football of their lives."

As always, Vermeil examined every detail of his team's preseason work. His program was very, very specific. He had particular demands for each position, for each aspect of the game. He asked his players to be stronger, tougher and smarter than their opponents.

"Notice, he always says 'smarter' in there," Saunders said. "He's a taskmaster, sure, but I think he believes you coach from the head down.

He was prepared, once again, to battle through growing pains with a team that had to start over.

He likes to say, 'I've never known a good football team that's a dumb football team.'"

Still, Vermeil kept his teaching techniques on the high road. As his first Chiefs camp progressed, he vowed there would be no burnout like he suffered in Philadelphia. As he proved during his Rams regime, he had learned to measure himself. His preparations were more efficient and he tried to tuck himself in before midnight to remain fresh.

He trusted his aides, though he hadn't worked with several of them before. Once again, he viewed himself as a CEO. "I came to St. Louis with that concept because I had been away from the game for 14 years," he said. "There was no way I could jump in and run my own offense. My offense was antiquated by then. The foundation of my offense is the foundation of this offense, same thing, same mechanics and everything, same terminology and same numbering system, everything. But in 14 years out of the game, that scheme coached by other people continued to grow. It's so much more massive today and complex and better. We get more work done today because we have more people doing it."

As always, Vermeil was prepared to stand up for his players as vigilantly as he pushed them. This is how he repaid their trust in him. One day at camp, an insufficient amount of food was prepared for breakfast. Those who came late only got scraps.

"We ask a lot of you," Vermeil told his players on the field. "The least we can do is provide you a good meal. What happened this morning will never happen again."

And it didn't. The Chiefs got hearty breakfasts from then on.

Before another morning practice, Vermeil told the team that it could work in shells instead of full pads in the afternoon—IF they had a crisp morning practice. He never would have used this tactic in Philadelphia, where the Eagles always worked in full pads.

"My point," Vermeil said, "was the ability to practice at that tempo existed before I said anything. It was there. But some kind of motivational tool stimulated them to work at that level. What we have to do is recognize that we shouldn't need some kind of extra stimulus to work at a level that already existed before we went on the field."

During the preseason, Vermeil continued giving Saunders high praise for his work with the offense. Trouble was, the Chiefs just didn't have the skill to play the Rams-style offense Saunders and Vermeil had in St. Louis. The No. 2 receiver, Morris, was gone and top receiver Derrick Alexander came into the season with a nagging Achilles tendon injury. Opposing defenses were able to double-team superstar tight end Tony Gonzalez with impunity, latching onto him the minute he came off the line of scrimmage.

So the Chiefs limped into the regular season. In their opener, they built an 11-point lead over Oakland in third quarter . . . only to allow the Raiders to storm back for a 27-24 victory. The Raiders controlled the ball for nearly 38 minutes of the game. The Chiefs rushed the ball for just 35 yards, Green was surprisingly scatter-armed in the pocket and the wide receivers did nothing until Snoop Minnis' late touchdown grab.

Todd Peterson's missed 37-yard field goal also hurt, as did a couple of botched snaps that the Raiders recovered. "When we have a third-down conversion, we can't get a call back," Vermeil said. "When we have a third-down conversion, we can't drop the ball and we can't have quarterback-center exchange problems. We left the defense on the field too long against a real good football team."

The Chiefs had a chance to acquire big-play receiver Kevin Johnson from the Cleveland Browns to pump up the offense, but concerns about Johnson's enigmatic play and the reluctance to spend another high draft pick prompted Peterson and Vermeil to take a pass on him. Johnson might have helped ease some of the heartache that was to come.

After the tragic events of September 11, 2001, the Chiefs' game against Seattle was cancelled. Instead, they played their next game two weeks later against the New York Giants. The Giants were understandably out of sorts, since they train and play across the river from Ground Zero, but they still beat the Chiefs 13-3.

The Giants were erratic on offense, with Kerry Collins hurling three interceptions. Vermeil couldn't believe his team would lose a game where it forced so many key mistakes. But the Chiefs' own offense was a mess, earning just 11 first downs. Green's first-quarter interception in the Giants end zone was especially costly; that was the only time Kansas City got near the New York goal line.

This defeat didn't fit Vermeil's profile of a loss. "I told them on my final visit with them Saturday morning that if we're plus in turnovers and harass their quarterback enough that will be enough for us to beat them," he said. "They're a former Super Bowl team and a former NFC champion and the only games they lost were ones they were minus in turnovers. We did a fairly good job of that, but we just didn't produce the points. I expect to be able to produce the points."

Green was especially awful. His surgically rebuilt knee still wasn't 100 percent, so he lost some mobility and his ability to throw effectively on the move was hampered. His overall arm strength has always been below average by NFL standards, but his lack of accuracy baffled the Chiefs. He started throwing off his back foot and floating his passes. His decision-making was flawed, too, since he was inclined to force throws toward receivers that were well covered. Smart alecks in the media would begin referring to him as Tr-INT instead of Trent.

But Vermeil remained fiercely loyal to his quarterback, as he would all season. "He's a guy who wants to be held accountable," Vermeil said. "He doesn't mind that at all. In fact, this whole squad shows a real presence in regard to accountability. They don't mind standing up and saying we've got to this better or I should have done that better. They don't point the finger at the other guy and say it wasn't me."

In the wake of this loss, however, some players did play the blame game in the media. Their frustrations were beginning to mount. Naturally, Vermeil wasn't going to tolerate any dissension in the ranks. A lack of team spirit helped sink Cunningham.

So he addressed the matter in a team meeting. To their credit, the offending players didn't claim that reporters misquoted them. "I read to the squad some of those quotes and all of them assumed responsibility," Vermeil said. "That is a tremendous tribute to the kind of young men we have on this football team. It didn't surprise me because I really expected it to be like that."

Vermeil continued to reach out to these players. When Minnis was hospitalized after the Raiders game with a severe concussion, Dick and Carol Vermeil visited him in the hospital. Carol followed that up with another visit, since Minnis' mother had yet to arrive to care for him.

The players took note of their coach's devotion. "Guys really have a lot of feelings for a coach like that because he does genuinely care and it means a lot to him," Green said. "Players want to perform for him."

Minnis' injury added to the team's receiver woes. Morris was done and Alexander was in and out of the lineup with his sore Achilles tendon. Naturally, fans wondered why the Chiefs were throwing so much with so little to throw to.

"I remember my first couple years with the Rams and we would throw the heck out of the ball and they'd be all upset that we weren't running enough," Vermeil said. "Three years later, we throw the first 12 or 16 plays and it's going like mad and they never say anything. We have an attack and an approach and it's how we play the game and I don't second-guess that."

Chiefs fans didn't see the relevance of what the Rams did in '99. Their team didn't seem to have the offensive playmakers. The Chiefs' overall passing efficiency was mediocre and they were especially feckless on third-and-long plays.

Vermeil's response to all this? The team didn't need a new system, it needed better coaching and execution. "We just have to keep searching our own coaching methods and our own approach and our own personnel—our utilization of things—to make sure we're giving them the best opportunity," he said.

Kansas City finally broke through with a 45-13 demolition of the ragged Washington Redskins. The Chiefs actually trailed 3-0 after the first quarter before breaking loose. Green silenced his critics for a week by passing for 346 yards and three touchdowns.

The Chiefs failed to build on that victory, however. They traveled to Denver and keeled over 20-6 to their arch-rivals. The good feelings generated in Washington evaporated quickly. "I thought, boy, we're over the hump," Vermeil said. "Then you come out and find out you're not over the hump, it's just a day the Redskins weren't ready to play, had some guys injured, and were all bitching and moaning. I thought, we're here, we've arrived.

"All of a sudden next week in Denver, we crapped in our hats. That was a maturing experience."

Green's favorite target in this game was Broncos cornerback Deltha O'Neal, who intercepted four passes. He seemed to have a better feel for the Chiefs' pass routes than the Chiefs did. Miscommunication abounded, as did sloppy execution. Vermeil's famous optimism was tested by this disaster. But he still had to keep his head up.

"You've got to go to your squad meeting like we did today and find some of the good things," Vermeil said. "We've got to build on those things, otherwise you go through seasons beating yourself down."

Was it time to scale back this offense, since Green wasn't passing to Isaac Bruce, Torry Holt, Marshall Faulk and Az-Zahir Hakim, as he had in St. Louis? Given all the injuries the Chiefs were battling, shouldn't the team get more conservative and just hand the ball to powerful running back Priest Holmes more often?

No they shouldn't, at least in Vermeil's mind. He didn't want his staff to back off, to reel in, to simplify. "You do that subconsciously sometimes," he said. "Sometimes you do that during ballgames and that's what you have to watch out for as a signal caller, allowing some negative that happened to influence you and make you pucker a little bit when it comes to making a similar call in the similar area of the field. I've been there. I've called enough plays in big games and I know exactly what happens."

The agonizing losses kept coming. The Chiefs fell 20-17 at home against Pittsburgh, in part because Green threw an interception that Chad Scott returned for a Steelers' touchdown. Green lost his composure during the game, unloading on Minnis after the rookie ran a wrong route. "I showed my frustration with Snoop and some of the guys," Green admitted after the game. "Some of the guys showed their frustration with me. When it gets going like this, there's a lot of frustration out there."

This game was quite winnable, but Kansas City found a way to lose. The Chiefs' run defense folded, allowing 203 yards. Only a late offensive push, with the game pretty much out of hand, kept the score respectable. The proud franchise fell to 1-4 for the first time since 1987, when a player strike marred the season. This was the first time the Chiefs lost their first three home games since 1980. These grim spectacles were more than many fans could bear to watch; Arrowhead Stadium began evacuating early on Sunday afternoons. The honeymoon was SO over.

Next up was a 24-16 loss at Arizona, to the annually dreadful Cardinals. The Chiefs somehow fell behind 24-9 before staging a late rally. The final Cardinals touchdown came after a roughing-the-quarterback penalty on Eric Hicks gave Arizona new life. This was a typical Chiefs mistake, the sort that put the team in a deep hole week after week. "Maybe we ought to just spot the other team 14 points right off the bat and get it over with," Michael Ricks mused. "That way we could start our comeback sooner."

This game ended with another mishap. The Chiefs reached the Arizona two before Corey Chavous intercepted Green with one second left. Back-pedaling away from a fierce pass rush, Trent could only loft the ball toward the back of the end zone and hope. The prayer was not answered, so the Chiefs fell to 1-5.

Around town, they were laughingstocks. Taje Allen, who rode high with the Rams during their astonishing 1999 season, had to go back to lying low. "It's definitely not fun looking at any sports news," Allen said. "The newspaper headlines are making jokes. On the radio, they're talking bad about your coach and your quarterback. Even your own family members are like, 'Why aren't you guys winning? I thought y'all were going to be good.' Stuff like that, man."

Additional failure came in the form of a 35-28 home-field loss to the Indianapolis Colts four days later. Green threw his third interception of the game into the end zone, helping doom his team. During the Chiefs' first seven games, they scored just eight touchdowns in 21 trips to the red zone.

Much of Green's trouble in this game was attributable to a lack of pass blocking by his team's makeshift line. Left tackle John Tait got turnstiled for a couple of sacks and multiple pressures. Also, his receivers had butterfingers. In the second quarter along, four players combined to drop five passes.

Vermeil had to mine the game video for positives, because few were readily apparent. "When you're a team like we are, you can dwell on the loss and the negatives but all it does is usually drag you down," he said. "You correct 'em, you coach 'em and go on to the next level."

Skeptics continued asking why Vermeil wouldn't scale back his offensive game plan and let Holmes do all the heavy lifting. But he resolved to stay course, making only minor adaptations while looking for better execution. Vermeil had to steer his program forward even as the exasperation built in the locker room. He had to find ways to ease the tension.

"This is a great group of kids," he said. "All we'll do is take the adversity that we experienced to get stronger and get better. We have two obligations . . . to assume some of the responsibility for not winning—coaches and players—and also assume some of the responsibility to get better and eliminate some of the bad plays. Eliminate a few bad plays and make a few more good plays and you win football games."

His personal resolve was being sorely tested as well. As in St. Louis, he took the first-year losses very hard. Once again, repetitive failure frustrated him. The enormity of the really bad losses overwhelmed him. The video review was depressing. Why, Vermeil often wondered, am I going through all this again?

"You think of everybody you ought to be mad at and everything you should have done as a coach," Vermeil said. "You look at the tapes, you're mad at a coach, mad at a player. But when it's all said and done, there's a process you go through to building a winning, championship football team."

In times like these, Vermeil welcomed calls for his old colleagues. Jim Mora, whose Colts also wobbled through the 2001 season, phoned to commiserate. "I normally call him from time to time just to pump him up when you need gas, when things aren't going too well," Vermeil said. "My way of relaxing—and I haven't done this as much as I did with the Rams—on a tough day is talk to a good friend in the same business. Find out they have the same problems, the same weaknesses, same thoughts. Then, I don't think you feel isolated in your own little world when you do that."

The crowds started turning ugly at Arrowhead Stadium. For years, football games had been a party in that place. Now the Chiefs were losing game after game on their own field. Vermeil understood the uproar. Kansas City had built one of the most impressive home-field advantages in the league. The franchise built a passionate fan base during the Peterson/Schottenheimer glory days.

"I can remember coming here in some early preseason games and you could have shot my deer rifle off inside the stadium and not hit anybody," Vermeil said. "But they changed that because of good football."

Bad football caused Chiefs fans to turn against Vermeil much quicker than Rams fans did. St. Louisans had grown accustomed to losing, but Kansas Citians couldn't remember the last time their team was this helpless. "I understand and expect a lot of criticism," Vermeil said. "I've never taken a job where you start out like we're starting out where you don't take a lot of flak. That's part of the job. If you can't handle it, don't take the job."

Yes, he admitted, the hideous start was a major disappointment. There were no excuses for what happened—not the injuries, not the new program, nothing. Just as the players were accountable for the team's failure, so were the coaches.

"I expected to be better than we are right now," Vermeil said. "Either I'm not getting the job done or we're not getting the job done or we aren't as I'd like to believe we are. I always see players as better than they are, I always have. Sometimes it's a fault and sometimes it's a blessing."

While he may have over-estimated the ability of these Chiefs, he insisted his belief in their character had been justified. "You won't see these guys lay down and hang their head and pout," he said. "You'll see them get upset and mad, but you won't see them pointing a finger at a teammate or a coach. This is a good group and that's what gives you a chance to get better. But we have a ways to go and some things are just glaring."

It's difficult to pinpoint where the team bottomed out, exactly, but the Colts loss left them 0-3 at home and 1-6 overall. The Chiefs tried not to mope, but it was difficult to find much joy in their work. Once players began to lose confidence, there wasn't much the coaching staff could do to restore it. In the face of such a calamity, each athlete had to do his own soul-searching.

Injuries just kept piling up, as the Chiefs lost Victor Riley from the offensive line and John Browning from the defensive line. These men had been bulwarks for this team in the trenches. With Morris gone and Alexander in and out of the lineup because of his leg problems, quarterback Green continued struggling within this ambitious passing scheme. Even Peterson began second-guessing the spending of a first-round pick to acquire Green from the Rams.

As the criticism intensified, Vermeil was forced to become more strident in defense of his passer. "I still believe in the guy," Vermeil said after the Colts debacle. "I'm not going to jump ship on him. I've been through this before with quarterbacks, with Ron Jaworski. They were going to boo him right out of town. The big thing is, Trent can't lose confidence in himself."

Vermeil stepped to the fore and tried to take some heat off his players. Rather than single them out for their individual failures, he stressed his own responsibility for the dreadful start. "Whenever you lose as many games as we have, you're just not good enough," he said. "That's all there is to it. That goes for me right on down. We've just got to keep working. Every time I've been in that situation, hard work is the only thing that's helped pull ourselves out of it. It shakes the confidence level and all that. My expectations are much better and greater. We're not getting it done. It starts me with me."

The Chiefs finally stopped the bleeding with a 25-20 victory at San Diego. Holmes, the offense's only reliable threat, pounded out 181 yards on the ground. As always, Vermeil tried a positive motivational message.

"Guys," Vermeil told the Chiefs before the game, "you aren't losers. You are on a losing streak."

In the locker room after the game, the Chiefs chanted "We're getting better! We're getting better!" It wasn't "We're No. 1!" but it was a start.

"If you were in the locker room after the game," Gonzalez said, "you would have thought we won the Super Bowl."

**Bad football caused Chiefs fans to turn against Vermeil much quicker than Rams fans did.**

But these Chiefs couldn't build momentum yet. They hadn't learned from their early-season fiasco in Denver, when they failed to build on a lopsided win over Washington. With Green throwing three more interceptions—running his total to 16 for the season—the Chiefs went to East Rutherford, N.J., and handed a 27-7 victory to the Jets.

They did everything wrong imaginable, including falling for a fake punt. They went looking for new ways to screw up. Vermeil was nearly inconsolable in defeat. "I'm pissed off at myself," he said after the game. "I'm mad at my coaches. I'm mad at my players. I think anybody who gets their ass beat like that gets upset. We're all responsible for a game like that. I didn't expect it. I thought if they beat us, it would be a tight football game. I was upset. Wouldn't you be upset if you were responsible?"

He couldn't help but wonder why he took on still another rebuilding job at this point in his life. He had been through the mill twice and he was getting ground up once again. He had left football on top after taking the Rams the distance. Why didn't he stay there?

Vermeil saw what still another miserable loss did to Carol. When he boarded the team bus for the flight home, his wife was crying. He had become better at handling defeat over the years, but he had never gotten used to seeing Carol suffer after especially bad losses. This was the only aspect of coaching that really bothered him.

When the Chiefs reached Kansas City, the town was buzzing about Green. Fans believed he had to go. But Vermeil stood behind him. He didn't yank him from this game and he wasn't yanking him as the starter. Many coaches would have bailed on their quarterback during a debacle of this magnitude, to remove the focus from themselves. The Chiefs had a capable back-up quarterback in Todd Collins, a former starter in Buffalo.

But Green kept his job and Vermeil manned the complaint window. "I want to be personally held responsible for some of his problems," he said. "I'm the head coach and I should be held responsible. I still believe in him and I really didn't even think about taking him out. I think he's the right guy and when everybody does a better job around him off the field and on the field, he'll be able to better demonstrate what he's able to do."

(Chiefs fans remained unconvinced. When the Kansas City Star surveyed fans around Thanksgiving to see whom they considered the biggest turkey on the local sports scene, Green took honors. A younger quarterback might have found such abuse hard to digest.)

Vermeil managed to keep his emotional grip. He did not want to be found wandering around the big Arrowhead Stadium parking lot, wondering if he should go on. He had gotten better at rebounding. The fact he had seen it all and done it all in football helped him cope.

He didn't feel like packing it in after reviewing the numbingly bad game video. "I don't let myself get as depressed as I did in Philadelphia, or my first couple of years in St. Louis," he said. "That drains you. I'm doing a better job of handling the disappointments now and keeping focused and going in the right direction. At 65, you look at things differently than when you were 45. You're more understanding, more patient."

He invited Peterson and several other staffers—and their wives—to his home for Thanksgiving dinner. For a night, they did their best to get their minds off football. This was another opportunity for Vermeil to get to know his people as people. This was another chance to prove himself as a leader, to prove that he could step back, catch his breath and maintain a long view of the program.

Such an in-season social event would have been inconceivable during his obsessive Eagles days. "Back then," Peterson mused, "he would have had Carol bring the turkey to the office."

Relief finally arrived in the form of a 19-7 victory over Seattle, the Chiefs' first home-field victory under Vermeil. Holmes stepped up as a leader before this game, speaking to the team about the need for accountability for himself and everybody on the team. Then he stepped up again as a leader during the game, rushing for 120 yards to pace the win.

This was a team victory. The Chiefs gave their strongest defensive performance of the year. Every aspect of Kansas City's game was solid, leaving Vermeil to rave about his team's character and resilience. The players refused to let the season get away from them, as the pitiful Detroit Lions and Carolina Panthers did in 2001. They fought through their earlier travails and became determined to get something out of this season.

When he looked over his team in the meeting room, he saw guys paying attention. Their eyes weren't dead. They still seemed ready to learn and willing to work. He didn't have a lot of guys milking marginal injuries to bow out of practice. "These kids are as good as you would ever want to be in regard to handling adversity properly," Vermeil said. "That's one of the keys why they've gotten better."

The Chiefs fell flat four days later, falling 23-10 at Philadelphia in a Thursday night game despite Holmes' 176 yards from scrimmage. The game started disastrously, with the Eagles executing an onside kick, and it didn't get a whole lot better for the Chiefs. Here was a typical play from this season: After Glenn Cadrez broke through the Eagles' line to partially block a punt, teammate Eric Warfield muffed it downfield and gave Philadelphia the ball back.

This defeat, which left Kansas City 3-8, left Gonzalez wondering if he should re-sign with the team. He was eligible for free agency after the season, although he expected the Chiefs to put a franchise tag on him to restrict his movement. Money would be an issue, of course, but so would the direction of the franchise.

A fourth straight dreary season had him at wits end. "It's unbearable, really," Gonzalez said. "Everyone on this team needs to look at himself. They need to look at the man in the mirror, as Michael Jackson says, because we can't keep playing like this. I feel like we're on a roller coaster. We've all got to work harder. We can be better than this. We have been better than this. We've all got to improve because I can't take this. This has to stop. This has to change."

By now, Vermeil realized that he would have to try to grind out victories with good defense and Holmes pounding the ball more. He and his staff finally had to take a step back on offense. Vermeil admitted his team wasn't capable of wheeling and dealing with an aerial attack. "We can't do that," he said. "We don't have the same type of talent we became spoiled by at the Rams. It's hard to screw those guys up. I couldn't. I'm sure as hell Mike Martz can't."

The Chiefs' inability to break big scoring plays prompted Vermeil to add receiver Eddie Kennison, who had walked out on the Broncos the night before a game. Kennison later tried to undo his "retirement," but the team sent him packing. Even though Vermeil had traded Kennison away from the Rams after the 1998 season—and even though Eddie had bounced around the league ever since—he decided to give the speedster a chance. A couple of family crises hit Kennison simultaneously and he unraveled.

Vermeil admitted that he wouldn't take a chance on a player like Kennison if he didn't have some history with him. "I know him and I trust him," he said. "We had a good relationship and a lot of people sometimes have a hard time figuring out how that could be when I traded him. 'How can you bring him in here,' they say. But he was a good person and he can play and upgrade out talent."

When the Broncos continued to rip Kennison for walking out on the team, Vermeil rushed to his defense. "I'm not saying Eddie hasn't had some problems, but they've had some other guys who have had problems who have been suspended from the league," Vermeil said. "What does that make them? I'd think they'd show more class evaluating their own people."

Ouch!

The Chiefs continued to show some heart, despite the mounting losses. Holmes continued his heroic play at Oakland, rushing for 168 yards and gaining another 109 receiving the ball. Kansas City won the yardage battle, 447-264. But the Chiefs somehow managed to lose to the Raiders 28-26 due to numerous errors and some glaring non-calls by the officiating crew. The Chiefs blew 10-0 and 17-7 leads in this agonizing defeat.

Kansas City missed a couple of two-point conversion attempts—with Raiders hanging onto a Chiefs receiver—and the Chiefs got stuffed on a critical fourth-and-one attempt in the middle of the field. They allowed Tim Brown to turn back the clock and return a punt for a touchdown. Perhaps worst off all, Todd Peterson missed a 28-yard field goal. This is the sort of stuff that happened to Vermeil early in his Eagles tenure. Champions don't make these sorts of mistakes.

Kennison played a small role for the Chiefs as they beat the Broncos in a 26-23 for their fourth victory of the season. Fans finally left Arrowhead Stadium buzzing about an exciting and meaningful victory. The players would be able to get out on the town without having fans yell at them. Vermeil sent them off with heartfelt, misty-eyed pat on the back.

"I got emotional talking about it because I was so happy for them," he said. "To see what they were able to do, playing together, playing hard and just sticking together all this season. To me, that's my reward and it makes it all worthwhile."

Although the Chiefs managed to outlast the dreadful San Diego Chargers 20-17 for their fifth victory, Gonzalez bristled at his lack of meaningful activity. He noted that he was better suited to play in the West Coast offense, which features the tight end more than Saunders' vertical attack. He wanted to win, of course, but he also wanted the football.

Gonzalez made some noise about going to the NBA to fulfill a lifelong dream, perhaps on a 10-day deal. He fantasized about earning a full-time pro basketball job, even as a role player. Anything would beat losing game after game while playing the role of decoy in this offense.

Vermeil and Saunders got Gonzalez's message. The Chiefs continued their late push by winning another thriller, 30-26 over Jacksonville. They sprung Gonzalez for a couple of touchdown passes. Green continued his accurate second-half passing and the explosive Kennison was a game-breaker in this game, repaying Vermeil for the opportunity.

The beleaguered Chiefs defense earned two red-zone stops in the last two minutes. As the final Jaguars pass of the game was batted down, Vermeil literally went airborne in celebration. "We felt they were the best losing team in football," Vermeil said. "If we can come down here and beat them, then we're the best losing team in football."

Well . . . that distinction wasn't exactly a Super Bowl title, but that was something. The victory was especially important for Green, who was able to spread the football around the field and put on a Rams-like show.

He and his receivers finally got in sync. "It's all been growing and swelling and his knee is so much better," Vermeil said. "He's a fine player and an outstanding person. When we went through the adversity, he never pointed a finger at anybody and never made excuses. He just went about his work."

Gonzalez sounded like he was finally warming up to the new regime. The invigorating Jacksonville victory helped, as did the pool table that the coach got the team for Christmas. That big new toy in the locker room helped turn some frowns upside down. It stood as a symbol of the coach's belief in his players. The Chiefs weren't calling their workplace "Shawshank," as the Jaguars did under coach Tom Coughlin's shrill command.

"With Coach Vermeil, I have had one of the best times I have ever had as an athlete, in this locker room, with the guys on this team, with the personalities on this team," Gonzalez said. "He's the kind of guy you want to play for. He's put TVs up, he's changed a lot of things around here and I've certainly enjoyed that."

The day after the Jaguars victory, Vermeil sent his coaches home early for New Year's Eve. He got home about 7:30 p.m. and enjoyed a quiet dinner with Carol. He couldn't recall when he was ever this exhausted in his life. "I certainly didn't stay up and listen to the bells ring and the horns blow," he says. "You know, I'm not as young as I used to be. I really feel it. Those games like that drain you, they really do. It catches up to you at the end of the season."

The Seattle Seahawks edged the Chiefs 21-18 in the season finale, keeping them from closing out with four consecutive victories. Had Gonzalez not gone down with a knee injury, the Chiefs would have liked their chances in the second half of this game. But, as Green noted afterward, "the game basically went as our season went. We did enough to be involved and stay close in the game. It was kind of flashy at times, but it wasn't the consistency we needed."

After vacationing immediately after the season—he made a getaway to the East Coast to get together with his extended family—Vermeil returned eager to get started on the 2002 season. A visit to his office on a February morning found him brimming with energy and optimism.

He woke up at 1:30 that morning. He lay awake in bed for three hours, replaying the season, his preparations and his approach. But rather than toss and turn and stew, he grabbed his tape recorder and began reciting suggestions to himself before catching a bit more sleep.

"I made 31 notes to myself with my little recorder," Vermeil said. "I took 31 notes off this morning. There's a process in building a team before you coach a team. There's a process in building a business before you run a business to be successful. Right now we're going through the process. That came up during the middle of the night because I started to recognize a few things, mistakes that I made since I've been here that's all part of the process of building a successful football team that, if I had the chance, I would go back and change what I did. I did that in St. Louis, too. You have to go back and keep evaluating."

The Chiefs went into their off-season on an upturn. They went 4-3 after their 2-7 start—and just missed winning a couple more games to reach .500 for the season—so they went into their off-season in a pretty good mood. They discovered that Holmes could be a far better running back than they imagined, since he piled up 1,555 yards rushing and 2,169 total yards from scrimmage—Marshall Faulk-like numbers.

Still, they had to ask a few "what ifs" as they went into their winter break. Vermeil began a thorough review of his first season in Kansas City. He examined why Green played so much better down the stretch, completing nearly 74 percent of his passes during the late three-game winning streak.

And how could the coaches help Green cut his league-high total of 24 interceptions? Vermeil's staff discovered that he was more effective in a play-action passing scheme than a straight-drop scheme. He got into a better rhythm this way. He is an excellent ball handler and Holmes' running success set up the play-action pass nicely.

"Maybe we could have done a better job coaching earlier, if we had known our personnel better earlier," Vermeil said. "Maybe we could have gotten things in sync earlier. I don't blame anybody other than my own self-evaluation."

# CHAPTER THIRTEEN
# PASSION

*"Do I have the same passion for winning? Yes. Do I have the same compassion for the guys I coach and work with? Yes. But sometimes, as a head coach, doing it the way I have to do it now, sometimes I feel a little bit left out. But I'm doing it the way I have to do it now, at this time in my career, having left the game for 14 years and come back. It didn't work too bad in St. Louis."*

-Dick Vermeil

A strong finish in 2001 brought no relief to the Chiefs in the 2002 training camp at River Falls. Vermeil wanted to build on his team's improvement, not step back from it.

The hitting quickly intensified. The veterans began to test the kids. The natural sorting process began, with the powerful offensive line banging on the overmatched defensive line. The Chiefs failed to land an impact veteran for this unit and first-round draft pick Ryan Sims, a potential cornerstone at defensive tackle, remained unsigned when camp opened.

Rookie Eddie Freeman quickly became a focal point during the full-contact drills. He had lots of ability, but he lacked composure and polish. So the veterans began goading him.

"Get out of here Freeman," Victor Allotey yelled at one point. "It's a man's world."

A week into the camp, veteran offensive tackle John Tait drove Freeman to the ground and pinned him there. Freeman flew into a rage and the two began fighting. Tait threw a punch and Freeman grabbed Tait by the helmet, tearing it off his head and then smashing him in the face with it.

The vicious blow broke Tait's nose and opened facial lacerations that required 17 stitches to close. "Fights happen and things happen in fights," Tait said afterward. "But I don't know about hitting people with a helmet.

"It's not like I'm going to wait for Eddie to get out of a meeting and then hit him with a baseball bat. It's not like I want to kill Eddie. I don't think Eddie is a bad person. He just made a mistake."

Vermeil didn't get a good look at the brawl. He believed Freeman hit Tait with his fist, not the helmet. That sort of thing happens all the time in training camp, especially a rugged Vermeil camp. He didn't believe it was a big deal and bristled when reporters kept bringing it up.

Finally, after a Wednesday night practice on "Family Fun Night" for fans in River Falls, Vermeil snapped. "If John Tait's helmet hadn't come off, nothing would have happened and you wouldn't be asking the (freaking) question," he barked. "I don't want to be asked that question any more, understand?

"Print it! All right? Good."

He stormed off without answering any more questions. But the next day, Vermeil felt sheepish about the outburst. His passion for training camp was as strong as ever, but he figured he should do a better with his temper at this point in his life. "I don't normally do that, but it's happened before," he said. "I'm human. I woke up in the middle of the night thinking, 'What an idiot.'"

After reviewing the incident—and listening to Tait's complaint that it went unpunished—Vermeil changed course and fined Freeman $2,500 for the attack. "John threw the first punch, but that retaliation was out of line for National Football League and the demeanor we want," Vermeil said.

He also held a team meeting to underscore the difference between battling hard and going postal. "What people need to understand is this: When players get in fights like that they go into an emotional state I call rage," he said. "At that point, anything goes. You can tell them to break it up and you can jump in and try to stop it. They won't do it."

Vermeil detonated again in training camp, after watching his team stagger through an especially sloppy morning practice.

"We were horse (manure)," he growled. "We coached horse (manure). We practiced horse (manure). Other than that, it was a good day."

Reporters wondered if it was just one of those days.

"(Shoot) no," Vermeil said. "No. I've got a philosophy about things like this. They do happen, but many times you allow them to happen. That's my fault. There were some breakdowns in communication on the practice schedule. Things were read wrong and guys making decisions on their own. We'll get it straight. I've been through this before. It pissed me off, but I've been through it before. It starts with me."

When defensive Nate Hobgood-Chittick went down with cramps

> His passion for training camp was as strong as ever, but he figured he should do better with his temper at this point in his life.

during a practice session, medical personnel swarmed him. This wasn't how Vermeil ran camps during his Eagles days.

"The reason he had so many people out there is everybody has to be so cautious these days," Vermeil said. "Nowadays when a guy has a cramp it's like he's on life transplant because everybody wants to overreact. Baloney. He had a cramp. I thought they were going to call a neurosurgeon."

Vermeil still cut players on the spot, if they clearly failed to measure up. Jason Baggett, a 322-pound undrafted rookie, threw up several times during a Friday morning practice. That was it for him. "It just looked like he didn't belong in a NFL training camp, so we sent him home," Vermeil said.

Clearly the head coach hadn't gotten soft. All questions about Vermeil's emotional stamina were answered. He still had the drive, the fire to coach as he always has. He could get up for the job . . . and he could still get down, too, whenever the team suffered a major setback. At those moments he wondered why he left the ranch in Pennsylvania to take on another rebuilding job.

"Sometimes I get worn out just like everyone," Vermeil said. "Sometimes I get upset with them. Sometimes I'm mad. Sometimes I'm down. I share all the same emotions in my job that everyone else does going to work on Monday morning."

But he always bounced back and hurled himself back into his work. This team did have some promise. The Chiefs signed veteran wide receiver Johnnie Morton to shore up the passing game. Receiver Eddie Kennison, a strong mid-season addition in 2001, mastered the offense during the off-season mini-camps.

All-pro tackle Willie Roaf was acquired from the New Orleans Saints to beef up the offensive line. Future Hall of Famer Morten Andersen was signed to clean up the placekicking mess. Sims and Freeman were expected to strengthen the defensive line, as did veteran John Browning, who was back from knee surgery.

"I like Browning anywhere you line him up," Vermeil said. "You know why? Because he kicks your ass. And we need that mentality."

Vermeil still believed in Trent Green, who struggled through an interception-filled 2001 season, and he knew that Priest Holmes and Tony Gonzalez were as good as anybody at their position. The rebuilding job wasn't complete, but it was well underway. Vermeil liked his team a lot.

And he especially liked how the Chiefs pulled together during his first season at the helm and grew even tighter during the off-season. He was moved when the players called Carol Vermeil out and presented her with a gift.

"That's the first time I've seen that," he said. "When a team gets together to buy a lady, my wife, a gift for all the nice things she's done for them. That just goes to show you what kind of football team this is. She was quivering she was so nervous when they called her up there. These kids know how to appreciate each other. That just shows you what kind of people they are."

As camp progressed, it became clear that Vermeil still had lots of work to do. Linebacker Donnie Edwards, a salary cap casualty, was clearly missed. Receivers Sylvester Morris and Snoop Minnis were still recovering from injuries. Sims missed virtually the entire preseason before finally signing. The same was true for Gonzalez, who dabbled with pro basketball over the summer and balked at agreeing to a "no-basketball" clause in a long-term contract. He finally decided to play under a one-year contract.

The absence of these two key players wore on Vermeil. He became especially vexed with the Sims situation. "It's time for him to come play football," Vermeil said. "Hell with negotiating. That's for agents, and the agent ought to get off his ass and get this guy in here and because he's hurting him and he's hurting the Chiefs."

The preseason schedule brought mixed results for the Chiefs. Green suffered a relapse of the interception woes that colored his 2001 season. The media continued questioning Vermeil's loyalty to the quarterback and his decision to spend a first-round draft pick to acquire him. Vermeil denied Green was getting special treatment.

"Everyone is held accountable," Vermeil said. "He was held accountable last year. Just because I don't get in the newspaper and say bad things about him doesn't mean he's not held accountable. We really don't operate negatively. We try to correct the mistakes as positively as we can and go on."

Green struggled through the preseason finale—a 23-16 victory over the Rams—and that put him and Vermeil under intense scrutiny as the start of the regular season arrived. But Green insisted he was fine. "If you are tentative as a quarterback, you might as well hang it up," he said. "You can't do that. Fortunately, I've been in the same offense or a variation of it my whole career, so I have a pretty good understanding of what we're trying to do."

Even with Gonzalez and Sims finally under contract, the Chiefs brought plenty of concerns into Vermeil's second regular season. "Sometimes, I think we're a lot better," Vermeil said. "Sometimes I don't have a clue. I think we're going to have to wait and see. I have my concerns. I wake up in the middle of the night with my concerns."

The season opener in Cleveland was shaping up as a fiasco. The Chiefs simply could not stop the Browns offense. When Cleveland's lead reached 30-17, all appeared lost for the Chiefs. But Green kept firing the ball, Holmes kept gobbling up yardage and the Chiefs kept coming back. They cut the lead to 39-37 and had one last chance to make the game-winning play.

Green dropped back looking to throw a desperation pass. The Browns closed in on him. He scrambled. Browns linebacker Dwayne Rudd wrapped him up. Green looked for somebody to pitch the ball to before he hit the turf. The nearest man happened to be the 6-foot-6, 323-pound Tait.

"I was just looking for a jersey," Green said. "I saw it was John and figured he had a better chance than me."

"We kind of made eye contact," Tait said.

"Man, you should have seen the look on John Tait's face when he got the ball," said guard Donald Willis. "He was looking at the football like, 'Man, what is this?'"

Rudd never saw the lateral. He believed he had sacked Green. He pulled off his helmet and began his celebration. "He was dancing like a little cheerleader," Freeman said.

"I thought he was down," Rudd said. "When I tackled him, he rolled over my facemask. I looked up and saw triple zeroes on the clock and thought the game was over, but I didn't get a chance to look behind me and see the game wasn't over. I shouldn't have taken it off, because it's against NFL rules."

As Tait started rumbling downfield toward the end zone, some 53 yards from the line of scrimmage, a penalty flag flew into the air. Players aren't allowed to remove their helmet on the field of play during the game.

Tait didn't see the flag. He figured he had to run all the way to the end zone for the Chiefs to win. "Your mind is a blur," he said. "I'm thinking, 'This is it. This is the last play of the game. If I don't score, we lose.' I could see the end zone, you know. I could see it. And all I thought was, 'get there.'

"I haven't really run with the football before. I've dreamed about it, you know. Every offensive lineman dreams about it. But I've never really done it."

Along the way, he picked up Holmes as a blocker, which was rich. "I can't remember what was going on," Holmes said, "but I just kept running into people."

Along the way, Tait encountered Browns safety Devin Bush. "I tried to give him a juke and I couldn't do it," Tait said. "Those little defensive backs are pretty fast. I tried to shake one guy and almost fell down."

Tait made it to the Browns 25 before getting knocked out of bounds. That would have been the end of the game, but Rudd was penalized for unsportsmanlike conduct. The game cannot end on a defensive penalty. The ball was moved half the distance to the goal line. The Chiefs got the opportunity to summon Andersen to kick the game-winning field goal and make Tait the most unlikely of heroes.

"As a kid, I always dreamed about doing something like that," Tait said. "In my dream I always scored a touchdown. But I'll take this."

The Chiefs won the game 40-39 on a 30-yard field goal with no time left on the clock. "This was one for the ages," Andersen said.

"Dwayne Rudd is our MVP right now," Tony Gonzalez said.

"I'm in shock," Chiefs guard Brian Waters said. "Absolute shock. I still don't know what happened. I think we won. I don't know how. But I think we won."

For the record, Tait's run was good for 28 yards, the longest Chiefs run of the game. "Well, I suppose I can cross that off my 'things to do before I die' list," he said. "Maybe now I should go see the pyramids or something."

This victory reminded Vermeil and Carl Peterson of the "Miracle of the Meadowlands" play that propelled the Eagles toward their first playoff berth under that regime. "I was at the Miracle of the Meadowlands, and I'm calling this the Miracle of the Dawg Pound," Peterson said. "This one was pretty special because more things had to happen than just pick up a fumble and score with it. We needed a little extra help with a defensive penalty at the end of the game. What that win did in the Meadowlands for the Eagles was propel us to our first winning season, 9-7, and our first playoff season. Good things came of it."

This game set an unpredictable tone for the Chiefs, one that would last the entire season. They could not get on the three- or four-game roll Vermeil was talking about. They followed that thrilling victory with a dud—a mistake-filled 23-16 loss to Jacksonville at Arrowhead Stadium. Their defense got burned for big plays and Green tossed two devastating interceptions.

With fans and media critics calling for Todd Collins to replace Green, Vermeil had to give his quarterback a vote of confidence. "The day I'm dissatisfied, all of a sudden you'll see a change made," he said. "I know more about the factors that control the performance of a quarterback. I can't be a bouncing ball, high one day, low one day, high one day, low one day."

The Chiefs rebounded with a frantic performance at Foxboro, Mass., rallying for two late touchdowns to tie New England 38-38 and force overtime. Unfortunately, the defending NFL champion Patriots extracted the victory with Super Bowl hero Adam Vinatieri's 35-yard field 4 minutes, 40 seconds into overtime.

Should Vermeil have gone for two points after Holmes scored a touchdown as regulation expired, cutting the Patriots lead to 38-37? Given the state of his defense, was it wise to kick the extra point and go into overtime?

"I did what everybody else would do because I thought it was the right thing to do," Vermeil said. "Right now, knowing what happened, I should have, because we never got to score. If I had gone for it and we didn't make it, you guys would think I'm an idiot. There's just no way to win in that situation."

Just as pessimism was reaching a crescendo, the Chiefs pulled themselves together and pounded the Miami Dolphins 48-30 at Arrowhead. Green finally shut up his critics by completing 24 of 34 passes for 328 yards and five touchdowns.

Vermeil gave Green a curtain call, sending in Collins so Green could hear an ovation as he left the field. Green had grown accustomed to hearing boos whenever he left the field. "I want them to appreciate that he's tough enough to handle the boos and all the criticism and the times I get upset with him," Vermeil said. "He's strong enough to come back and play.

"The thing I watch is what he does after adversity. What does he come back and do in the fourth quarter? If he's a tanker in the fourth quarter, he goes right in his pants. If he's a tough guy that has emotional security and confidence to overcome his own personal mistake, he'll start throwing strikes again. Has he not done that?"

The fun continued the next week, with the Chiefs rallying to topple the New York Jets 29-25 at the Meadowlands. Green connected with Holmes on the winning 19-yard touchdown pass with 27 seconds left in the game.

The Chiefs offense took the field with great confidence for their final 10-play, 78-yard drive. The players were all business in the huddle. "There were no jokes," Green recalled. "And there really wasn't a whole lot said. Everybody was very calm. Nobody was stressing out or freaking out."

The Chiefs collapsed at San Diego the following week, allowing three fourth-quarter touchdowns during a devastating 35-34 loss. Chargers quarterback Drew Brees threw the game-winning touchdown pass to Reche Caldwell with just 14 seconds left.

Kansas City somehow fell despite recovering three fumbles, picking off two passes and blocking a punt. "We came up with 14 points on special teams and finished plus-four in turnovers," defensive end Gary Stills said. "We should have won this game. I don't know how we didn't win this game."

Compounding that defeat was the loss of defensive tackle Ryan Sims, who suffered a broken elbow. An already suspect defense got appreciably weaker. The tension continued to mount in the defensive meetings as Vermeil pressed his staff to find solutions.

"To be honest with you, those defensive meetings with the head coach aren't a lot of fun," Vermeil said. "I don't like them because I'm real honest and blunt. Not cruel or mean, but point out the things I think and compare them with defenses I see and the situations I see that we handle well and don't handle well."

All efforts to inspire the Chiefs defense failed. Kansas City blew a 14-point lead over Denver at Arrowhead Stadium and lost in overtime, 37-34. Among the mishaps was a 43-yard field goal attempt Andersen missed when the Chiefs were leading 34-27. More blunders followed.

In overtime, Kennison dropped a third-down pass that could have kept the Chiefs driving. The Chiefs allowed punter Dan Stryzinski to get a kick blocked. Then cornerback Eric Warfield contributed a pass interference penalty to give the Broncos a chip-shot field goal for the win. They searched hard for ways to lose this game.

It was almost too much for Vermeil to bear, especially when he saw Carol's tears after the game. The scene in his Arrowhead Stadium suite Sunday night was bleak. The entire coaching family was suffering. How much more losing could these people take?

"When I walked into my office and saw my wife and saw my coaching staff's wives, I'll tell you, whew, it ain't worth it," he said. "You can't do it too long. Because you are not the only one that suffers. You're not the only one that dies, but you know that it is your responsibility. And you're conditioned, you've coached yourself to handle it. But the other parts of your life, you're not coached."

The Chiefs screwed up in every phase of the game while falling to 3-4, but this time the brunt of the criticism fell on defensive coordinator Greg Robinson. During Vermeil's weekly news conference, Kansas City Star beat writer Adam Teicher pressed the issue. His exchange with the coach went like this:

"You're still happy with the job Greg's doing?" Teicher asked. "You're seeing the necessary adjustments and things? I look at the New England game and the game yesterday and the San Diego game . . ."

"What would you like me to tell you?" Vermeil snapped. "That's he's all (screwed) up or something like that? He's my defensive coordinator. I brought him here. He's a damned good football coach. The other coaches that we work with are responsible for the performance of the defense and I am, number one, responsible for the defense. I'm not going to sit here and criticize my coaches for you and if you already have your story written write it."

"I don't," Teicher said. "I want to know how you feel . . ."

"I told you," Vermeil said, glaring at the scribe. "I have a lot of respect for Greg Robinson and that's why I brought him here. We have problems on defense but they aren't all coaches problems."

"I'm not suggesting they were," Teicher said, "but I wanted to know what you believe Greg Robinson's responsibility is in all this?"

"I'm responsible, number one, because it's the Kansas City Chiefs defense," Vermeil said. "He has the authority to coach along with the help of the other people. Whatever we're doing, it isn't good enough. Whether it's coaching, playing, or whatever I'm doing, it's not good enough. We know that. But there's a process to go through to go and make them better and it's not blaming the defensive coordinator, believe me."

Vermeil went on to lament the negative nature of media coverage in the NFL. "I think we have a group that sits in this meeting room after a disappointing loss that assumes some of the responsibility for the loss and doesn't blame or point the finger at somebody else," he said. "It's so easy to do that. There are people who make a living as journalists beating up people when they're down. That's what they do for a living. That's our society. But we don't do that in a program run by me or my coaching staff. We don't do it. We don't do it within the locker room. We don't keep them on the roster if they're that way because it makes it really tough."

He vowed that the Chiefs would someday benefit from playing these harrowing games. "I think—and you guys can tell me I'm full of crap when it's all said and done—that we will use our adversity, our setbacks and our disappointments as tools to get better," Vermeil said. "We will line up and keep getting better and some of the guys will be the same guys. They may not go to the Pro Bowl and they may not put us in the playoffs right now, but they will end up using those negative experiences to get better."

Sure enough, the Chiefs pulled themselves together and upset the Super Bowl-bound Oakland Raiders 20-10 at Arrowhead. The beleaguered Chiefs defense forced a pair of critical turnovers and held firm in the fourth quarter.

Robinson praised Vermeil for standing by him and his unit. "In 27 years of coaching," Robinson said. "I've been in hostile situations where it can get very negative. But I've never been in an atmosphere like the one Dick has created for us. He did nothing but support us. He removed any dark cloud that was hanging over us and let us go do our thing. He hangs with people. He lets people grow."

The defense delivered a solid effort next time out, too, but the offense sputtered during a 17-13 loss at San Francisco. "We weren't high-powered today," Vermeil said. "We were not the leading team in football today. We couldn't beat a junior high school team today."

Forty-Niners linebacker Julian Peterson literally put the cuffs on Gonzalez, holding him to one catch for six yards. "Somebody in high school could have guarded me the way he was guarding me," Gonzalez sniffed. "He was holding me all the way down the field. Just look at the tape."

Vermeil was furious with the officiating crew. "The guy in the deep position ought to donate his check to charity," Vermeil said. "This will force us coaches to work on release techniques – fist fights, clubbing, kicking, biting and scratching and everything else. Then we'll get called for holding."

This was a terrible week for the Vermeils. Carol was robbed while shopping in the trendy Country Club Plaza area. She had her hands full with packages when a man approached her, asked a few questions and then grabbed her purse. Carol refused to let go and started screaming. She fell to the sidewalk during the struggle, scraping her knee. "I hung on for dear life," she said.

Her purse came open and the robber grabbed the wallet and raced to a waiting car. In the wallet was $70 in cash, credit cards and Carol's favorite picture of Dick—one when he was coaching at Hillsdale High School. "He looks like he's about 19 years old," she said. "I've always loved that picture."

The Chiefs brightened Vermeil's mood with a 17-16 victory over Buffalo at home. Green scrambled nine yards for the game-winning touchdown, then oft-maligned cornerback Warfield made the game-clinching interception at the Chiefs' three.

In the locker room afterward, Vermeil got misty-eyed as he presented a game ball to Warfield. And Warfield glowed when he discussed his relationship with his coach. "He's been my No. 1 supporter," Warfield told reporters. "You guys have bashed me, put me in a hole. He's been the number one guy who's been there for me. I'm glad he's on my side. It's been rough, really rough. If he hadn't been there to help me, I could have easily gone in the tank."

The good feelings didn't last long. The defense collapsed again the following week in a 39-32 loss at Seattle, which dropped the Chiefs to 5-6. They blew early 10-0 and 17-7 leads and allowed the previously inept Matt Hasselbeck to pick them apart for 362 yards and three touchdowns. They wasted Holmes' 307 yards from scrimmage.

"When you lose to a 3-7 team," Chiefs center Casey Wiegmann said, "there's not much lower than that."

The flight home was miserable. "I get on an airplane flying home from Seattle after being embarrassed and say to myself, 'What the hell am I doing this for? Who needs it?'" Vermeil said.

Carol had the same thoughts after this latest fiasco. "She dies with the losses," Dick said. "She'd rather be in Pennsylvania. She'd rather be there and she has her second thoughts in regards to us being here."

There was more tension in the defensive meeting rooms. "All week the defensive coaches worked like they were in the city morgue," Vermeil said. "There was a tremendous sense of urgency the entire week. When our defensive coaches turn pale green, you know how bad they feel. Doubt starts to creep into your decision-making process, and it becomes infectious."

Once again, Vermeil had to preach perseverance. Most of the Kansas City media wrote the Chiefs off after this loss, but Vermeil refused to concede. He noted that his "Miracle in the Meadowlands" team in Philadelphia reached the playoffs with a 9-7 record. "When you have hope and desire, it creates motivation to keep striving. But as soon as you lose that, it's tough to compete," he said.

"We're not out of this yet. I've been in this environment before. I've been written out of it before. I've been written in too soon, and then lost out. That's what this league is all about."

The Chiefs evened their record at 6-6 with an overdue blowout victory, 49-0 over the hapless Arizona Cardinals. This was the second-most lopsided victory in the franchise's history and it allowed Vermeil to let everybody on the active roster have some fun.

That prepared the Chiefs for their crack at a reeling Rams team. During their third post-Vermeil season, the Rams had fallen on hard times due to injuries and surprisingly sloppy play. Coach Mike Martz, Vermeil's successor, was under heavy fire because of the team's collapse, especially since they were the defending NFC champs.

Ever loyal, Vermeil spoke with Martz frequently during the season, offering advice and encouragement. "I talk to him every week," Vermeil said. "Either he calls me or I call him. We cry on each other's shoulder from time to time. I sympathize with him. I, personally, have coached as a head coach longer than he has and I've never been put through a season like he's been put through injury-wise."

There was no sympathy expressed on the field, however, as the Chiefs put a 49-10 beating on the Rams. Their defense dominated, sacking Rams quarterback Jamie Martin six times and forcing one fumble and two interceptions. The resounding victory lifted the Chiefs' record to 7-6 and revived their playoff hopes.

In the locker room afterward, Chiefs players presented Dick and Carol Vermeil painted game balls. Green and fullback Tony Richardson had come up with this idea during the week. "We knew it was going to be very emotional for coach," Green said, "and it was something we wanted to do for him and let him know we appreciate him not only for being a coach, but for the person he is."

Naturally, Vermeil's tears flowed again when his players honored him. "Name the last NFL team ever to give a game ball to a coach's wife," he said. "Plus, it's already painted. I told them I would have slept better if you would have told me we were going to win before we played."

The Vermeils were ecstatic as they went to a staff Christmas party hosted by Peterson. "It was a nice event," Vermeil said. "What made it even better was the win."

Had the Chiefs been able to build on these two impressive victories by winning in Denver, they would have earned the inside track on a playoff berth. But the defense suffered a relapse, allowing the Broncos 482 yards of offense, and the Chiefs' frantic comeback bid fell short.

Holmes and Richardson got hurt in this game, joining receivers Morton and Marc Boerigter on the injured list. Green, who threw 49- and 75-yard touchdown passes to Dante Hall, simply ran out of weapons as the game wound down.

"There was a lot of chaos," Green said. "Anytime you lose one of your starting receivers before the game starts, then you lose both of your backs and another starting receiver . . . and all of a sudden we have guys out there playing positions they hadn't played before."

Hall's heroic play justified Vermeil's unwavering faith in him. From the start of training camp, Vermeil believed Hall could be much more than a kick returner and a situation receiver. Sure enough, he blossomed into a big-play threat.

"The last time we played San Diego, he dropped two balls," Vermeil said. "If he catches one of them we win. So what do we do? Crap on him right there and say, hey, he can't play? You know something? That happens. I've been in that environment. I've learned from that kind of environment that what you do is shortchange players on the negative plays that they make. You don't allow them to grow. Use the mistakes to let them get better."

How grateful was Hall? He invited Dick and Carol to attend the Pro Bowl in Hawaii as his guest.

The Chiefs had one more thriller in them. They rallied for a 24-22 victory over the Chargers at Arrowhead Stadium, ruining the homecoming for Chargers coach Marty Schottenheimer. Green threw three touchdown passes, including a 99-yard strike to Boerigter. But the Chiefs needed a 38-yard field goal from Michael Husted, in place of the injured Andersen, to squeeze out the victory.

With the game clock ticking toward the final minute of play, Saunders wanted to take one more shot at the end zone. The Chiefs had marched from their own 3-yard-line into scoring position, despite missing Holmes, Richardson and Morton because of various injuries.

Saunders called a passing play. But Vermeil overruled him on the sideline and sent in a running play instead.

"Hey," Vermeil told Saunders, "let's just run the ball and put it in his hands and let him kick it."

And Husted came through, nailing the game-winner with 68 seconds left.

"I took several deep breaths and relaxed," Husted said. "I basically got out of my own way and let my body do the talking."

The Chiefs finished their home schedule on an appropriately dramatic note. "It was time," Vermeil said. "We've lost some tough football games this year, some one-pointers, some overtimes, some three-pointers. To be able to win one in the final seconds, hey, we deserved it."

At 8-7, Kansas City remained mathematically alive in the playoff race heading into their season finale at Oakland. But with Holmes still injured and the Raiders on top of their game, the Chiefs took a 24-0 thrashing on a muddy field to end their season.

"Never in my life did I think this team could get shut out," Waters said.

The pass-happy Raiders stayed on the ground and pounded out 280 yards rushing. Once again, the defense failed miserably. Once again, reporters wondered what Vermeil would do about this problem in the off-season.

"I'm not going to talk about what needs to be fixed," Vermeil said after the game. "I just got my ass handed to me. I don't feel like talking about next year now."

Vermeil regrouped by the next day. He and Peterson convened one final team meeting. One more time, the coach gave his team a pep talk. According to the Kansas City Star, Vermeil talked about how close the Chiefs came to reaching the playoffs. He talked about the commitment the players had to demonstrate with their off-season conditioning. He talked about the pivotal third year of his regime, looming in 2003.

"The biggest room in Arrowhead," Vermeil told his players, "is for improvement."

There was much ahead, mostly on the defensive side of the football. Robinson took post-season beating from the local media. It wasn't hard to find players willing to express skepticism about their boss. "Guys have hated his system all year," one unidentified player told the Star. "That's no secret. Obviously, some changes need to be made for us to get where we want to be next season."

Vermeil elected to retain Robinson, but demanded that he create a more robust defense. "We could use more violent attitude players, and I think we've got to coach that, starting with (Robinson)," Vermeil said. "We were not a good tackling team. Period. That we can improve. We can't do it with two-hand tag below the waist, we can't do it with feather drills or in light tempo, warm-up drills and all that B.S. We've got to get back to some things that will make us better."

He noted that his record of 14-18 in two years is worse than the two years (16-16) that got his predecessor, Gunther Cunningham, fired. "That's a negative reflection on me," he said. "I'm not as tough on the players as I used to be, not as demanding as I used to be—almost too understanding. I've got to toughen up or else they've got to replace me."

Vermeil promised to be tougher on himself, too. His passion kept him moving forward in 2002, but his body didn't always hold up. "I've got to get in better shape," he said. "I run out of gas. You know, it's a long, long season. The stamina it takes to go out on the field and push and drive and then come back in and work late nights takes a lot of energy. I run out of energy quicker than I used to. I never used to run out of energy.

"I cannot be what I was. I wish I could."

But, ultimately, his approach would remain as positive as it's ever been. "I'm not going to spend the off-season hours feeling sorry for myself or believe we've failed," he said. "I'm going to appreciate all the good things we've done and attack our problems and go from there."

The Chiefs reloaded for the 2003 season, regaining injured players and adding impressive talent on both sides of the ball. They selected Penn State running back Larry Johnson in the first round as insurance against Holmes' hip injury. The beleaguered defense gained new leadership in former Eagles linebacker Shawn Barber, former Packers defensive end Vonnie Holiday and former Rams cornerback Dexter McCleon. Linebacker Kawika Mitchell and cornerback Julian Battle arrived in the draft. Defensive tackle Ryan Sims returned after missing 10 games with his elbow injury and safety Jerome Woods was back after missing the entire 2002 season with a broken leg.

When the revamped defensive unit gathered for its first mini-camp meeting in May, the words "2002 season" were scrawled on the grease-board. When Robinson entered the room, he erased those words. It was time to start over with new players and a new attitude.

"This is the year for us to lay it on the line," Barber said two months later as the team went to training camp. "This is not the year for us to worry about the future of the team. This is not the year for us to be trying to develop players. We need to make our Super Bowl run this year."

Vermeil prodded the Chiefs through another demanding camp. This time, the team looked especially sharp in the early drills. "I think it's a reflection of their concentration in the off-season," he said. "I thought we had a very good mini-camp routine. I thought we had very good organized team activities, the 12 of them we had in our off-season program."

That didn't lead to total serenity for the head coach, however. Vermeil proved, once again, that he had lost none of his fire. He reached his boiling point during at River Falls during a contentious session with the visiting Minnesota Vikings.

When a Vikings camper Rushen Jones took out the legs of Chiefs camper Dameane Douglas during an intersquad scrimmage, Vermeil snapped. When he saw Vikings scout Kevin McCabe, who worked for him in St. Louis, Vermeil yelled that he should take a shotgun and "shoot (Jones) in the head."

Whoa! When the two teams met again, the Chiefs pounded Minnesota 26-16 in its third preseason game. The Chiefs rolled up 429 yards in that exhibition, reminding everybody that they were still an offensive juggernaut.

Their '03 preseason was a glowing success. They finished 3-2, avoided catastrophic injuries to key players, got Holmes all the way back from his hip injury and then locked him into a long-term contract extension. Roaf looked much stronger than the year before, when he was coming off knee surgery. Gonzalez set aside any bitterness over his earlier contract squabbles and brought a new attitude into the season. Morton looked like a different player, too.

The rebuilt defense appeared much quicker and far more aggressive. Since Vermeil took the Rams to the Super Bowl in his third year in St. Louis, the third season of his Kansas City regime brought great expectations.

"I think we've earned the right to be optimistic," Vermeil said on the eve of his regular season opener. "We've improved in everything we've done in the first two years except for the defense and I think we've made the move on defense right now. All we have to do is go out there for 16 weeks and prove that we're better. We can talk about it, we can brag about it, we can pat each other on the back, but now we have to prove it.

"We have a mountain to climb. Maybe not Mount Everest. But I've been to the mountain before, and I've heard stories about climbing Mount Everest, and the one thing I know: You don't get any helicopter to drop you off at the top. You climb and you climb. We've been climbing for three years."

Convincing season-opening victories over San Diego and Pittsburgh kept the program moving upward. But Vermeil kept reminding his troops that bigger challenges loomed. "In this league," he said, "until you play in a playoff game, you're a contender and that's all.

"It's our job to move into that upper echelon. Move into that respectful level in the National Football League when people say, 'Here comes Kansas City, they are a playoff team.' You don't earn that right until you play one in January. But you don't become one until you play like one for 16 weeks. We have it pretty well defined by what we have to do."

Improbably, the victories kept coming. The Chiefs went to Houston and routed the Texans 42-14. They slugged out a 17-10 win at Baltimore. They edged the Denver Broncos 24-23 in a thriller at home, thanks to Hall's breathtaking 93-yard punt return. Down 31-14 in the fourth quarter at Green Bay, the Chiefs roared back behind Green's 400-yard passing day to steal a 40-34 victory in overtime.

"I'm not surprised we're 6-0, but I also know we're fortunate to be 6-0," Vermeil said. "But you still have to play every down, every quarter, every half, every game to keep yourself a winner. Something good can happen and you can take advantage of it and you are playing hard enough to create some good things to happen to you."

Vermeil scoffed at the suggestion these Chiefs were a team of destiny. "I've heard those kinds of things, but destiny doesn't line up and take on double-team blocks and protect good pass rushing ends," he said. "I've said to the squad that's there's a spiritual innuendo sometimes. I told them a monsignor who used to be the team chaplain for me in Philadelphia, who was a great man and jumped out of an airplane with paratroopers during World War II. He was a man's man. He used to say all the time, 'the good Lord doesn't choose which side of the line of scrimmage he plays on. He leaves it up to you to win or lose the football game and take advantage of your God-given talent."

Vermeil's goal is to restore the Chiefs to their old prominence, preferably by getting the franchise back to the Super Bowl. Then, once his services are no longer needed, he can finally retire for good.

Did he need to meet this final challenge to complete his coaching legacy?

"That's for guys with huge egos," he said. "First off, no one can ever take away the relationships that I've been able to establish with the teams I've coached and the victories and the losses we've shared and the Super Bowls, the Rose Bowls, the high school championship games, in losing a Junior College championship game. No one can take those experiences away from me. I don't need someone to come up and tell me how good I am. I've never put myself in the upper echelon of anything, other than I'm doing what I like to do."

# A P P E N D I X

## DICK VERMEIL ON COACHING

Every time Dick Vermeil talks, there is a good chance he'll lay some coaching wisdom on his audience. Here, in his own words, is a guide to successful coaching culled from his various media addresses:

### SETTING THE BIG GOAL

"You've got to be careful that within your franchise and your organization that you don't allow things to distract you from what the number one thing is you're supposed to be doing. That's winning football games. The total organization's focus has got to be on winning football games. You can always point fingers at things where you wonder why they do all this stuff: marketing, all this selling tents, barbecues, pre-game. It all comes down to getting football players and an organization put together that can win football games. Then a lot of things start taking care of themselves."

"Before you become a playoff team, you have to play like one. Once you get playing like a playoff team through four quarters of a football game, then you start beating people."

### DOING IT YOUR WAY

"In the National Football League you're going to get fired anyway, most of the time. You might as well do it your way. George Allen told me that a long time ago when I was going to be a rookie coach."

### BUILDING AN ORGANIZATION

"The No. 1 key to longevity in the National Football League normally is a fine organization—a fine base of people that you're surrounded by. It all starts from the leadership from the owner to the president right down through the head football coach. Any time I've ever had any success it's been a direct reflection of everybody working together in the total organization."

"Leadership is training. You'd better develop other leaders. When an organization gets so big, you have to develop a footprint that extends from you and your philosophy of leadership."

"I want to give everyone a piece of the action. I want to get everyone involved. I'd like to have the person who works in community relations feel as badly as I do when we lose. I want that person to share in the joy when we win. I'd like to have a group of people in the organization that anticipates what needs to be done. We need to get it to the point where they'll know what we want without asking, and we don't have to tell them what to do. They just do it. I want everybody to be that way. That's the only way we'll catch up."

## MAINTAINING STAFF HARMONY

"What we want to build on our staff is the same feeling that we want to build in our locker room, where it's important for one coach to help another coach. My job is to provide these assistant coaches with an environment where they can build that bond. Before it can be built with players, it must be there on the coaching staff."

"I try not to hang assistant coaches out to dry. I just don't believe in doing that. When it becomes obvious I'm wrong, then I've got to do what I've got to do, and I've done that before. When I've done that, I've had all the information and all the reasons I needed."

## THE VALUE OF TALENT

"You want to know what the essence of coaching is? John Wooden told me a long time ago, when I was at UCLA and my office was right down the hall from his. He said, 'Dick, players win games, not coaches.'"

"Normally when a football program changes leadership it's because they didn't win enough games. Normally in the National Football League when you don't win enough games, you don't have enough good football players. The reason the guy was fired was he didn't have enough good football players, not because he couldn't coach. That's nine times out of 10, maybe more than that."

"It doesn't matter how good you are as coach. There's some teams that aren't well-coached that win more games than teams that are better coached. They have better players. The big thing is to make the right decisions in personnel. Absolutely critical thing."

"People make systems work. Players make systems work. Coaches coach systems and discipline them and teach the fundamentals within the system. But it's players."

"In today's game, if you don't have those skilled people that can do something beyond your coaching or design, you aren't going to score enough points through 16 games to be a real solid contender for the Super Bowl."

## BUILDING A TALENT BASE

"I believe this: There's a difference between building a team and coaching one. The first thing you've got to do is build it and then you've got to make sure you're doing a good job coaching it. There's got to be a philosophy behind your building process, the mechanics of how you want to do it and the kind of players you want to do it with and the kind of people you want to do it with."

"You draft players and hope they become good football players. You sign some unrestricted free agents and hope they make winning contributions. Then you have to develop those young players who aren't drafted or were inexperienced guys who were low draft picks. If you can build two or three players a year that two or three years down the road can end up starting and make a contribution, then you have a chance to build a championship football team."

## WHAT TO LOOK FOR IN PLAYERS

"I like a person who has an overall deep level of character. Someone who cares about his teammate, someone who is humble and appreciates what the other guy does for him in helping him do what he does for a living. I look for a guy who trusts, who has integrity, a tremendous work ethic, that will share responsibility for winning, will share the responsibility for losing. They're out there. People who appreciate their opportunity, unselfish guys."

"Every guy we visit with, I always say to him, 'I'm looking for a kid who's not motivated by his contract, someone whose performance will control his contract.' And someone whose mom and dad built within him an intense desire to excel, to be successful, and it's not wrapped in dollars. The dollars are rewards. It starts with their work habits, their off-season habits, their self-discipline. Are they there when they said they are going to be there, and do they do what they say they are going to do? Like I say, instead of them wanting to be the best player on the team, they want to be the best player for the team. When you start getting enough of those guys, then other people who don't automatically fit that mold fall into line. Or fall out. Once you start getting that real core group that fits what you want from a philosophical standpoint, the new people who come in have to conform. Then, gradually, it becomes infectious."

"I notice certain things and how they work and how they take coaching and how they prepare, how they come out and service scout team work, how they work in improving their own individual skills. When you see somebody who does it without being pushed at all, then you want to make sure you keep him around long."

"If you have five guys linked together and you draft the guy with the most passion, you're going to win almost every time. Even if you reach for a player—which I've done before—you reach and he'll play 10 years. He may not play in the Pro Bowl, but he'll play on a championship team as long as you've done the right things with the other players that surround him. That applies to all draft choices."

## HOW TO REACH THE PLAYERS

"I think even in the National Football League you have to coach the total person. You have to coach him as a person. First off, he has to know you believe in him; chances are, he will believe in you. First off, he has to know that you care about him; then, chances are he will care. You have to give to him, then he will give to you."

"Good coaches shape player opinions and win their enthusiasm by using every available opportunity to send their message and win their support. When as a coach, you can move that commitment from their heads to their hearts, you've got a truly motivated player."

"I've always tried to treat people the way I want to be treated. It's not very complicated. If you've done things a certain way over a long period of time, you can establish credibility with people."

"The better I know somebody, the better I understand, the more I can help him to be what he has the ability to be. The more I can help him solve his problems that are preventing him from being what he ought to be. I'm talking about taking the good player to a better player, the better player to the Pro Bowl level. When you get to see young people meet expectations and go beyond to see what it does for their whole profile as a person, it's really a warm, warm experience."

## PUSHING PLAYERS TO ACHIEVE

"That's the number one thing I work on every day, whether it's for the staff or for the players, trying to create a situation that makes it possible for them to go beyond what they think their capabilities are."

"People need to be pushed. If you don't push, they loaf. They need to be driven. They thrive on it. They need to be disciplined even if they bitch. It is no different in high school than it is in college. In fact, in my experience in the National Football League, motivating and driving a guy to be better is more important than on any level. Why? Because there is no such thing as a bad football player in the National Football League. Now there's some better than others, no question about it. But you've got to find a way to make the average guy better, and the great guy better. And the third stringer, he's got to be good enough to play on Sunday if some guy's hurt."

"When you take over a losing organization, every team that's been beating you, they have the same access to talent—the draft, free agency and everything else. And the only way you can gain an edge is spend more time, invest more time on the practice field."

"If you don't invest much, then defeat doesn't hurt very much and winning is not very exciting."

## PRACTICING TO WIN

"I like high-speed practices. The game is played fast on Sundays, or Thursday night, or Sunday night, or Monday night. If you practice at a mediocre tempo I've always believed you're conditioning yourself to play at that tempo. Things happen so much quicker when you're moving faster like a ball game that you have to duplicate it as close as you possibly can on the practice field."

## THE IMPORTANCE OF FUNDAMENTALS

"A lot of times things break down not because the design's not good or it's called at the wrong time, it's just that something broke down fundamentally. A lot of things break down because the fundamentals break down. You're able to correct these things as you go."

"A fundamental breakdown is every bit as critical as a mental breakdown. The wrong pass set on a good defensive end can get your quarterback sacked. Now, what's the difference as long as you block the guy? It matters because a fundamental mistake can kill you.

"Fundamentals have to hold up against the best players you play against. If they don't hold up against the best, then they weren't good enough."

"That's what this league is, technique. When you break it down, it's nothing but technique combined with quickness and speed.

"Kids don't come out of college as far along on fundamentals any more because of the restrictions on (practice) time and those kinds of things. So their fundamentals aren't always as good as their athletic ability."

"All the little things have to happen for the big, obvious things to happen. I mean, for example, for us to execute big plays, it all starts with the center. He better get a good snap. All the pass sets better be proper, all the placing of hands, all the first steps, all the stunt pick-ups, all the routes run precisely."

## THE VALUE OF GAME-DAY MOTIVATION

"Let me tell you this: When momentum changes in a football game, how many different players are in those uniforms? Not one guy changes uniforms. The only thing that changes in the frame of mind. We coach with the attitude that we want to play a football game as though we've already gained momentum."

## THE NEED FOR CONSISTENCY

"I don't believe in this stuff about not being able to get up every week. The paycheck is the same every Monday. We compare it to a sprinter. If you have the ability to run 9.3, then you better be able to run a 9.3 every Sunday, and at some point strive for a 9.1. That's what we try to impress on our players. If you run a 9.7, you can't win with that. Those are the kind of people who get coaches fired. That's why you have to find those people early. I know we do."

"I lost a division title in 1979 because we lost to a losing team on the road that had one win. To me, I always thought I didn't do a good job getting us ready to play because I didn't truly know how to evaluate what confidence in football is all about. Toughness in football is playing well regardless of the environment, regardless of the record of a football team."

## THE DANGER OF COMPLACENCY

"The one thing that is a constant regardless of how long you've coached and what years they were, in this league you have to get better. You can't remain status quo from week to week. When you drop off, you really get beat. When you fail to improve, you end up getting beat."

"In the National Football League, every time you turn the corner there is a bigger turn in front of you."

## REMAINING POSITIVE WITH PLAYERS

"My leadership attitude is to keep doing it. We don't criticize. We don't blame. These are our players. We aren't going to go out and create a whole new roster. The only way we're going to solve any weakness on the roster is to coach them better, define for them opportunities to get better and keep in the right frame of mind to be coached. If you recognize somebody that doesn't fit that mold, then you kick their ass out of town. That's the only way I know how to do it."

"Mistakes made by players are coaching opportunities. They should not be causes for punishment. People have unbelievable tolerance for praise."

"I do the same things when we win as I do when we lose. Look for all the good things that we do and correct all the wrong things we do. It's just when you lose, you have more things to correct."

"I always see the best in players. When I see somebody do something well one time, I think all we have to do is coach him and get him in the right frame of mind to do it consistently."

"If you're always working on what they can't do or what they don't do, you're setting mental limits for them. A high percentage of the athletes you work with in the professional field today come out of dysfunctional homes or homes where there wasn't a male figure. Even though they're gifted athletes, sometimes their confidence isn't as deep as the image they present."

"It's so easy to beat somebody when they're down. Beat on them. But then they never come out of the hole you dig for them. I've never coached that way and have had some luck in turning some things around within a season. I've seen quarterbacks turn around within a season and I've seen one side of the ball or another turn around within the middle of the season."

"The thing about coaching is you have to believe in people. That's the most important part of the job. Trust . . . what I try to do is see something in a person that he may not see in himself. That's when you're a good coach – when you can convince a player that he's better than he is."

### WHY PLAYER CONFIDENCE IS CRITICAL

"I think it's tough to play well afraid of doing something wrong. I think you've got to turn it loose and play and not be in fear of making a mistake, not fear of making it less than 100 percent right. If all you ever hear is all the negative things you do wrong, you usually end up meeting that description somewhere down the road. Then you never get better."

"We can't be afraid to lose. You can't go into a ballgame afraid to make a mistake. You've got to go play and rely on the confidence and the knowledge in what you've gained in practice. My analogy has always been: You take the take great hitters of our day. They don't go up to bat worrying about striking out. They get up and swing the bat."

### THE VALUE OF COACHING

"If you work and you can teach and communicate, that's coaching. I think we can raise the level of performance and maybe in some circumstances raise an individual player's level of expectation."

"I like to think I can lead people. I think I can get more out of some guys than others have, make them play better than they have played before. To me, that's a coach."

"What you want to strive to be is a coach who can win more games with the same players than somebody else could win with those players.' That's what I've tried to do. "

"Every coach has a purpose, and I think one of my most rewarding purposes in coaching is to help young people mature and become what they have the ability to be. That's coaching and that's teaching. I get the biggest thrill out of that. I really do. "

## THE RISK OF OVER-COACHING

"What I've learned about coaching is coaches lose more games they should win and than win games they should lose. I recognized that even more in broadcasting sitting up there when you're not emotionally attached to the two teams playing. I really believe that's true. Through a season or your tenure, somewhere you end up losing more games that you should have won than winning games you should have lost. "

## THE BONDING OF AN ORGANIZATION

"I think when you bond between a coach and a player, a head coach and an assistant coach, one assistant coach to another, the relationships you develop in those situations, it goes beyond respect. What's beyond respect is love. I know their feelings go beyond just respect for me as a coach. That's why I have no trouble saying, 'I love you.' I don't use it unless I feel it, but I use it when I feel it. "

## STAYING THE COURSE

"A new program always has a fragile profile, a fragile personality. When things go well, they get very excited and when things don't go well, what I call the doubting Thomases get more vocal, especially the older veterans who haven't been forced to work like the younger players have, then that's the reason they're losing, it's because they can't quite play like they're used to play. "

"The worst thing you can do is vacillate because if you really believe in what you're doing, you keep doing it until everyone does it well. Believing in something gives you a chance to make it work; it doesn't make it work, it doesn't make it easy. You hang with what you believe in. "

"Sometimes you get worse before you get better. Just like if we took any one of you that's a pretty good golfer and changed your swing. That ultimately will make you a better golfer, but for a while you don't score as well. Sometimes that happens to a football team. It happened to about every football team I've ever coached."

"You have to, in rebuilding a football team, you have to be able to use adversity to grow. If you can't, you'll never make it. That's why some teams keep firing coaches and never go to playoffs. That's why there are 10 teams who have never been to a Super Bowl."

"I believe it's good for a quarterback to go through adversity and fight through it. I've been in situations where I really felt a quarterback going through a bad game would just as soon be taken out. But how he gets better is to stay in there and play."

## DEALING WITH PLAYER TURNOVER

"That's the modern world. Free agency has created movement within the league and in the normal rotation of a player he'll have the right after four years or maybe five to move to another club and become a free agent. Some players move and some players don't. I don't hold that against them. In the corporate world today and big executives making a lot of money, if they get a chance to go somewhere else for more money, they normally go. But yet a football player does that and he's looked down upon as selfish and not loyal. I don't look at it that way. I just look at it as a part of the business. I would rather not have it that way, but that's the way it is. You accept it, but you try to build a program that the environment and the atmosphere there is so conducive to staying that they don't want to leave and they'll play there even maybe for a few dollars less. Not a lot. I wouldn't expect them to play if it were for a lot less."

## TURNING THE PAGE ON PLAYERS

"I really enjoy people. But I have a hard time coaching somebody I don't care about or I don't trust. I'll give them a year, but probably no more than a year. If I don't feel comfortable coaching somebody, I let them go."

"I have no trouble cutting someone I can't develop a relationship. But someone I have a real great relationship with . . . I've cut kids who played three or four years. I was there when their first child was born. That kills you. But if you're always honest with them, and you have the right communication system going, they understand because you never misled them. They always know that the bottom line is the bottom line. Security is based on performance, not on how much I love them. He still has to play well."

## DEALING WITH FAN DISPLEASURE

"They reason they yell is because they love them. It's like getting mad at your own kids. You get mad at 'em because you love 'em. This is an instant gratification business. We're in show business and when the show isn't very entertaining, people don't like it. It usually starts with the quarterback. It goes from the quarterback to the head coach on through the coordinators. Better the fans be there and boo than not be there at all because they pay our salaries."

## CONFRONTING ISSUES HEAD-ON

"I don't hide my eyes behind closed doors and make up stories. We attack problems, address problems, evaluate where the breakdowns are and what we can do different in coaching and in scheme and in personnel changes."

## THE URGENCY TO WIN

"Anybody with three losing seasons is going to get fired in this league. It doesn't matter if you're working for your grandfather, your uncle or your best friend. In this league, it's tough keeping your job if you lose three years in a row."

"Someone's going to take the blame for losing and someone's going to sell tickets for next year. Sometimes they fire the guy after three years and it creates a whole new level of enthusiasm. And if he's not successful, they fire him. It's just a constant, vicious cycle."

"It's an instant gratification business and it's a marketing business much more than it used to be. In fact, I think some organizations get so focused on marketing they forget the business we're really in. You win football games, it will market itself."

# ABOUT THE AUTHOR

Jeff Gordon has been a sportswriter at the St. Louis Post-Dispatch since 1986. Previously, he worked at the Baltimore News American, Kansas City Magazine and the St. Joseph (Mo.) News-Press and Gazette. His work has appeared in several national magazines during the last two decades, including The Sporting News, Sport and Inside Sports. He is the author of several books, including "Keenan, The High Times and Misadventure's of Hockey's Most Controversial Coach." He lives in Manchester, Mo., with his wife and two daughters.